Chicken Soup for the Indian Teenage Soul

Chicken Soup for the Indian Teenage Soul

101 Stories To Celebrate & Learn From Our Growing-Up Years

Jack Canfield
Mark Victor Hansen
Raksha Bharadia

w

We would like to acknowledge the following publishers and individuals for permission to reprint the following material. (Note: The stories that were penned anonymously, that are public domain or were written by Raksha Bharadia are not included in the listing.)

Is She Really Me? Reprinted by permission of Shobhaa Dé © 2009 Shobhaa Dé

Rising Hormones, Setting Sun. Reprinted by permission of Anurita Rathore. © 2009 Anurita Rathore

(*Continued on page 330*)

westland ltd
61, II Floor, Silverline Building, Alapakkam Main Road, Maduravoyal, Chennai 600095
93, I Floor, Sham Lal Road, Daryaganj, New Delhi 110002

15 14 13 12 11 10 9

ISBN: 978-93-80032-63-4

Cover design by design on u

Inside book formatting and typesetting by SÜRYA, New Delhi

Printed at Repro India Ltd., Navi Mumbai

Contents

Introduction

Chicken Soup stories have the power to change lives. During the course of compiling, editing, and writing *Chicken Soup for the Indian Soul*, I know they changed *my* life. Working on this volume, *Chicken Soup for the Indian Teenage Soul*, has influenced my relationship with my own two teenage children. Re-visiting my tumultuous teens, I understood much better the experience my children were undergoing. Manuscipts would be lying around or my laptop would be open on a story and I'd see one of them reading. A slight widening of the eyes, a smile, or a titter, an expression of understanding, of revelation—all these and more are what I saw on their faces. At the conclusion of my work on this volume, I know we have a deeper, stronger bonding.

Teens everywhere, across space and time, are plagued by the same basic issues. The mileu may change, the materialities may differ, but the issues never do. Teenage is the time where everything is in a state of transition, in the process of building. Teenage is a distinct phase when you're no longer a child, but nobody will treat you as an adult. It is a phase during which you are trying to come to terms with everything and everyone, yourself, others, the world. As the author of the bestseller *Teenagers*, Dr David Bainbridge says, 'Our teenage years are the most dramatic, intense and exciting of our lives.'

But teenagers also have to grapple with physical and other changes—suddenly storklike legs, a cracking voice, pimples, developing breasts and biceps; anxieties over peer pressure—from friends and other teenagers, from parents and relatives, from our icons; awkwardness with the opposite sex; the ecstasy and agony of the first crush; the urge to explore new sensations, the irrational thrill of risk-taking; dealing with teasing and bullying; the pleasures of discovering new interests and whole new worlds.

As you go through these stories, dear reader, you will realise that you are not alone in feeling, behaving and reacting the way they do. You will see that your issues are not unique, but shared by many.

You are not the only one with gangly limbs, you are not alone in trying to get rid of non-existent fat even at the risk of becoming anorexic. You are struck no less fiercely than the others by your first crush, when you want to conveniently put aside the rest of the world. And when the world becomes important again, they will be there with you, feeling the same way.

Through the struggles so candidly shared in these stories, you will not only understand your own issues but find a way to deal with them. It is difficult to rise above another's opinion of you, or hoist yourself out of the occasional pit of despair, but the rise in self-esteem that follows is the greatest feeling.

There are personal stories here, of physical, emotional and verbal abuse, and they teach a lesson about not going into self-denial. If you are in such a relationship they may perhaps inspire in you the courage to fight back.

You don't have to be a teenager to enjoy these stories. As they have already helped this mother, they will be relevant to all parents of adolescent children, too. In our own teens, we too shut ourselves up in our rooms for hours, ignored any age group that wasn't ours, been unkempt, lazy, irresponsible, selfish. In *Chicken Soup for the Indian Teenage Soul*, you will find many parallels. Your children too are going through the same concerns, anxieties, worries, pressures you did as a teen. You might become a more understanding, caring parent.

For some of these stories we went back to the original source and asked them to write it or tell it in their own words. We have attributed every story we could to the original source. We have included a contributors section in the back of the book where we have listed their names and email ids so that you can contact them yourself if you wish.

Help yourself to some more *Chicken Soup*!

Raksha Bharadia

the shut ourselves up in our rooms for hours, ignored any [illegible] impossible selling in London and/or [illegible] Mumbai or the South, you will find many parallels. Your children are going through the same concerns, anxieties, worries, pressures, yet, and [illegible] teen. You might become a more understanding parent [illegible]

For some of these stories, we went back to the original source and asked them to write it or tell it in their own words. We have attributed every story we could to the original sources. We have included a contributors section at the back of the book where we have listed their names and email ids so that you can contact them too if you wish.

Help yourself to another Chicken Soup!

[illegible] [illegible]

1

ON CELEBRATION

'One of the extraordinary things about human events is that the unthinkable becomes thinkable.'

—Salman Rushdie

Is She Really Me?

It is my daughter Anandita's birthday today. She is the baby of the family and my youngest child. Last night, when she came home from a mini-date, I was waiting to bring in her special day. I had arranged a small mother-daughter celebration and made her two cards. The one that made her cry had to do with the message I'd written across a photograph of hers taken as a teenager in Goa. A TEENAGER! We were both acutely aware of the significance of the moment—these were her last, very precious minutes before she left that magical, mixed-up, exciting and exhausting teen world behind and stepped into 'official' adulthood. I lit the birthday candles and asked her to make a wish. As Anandita turned twenty at midnight, we hugged each other.

'I want to remain a teenager forever,' sobbed Anandita, as a river of mascara streamed down her cheeks. What I didn't say was, 'So do I, darling. So do I.'

I never wanted to grow up. Does anybody? My own teenage years had been spectacular. Oddly (and very fortunately), I'd skipped the customary angst, the gawky growth curve, the acne and heartbreaks altogether. I'd actually enjoyed being a teenager. And I do hope my mother (if not stern father) would agree it wasn't all that traumatic for her either. I'll never know. I never asked. And now she is no more. I think she enjoyed my teenage pangs (such as they were) as much as I did. Just as I enjoyed Anandita's. Of course, being a teenager in the 21st century is an entirely different ball game. But hormones remain hormones, even if the century changes.

As Anandita and I dried our tears, opened her gifts, and took pictures (for Facebook, of course!), I felt a twinge of regret . . . no more teenagers to deal with in my life . . . till the grandkids arrive. And wasn't that a pity?

Anandita had given me a harder time than all the older children, no getting away from that. I doubt she'd argue the point! As the youngest, she had extracted the sort of privileges out of me that the others wouldn't have dreamt of. Extended deadlines, more money, less nagging. Frankly, I understood what she was about. I grew up as the youngest child of my parents myself. It was a space I could totally identify with. So many decades on, my siblings still feel I had it easy as compared to them, that I was pampered silly and worse—that I took full advantage of my parents and my privileged position.

Ah well . . . there is some truth to that. Why challenge the obvious? Anandita's story is different. She has grown up in such a rapidly changing world, it was difficult for me to keep pace with all the dramatic and radical shifts in it. Anandita often left me gasping at the gatepost, angry and unsure, helpless and frustrated. My concerns were conventional (studies, boyfriends, bad company, bad habits). But hers had to do with brands, clubbing, gymming and getting to be a size zero!

Did I get it? Not always. Besides, I knew I had to be eagle-eyed at all times, looking for signs of drug abuse, anorexia, bulimia, smoking weed, alcohol consumption, to say nothing of sexual activity, unwanted pregnancy and other similar, and terrifying, issues that today's parents have to cope with—

embarrassedly, apologetically, guiltily, stealthily, sensitively. Damn it, we were left with no option but to 'understand' and eventually accept whatever came with the teenage turf. It was almost as if I was the one being tested. 'Are you a cool enough mom?' 'Can you handle it?' More importantly—'Do you get it?'

Often, I couldn't and didn't. The failure had to be mine! But as my older children frequently reassured me, 'If there was something to worry about, we'd intervene and tell you. So just chill, Mom. You're being neurotic, paranoid . . . a control freak. Anandita is just fine. She is like any other teen. It's normal to want all that stuff. That's the world.'

Oh. Now that, too.

Several times during this intense period, I sat Anandita down, pulled the iPod headphones off her ears, and prayed. I didn't want to preach, but I did want her to pay attention. What I was saying was important. To her, to me. It concerned her health—physical and emotional. I wanted her to know I wasn't judging her or her friends. But I sure as hell had to make sure she was safe at all times. Was that asking for too much?

Strange, through all this turmoil and turbulence, there were times when a reversal of roles would take place—it would be Anandita advising me on how to cope with her life! But the good thing to emerge from this insane period was that our lines of communication stayed open at all times, and gradually I found myself easing up, gaining entry into her world, her mind, and most importantly, her heart. I still wait up nights for her (old habit!), and I can't always stop myself from asking, 'Who was that?' each time she answers the phone. But these days, she doesn't leave the room to take that call, nor turn her back on me—Anandita winks and asks cheekily, 'Guess?'

Bingo! Nine times out of ten, my guess is bang on. She

sleeps better at night, and so do I. We've discovered a beautiful word. It is called 'trust'. But sometimes, only sometimes, I miss Anandita—the teen princess. Or maybe, I miss the old me.

Shobhaa Dé

Rising Hormones, Setting Sun

Whatever I am today, is because of those numerous sunsets I grew up watching. Because watching the sun go down invites introspection.

I'd say my childhood years were all about such things: sunsets, sunrises, innocence. I had a book of T.S. Eliot's poems that was my dearest companion. I really believe that when the sun sets, the earth begins breathing again. I used to take time out to see it sink into the horizon. I'd take my cycle, pack a thermos of coffee and take along a friend/companion to the sunset point five kilometres to Pashan Lake, on the outskirts of Pune.

I must tell you more ... I was this gawky-looking guy in glasses who went ahead and asked girls to dates. There were lots of girls I rode with, in fact. Those who liked me sat in front; the others would feel safer sitting behind. There would be a place nearby that was pretty secluded, with old boats lying about. We'd sit there and watch the lake turn into a sheet of gold.

My family had chalked out plans for me. They wanted me to pursue the IAS or IFS, but I never got into arguments with them over that. I just kept doing what I wanted. Not that I knew then what I really wanted to do! All I knew was that I wanted to be surrounded by ladies (and that's something I managed, too). I spent 90 per cent of my waking life as a teenager thinking about getting laid, and the remaining time trying to do it—apart from juggling parental expectations and studies. Women were all I thought about. But one thing I never did was lie in order to get them.

We were a group of largely outdoor kids, into games of hockey, horse riding, football and squash, but because I wore spectacles, people mistook me for an intellectual. Truth is, I was a duffer. Being dyslexic, I was brilliant at what I was good at, but in areas I was bad, I was worse than the others. I was good at poems and literature, though, and I was also blessed with natural leadership. It's ironical how I used to be punished for day-dreaming in school; today I'm paid for it!

But I particularly attribute the course my life took to my school days, first at St Thomas in Dehra Dun, and from class VIII and beyond at Sainik School, Kunjpura, near Karnal. It was a tough military school (my father had been in the army although he passed away when I was nine, and my mother brought my sister and I up) where the principal, Lt Col E.J. Simeon, was known to my parents. The colonel and his wife, who we lovingly called Mater and Pater, played a big role in shaping our lives. They spotted and honed each child's individual talents. The cadets of all four years who passed out in my time there have all done well. Some are generals, brigadiers, even high-rankers in civilian life.

When the time came to pursue a career, I decided to play polo since I was a good horse rider, but my eyesight prevented that plan from forming. Fate had other ideas. I got into an ad agency in Delhi, and then a multi-national bank where I topped my way through. The job was good but the women around were unattractive. That was reason enough for me to leave, believe it!

One day, as I was wandering around the reception area of an advertising and sales promotion firm, I chanced upon the most beautiful pair of legs. Her name is Farida Pandey and she was the one responsible for inflicting me on an unsuspecting advertising world! I always knew my life would be spent around beautiful women. I sported long hair to indicate I was a rebel, but even cut that off for a woman I wanted to marry—but couldn't!

Today, when I look back at my teen years, I realise how they are the most important years of our life because that is when we form our impressions. Our likes and dislikes take shape then; our ideas take shape. I do feel my teen years prepared me to expect what the world could be. It made me deal with people. It's not formal education that helps us as much as direct dealings and relationships do. And I think I realised that very early in my life.

Prahlad Kakar
(As told to Anurita Rathore)

Becoming Indian

I was not always the confident, content young woman I am today. I was not always this comfortable in my own skin. There was a time when I wished my golden-brown skin was a creamy shade of white. As a young Indian growing up in the West, I was always self-conscious about who I was, conflicted about who I wanted to be, and instead of embracing my uniqueness, I was insecure about it. I was born in England and raised in the US and New Zealand. Deep down, I just wanted to blend in among a sea of white skin, blue eyes, and blonde hair. I took for granted the fact that I come from such an amazing cultural background that is so full of beauty, magic, colour and passion.

Looking back now, overall, I had a good experience in each Western country, but there is always more to every story. I felt displaced. You could call it a crisis of identity. It was necessary to act like the Westerners around me, but at the same time, I felt I always stood out physically. I remember feeling uncomfortable when the kids at school in America questioned me as to why I looked different from them and where I was from. I'd say, 'What do you mean? I'm American, just like you.' But, they never bought it. And come to think of it, neither did I.

Not only did I feel internal pressure to act like the kids

around me, but also to *look* like the kids around me. Living in New Zealand, I was surrounded by light eyes and light hair and became conscious of my dark hair and eyes. I went through a stage of dyeing my hair a startling shade of blonde and wearing coloured contact lenses to lighten my eyes. I was very confused about who I was and who I'd rather be.

After spending years of confusion as a diasporic youth in America and New Zealand, I somehow started coming into my own. With age and maturity I began to appreciate my ethnicity—the identity gifted to me by God. I guess you could say the turning point was on my first trip to India in 2003 which made me truly realise who I am, where I come from and what I want to be.

My dada and dadi, who live in Chandigarh, invited all nine of their grandchildren who live in New Zealand, to come and stay with them in India for a couple of months. They wanted to teach us about our culture and to that end took us on an extensive tour of the country. It was that trip that exposed me to India, which taught me about the history, culture and tradition of an ancient nation. It was that trip which left me on a high; which made me fall in love.

We began our travels through the motherland in our ancestral village, Duneke, located in Punjab, and saw the old village house where my grandfather was raised and the room in which he was born. We then visited the spiritual abode of the Sikhs, the Golden Temple in Amritsar, and all of us cousins were emotionally stirred by the experience. To witness people coming together from all walks of life with one common goal—love for, and devotion to God, was indescribable.

Our family continued on our journey and the next stop was Delhi, where we soaked up much of India's history and tradition as we explored the temples and monuments. From there we went to Agra and saw for ourselves India's mystery and majesty when we laid our eyes upon the Taj Mahal. We indulged in the magic of Rajasthan, and even took a two-day train journey to Goa, discovering a completely different side to India. The entire experience was life-changing.

Being raised in different countries I have had the opportunity to travel the world, but in all my expeditions, I have never seen as much beauty as I have on my journeys through my homeland. Meeting all of my family here, many for the first time, and experiencing such hospitality, love, and a sense of community, left me speechless. Customs and qualities fundamental to Indians are absent in Western society.

One aspect of our country which really stood out for me is how spiritual the people of India are. Deep-rooted belief in God is essential and a part of daily life. Spending time with my nana and nani helped me realise what was always inside of me, which I had previously turned my back on. I found God within me and have never looked for Him elsewhere. From that moment on my life was changed and I was awakened within.

After two-and-a-half mesmerising months, the trip was over and reality set in. I had to return to New Zealand to continue my studies. I was overwhelmed by sadness, but resolved to integrate all I learned in India into my life in the West. I was, finally, happy to be just me.

And I also came to a decision—I would one day return to the motherland. Time ticked on and more than three years later, after finishing my studies and post-graduation, I packed my bags and came to India in early 2007. I have now been here for two years and I'm hooked. You can't really know yourself until you understand where it is you came from. I have come to realise that my brown skin, dark hair, and brown eyes, are beautiful, not only in India, but wherever in the world I go.

Priya Kaur Gill

Celebration

If life were a celebration,
would I have it in me to be happy?
Wouldn't I have tired of your perfection long before
perfection would have rejected an imperfect me?
It is cold outside
but that is not what freezes my soul,
it's the lack of warmth in the smiles of those around.
Searched the highs and lows
but still haven't got what I was looking for.
Maybe just need to figure out the worth of what I found.
If I were to love
only when someone were to love me first,
would I be in love only because I long to belong?
If only I could sing
a melody which would bring a smile to bloom.
If only I see just one face before it fades into another song?
If life were a celebration,
would I have it in me to be happy?
I rejoice because unhappiness is the eyes with which
I recognise happiness when it knocks at the door for me.

Malcolm George

Colour Me Everything

Sometimes I think festivals are a necessary result of the terrific life force that lies in the hearts of millions in this country. Over the past eight months, I have caught glimpses of this dormant energy waiting to explode in the eyes of street children refusing to be cowed by poverty, the strong hands of labouring village women, the laughing feet of spontaneous dancers, the intensity of voices rising in a bhajan, and the quick strokes of someone kneading dough for chapatti. There is passion in all these vignettes of a country holding 1.1 billion people together.

But life is most palpable on the annual festival of Holi.

Though there are various fables and legends concerning the festival of Holi, it is primarily a celebration of spring, and because it hails the arrival of a new agricultural season, it receives greatest attention in the villages and pastoral regions of India. The means of celebration are colours—the intense colours of hot red, sunflower yellow, parrot green and turquoise blue that people gather to douse each other with, all social differences cast aside, on that magic day.

I have had the privilege of being in India on three occasions of Holi. I spent my first Holi with my relatives in Delhi, when I was maybe fourteen years old. They did not allow me to venture far beyond the family complex because of the 'bad elements' that roam the city during this festival, rowdies who use the freedom associated with the occasion as an excuse for mayhem. Jaipur was the site of my second Holi in India. I was in a 'semester abroad' programme and spent the day with the fifteen or so other Americans that were part of the project. We played with one another in a small courtyard in front of our hostel. Once again, access to the outside was forbidden due to the possibility of unruly crowds.

Then, a few weeks ago, I celebrated my third Holi in India, and the experience was one that surpassed all my expectations.

Though there were many events on, emotions around, and impressions of that hot March day that are memorable, one memory in particular stands out in my mind and represents a piece of what I wish to take back with me from this year in India.

It was still early in the Holi festivities, around 10 o'clock in the morning. We had played with the neighbours, spraying each other with coloured water across the fence that separated our lots. Some friends came over afterwards, and we had another round with them. By the time we made our way down the street, we were already splashed with a rainbow, various colour combinations running down our legs and dripping from our hair.

We travelled down the street in a pack, with two dholak-players leading the way, beating out an infectious rhythm. We stopped at a friend's store to ambush him and his family, but ended up being greeted by bucket after bucket of water. After this embarrassing encounter, we moved down the street in the direction of the slum area to play with the children. As we passed by the makeshift huts erected on the side of the road, it never occurred to me that the people living inside belonged to an entirely different world to the one I'd grown up in. For the most part, they were squatting illegally on government land, living in lean-tos or shabby brick houses with no (legal) light or toilet facilities. Most of them performed menial jobs as ragpickers, shoeshine boys and vegetable-vendors. Some lived hand to mouth, supporting a family of six or eight. The vast majority could not read or write their names.

As we marched through the area, following the sound of the dholak in front of us, I smiled at these individuals that I walked past every day on my way to the bus stand. My eyes caught those of a lady sitting on her woven cot, watching our little procession. She was dressed in a faded pink sari, which was in stark contrast to her ashen brown skin that hung in small folds across her body. She rose to her feet when our eyes met, and advanced to meet me.

Unsure of how to react, I stopped and waited while the procession in front of me went ahead. The woman raised her hands and began to dance. She moved her hips from side to side and swayed her arms above her head. Her deep laugh summoned me forward, and I began to imitate her movements. She motioned for the dholak player to return, and grabbed my hands. We began to dance and managed to communicate with each other and the music without once saying a word.

It could not have lasted more than two minutes, but that small experience captured the essence of what this country has to offer the world: a diversity of passion. For two minutes, two strangers from entirely different worlds united through a common urge to dance and celebrate something good and beautiful. For two minutes, parallel life forces converged to where nothing existed outside of the moment. For two minutes, I lived the bond that ties people of different classes, castes, religions, ethnicities and linguistic groups together. All you need is that moment to give you hope for India's future.

Sandhya Gupta

My Taste of India

I was born in the US, studied there till the fourth grade and knew it to be my home. One summer, when we were visiting my paternal grandparents in India, Dad suddenly announced that we would be staying on. To say that it was a shock for my brother and me is an understatement. The American way of life was the only one I knew and my friends were American too. But, Dad had made up his mind and 'stay on' we did.

I found everything here different and alien. Not to mention that I was treated as an outsider as well. Kids here found me as weird as I found them strange; they kept away and I didn't make an effort to fit in either. All the while I kept praying that this was a nightmare and I would soon wake up and find myself back in the familiar surroundings of the place that I knew as home—the US.

Language was definitely the biggest barrier. My peers spoke Hindi and Gujarati, while I barely knew the basics of the two languages. Kids here played games on paper, not board games like I was accustomed to. Hide-and-seek had a new name—'Thuppo'. Junk food wasn't the same, the movies they watched were in Hindi, even TV shows were in that language! And cartoons?! Whatever happened to *Rugrats* and *Hey Arnold*? Here it was all *Shin Chan* and *Power Rangers*. The game everyone talked about was cricket, which I knew nothing about. I had grown up playing baseball. Even the music they listened to was foreign to me. I liked some of the tunes, but I never understood the lyrics. I just couldn't relate to anything or anyone. And it all made me miserable.

I found books to be my only comfort in this strange country. I became an introvert and hardly spoke to anyone. Four years passed in this manner, and though I still did not care about the Indian lifestyle, I had more or less settled down, and my fervent prayers to go back to the US had stopped.

In the eight grade, I shifted schools and met my best friend Bianca. She was this spark of energy that just never died down. Slowly, but surely, she brought down my inhibitions, doubts and prejudices and introduced me to her way of living—the Indian way. Soon we became a bunch of five friends. Through them my entire world changed. I finally began to open up. I became garrulous and confident. Most importantly, the way I perceived things changed. Everything that till now had been 'different', became an adventure or a challenge.

My new gang introduced me to the famous dhabas, and food from Lari's filled with many different yet interesting spices. After initial protests, my stomach also adjusted and I finally shattered the myth that a single pani-puri would land me in the ICU section of the hospital. My friends took me shopping at Law Garden, where I haggled for the first time in my life. What a unique and fun experience! I made my acquaintance with Indian dance. To my mind Indian dance forms were just Bharatnatyam and Kathak, but I discovered funky forms and freestyle moves through Shiamak Davar and other dancers. I found a new passion for dance, thanks to this. I had only done ballet in New York before, and this was so different yet really great fun.

I saw tons and tons of Hindi movies. *Munnabhai MBBS*

made me realise that Hindi movies aren't all serious or about deception, and that they can be funny too, yet carry a message. I recently watched *Jodhaa Akbar*, and even though I didn't understand most of the language, I still understood the story, because of the action. I finally understood that language is a barrier only if I allow it to be. Thank you, Ashutosh Gowarikar, for making me realise this.

I also noticed this warmth and camaraderie whenever I visited my friends' places. Their aunts and uncles would join us for a quick chat, cousins would exchange their news, someone would cook us *thepla* . . . I just loved the feelings that bound the extended family together. I especially appreciated the fact that people here actually do have time for each other.

When I had first moved here, I was sheltered from the outside. I had no idea of the world around me, but my friends introduced me to it. I also introduced them to certain American traits as well. Kids in the US, on the whole, are more rebellious than their Indian counterparts. They argue for what they want. I think I might have inspired my friends to change a little in this regard, as they began to argue for what they felt was right. If they were told to first study and then later to take a nap, they would protest, saying that since they were tired now, they wanted to take a nap first, so that they could study more effectively later.

Tuitions were something I had never heard of, and when my friends told me they took them I was shocked. I told them if they simply paid attention in class, they wouldn't need all the extra help, and I think I might have changed them in that way as well. When I lived in America, we had to help out around the house a little, do simple chores like putting away board games away after we were done playing and things like that. I found that most Indian children aren't used to that as they have hired help around them all the time. Since I still help out at home, some of my friends have picked up on that.

RSVP-ing was another thing that my friends did not do with sincerity. There was always a 'maybe', never a definite 'yes' or 'no'. If I planned an event, I made my friends tell me if they were coming for sure or not. Now, they've all started doing the same.

I didn't have a large group of friends, but the ones I did have loved me for who I was, and I loved them. I opened up even more in the ninth grade, when I changed schools yet again, following the IGCSE system. Here, boys and girls mingled freely, without fear of judgement. It was a blast of fresh air, something about America that I had really missed. I explored new hobbies, discovering what best suited me. Everyone was so different and unique in their own way, and yet they all loved each other. That was such an interesting dynamic. I was more talkative in school. I quashed my doubts and raised my hand when confident about answers, willing to express my thoughts.

I don't always follow my friends around the way I used to, because I am no longer afraid that I will become an outcast if I don't conform. I am confident my friends will always be there for me, accepting me for who I am. I used to be afraid to show my true colours, to show my spontaneity, to make jokes that I was afraid no one would laugh at, but now I do, regardless of how people react, because that is me. The fear of becoming invisible has vanished. I am no longer compliant, and I am truly myself. I have found myself a comfortable place in the cultural jumble that is my world.

Anjali Ambani

Oporajito

It was a perfect spring day for our date in the park. We sat in the shade of the trees, my hand in her hand and her hand in mine. We were enveloped in each other's thoughts, and we were one. And then it came to us out of nowhere. It was supposed to be an ill omen, but it was the greatest talisman we could have.

The shalik landed gracefully on the fallen leaves and stood still for a while. And then it turned to face me and I was transfixed.

'Look, sweetheart,' I said in wonder. 'This is the most amazing bird I've seen . . .'

'Why do you say so?' she asked.

And I answered, 'Look at it carefully and you'll know.'

She took a close look and exclaimed, 'Shubho, it's got only one leg.'

'Yes . . . and yet it's standing strong.'

The bird turned and hopped. Remembering the one-legged games of childhood, I wondered if it would be able to maintain its balance.

But the bird was stronger and more stable than I expected it to be. It pecked the ground and lifted something with its beak. And then it leaped once again . . . and again . . . and again.

Not once did its solitary leg tremble; not once did it double-hop to regain its balance. It seemed as if the bird was the embodiment of the word perfection. It was a bird from heaven. It was a bird of light. It was a bird that cannot be beaten.

And I asked my love, 'I think we should name the bird. What do you suggest?'

And she answered, 'Oporajito.'

'Yes', I said, 'Oporajito is a perfect name for a perfect bird.'

The bird hopped around for a while, steadily going away from us, minding its own business in a way that suited it; and it minded its business more carefully and precisely than any other bird could have. Maybe its handicap had something to do with it. But what mattered in my young mind was that it showed me what can be achieved in life only if there is a will and an indomitable spirit.

The bird hopped and with each hop, it defined the divinity of creation. And then it spread its wings. And within the span of its wings it held the universe, for the universe was not without it.

As I stared in its wake, I felt more energy than I'd felt in all my young life. I looked at my hand. The bird was hardly any larger than my palm and yet it held more courage and determination than this six-foot-tall body of mine did.

I thought to myself, 'Goodbye, Oporajito, king of birds. No eagle can ever challenge you; no hawk shall ever defeat you . . . for you are the messenger of God. Show everyone the way. Teach them never to give up. Teach them the meaning of your name, The Unvanquished.'

This was the story of a bird named Oporajito. This could be the story of so many Oporajitos around us who don't let failures get them down.

Shubhabrata Dutta

Personal Style

If I have to tell you about my teenage years, all I can say is that I was a quiet boy, plain shy. I remember myself as a person content in his own world, reluctant to enter any other that contained too many people. I had no clue to what was happening with others around me and I had no sense of humour. It wouldn't be an exaggeration if I said I had no sense of anything.

I was the oldest of three brothers. My father worked as a hair stylist at the Oberoi in Delhi, the city in which I grew up. We would often accompany him to the hotel. We had a Rajdoot bike and would ride on it to the movies on Tuesdays, my father's day off. Those were the occasions we most looked forward to.

Otherwise, I remember being pretty much by myself, the kind of teenager people would call 'vague'. (I am a quiet person now too, but on the professional front, my dealings with people require me to be interactive.) The one thing I held dear even then was my self-confidence, although I'd never imagined I'd be famous. I guess it was all about being real, about having no pretentions, about never wanting to project a picture of my life that was not.

My school days were another battle. I wasn't the best student; I wasn't bright and would barely manage to pass my exams. Since my dad was working, and my mom did tailoring, I knew I had to find an interest I could work hard at. I started on cricket when I was about thirteen and played at the Madras Cricket Club. Hair-styling was still far from becoming my idea of a dream and a profession. Both my younger brothers went abroad to study but I never even planned to go. I considered hotel management but the plan fizzled out.

It was my final year at JNU, where I was pursuing my MA in French (only because I was told that learning the language would increase my chances of getting into a good hotel management institute manifold) that something decisive happened that brought a twist to my tale. My father got me admitted to Morris Master Class (London) for a nine-month course in hair-dressing. That would make me a regular master of style! I think that changed my life, my personality. I became expressive, even outspoken. Maybe the girls there spoilt me! I must admit, London made me more outgoing.

Today, I'm sure of myself. I am married and have grown-up children. I do believe that being true to myself has helped. Telling things as they are and believing in one's natural capacity normally doesn't fail you. My youthful conviction was a strong foundation, and that's going to stay.

Jawed Habib
(As told to Anurita Rathore)

So Very Young

Everyone's life is built on their experience of childhood. And there is always something that we credit our life's chart to. The one incident that changed me, or rather, made me what I am, is the time I decided to leave home at thirteen. Not many would take a decision like that at such a young age. That is the time when, normally, teenagers have a social circle of those they regularly meet up with. All I cared about—was addicted to—was music. I knew I wanted to be a vocalist. My father was a pandit, and early in my childhood, I took up singing. Come to think of it, I was all of three when my father began to train me in *shastriya sangeet*. When I was four I knew I'd have to work hard to achieve perfection. It was also then that we shifted from my town of birth, Meerut, to Delhi.

Time did not diminish my passion for music. When I grew older, I realised I would ideally have to stay away from family and isolate myself enough to truly understand music in depth. Everyone objected; my mother cried; my father said I'd bring disgrace upon us; but I left home all the same. I decided to earn while I educated myself. Living alone, I grew mature in my early teens.

It wasn't just music for me then. I studied, worked, did creative arts—I had to, I was supporting myself. I assisted a C.A., maintained his cheque books and helped in his paper work. He was a stock exchange broker as well. Imagine, I was only fourteen then, and I was writing notes for him! All this made me realise that life wasn't a bed of roses. At an age when children read comics, I was absorbing lessons in real life.

Today I have fans aged four to ninety. They don't just share my music but my thoughts too. However our lives may differ, our journey on earth is planned by God, and we pick up new knowledge all along the way. Every moment of the earth's revolution, we are changing from what we were at birth.

There used to be times I would get so scared I contemplated going back home. People in north India are aggressive. If I so much as looked at someone for more than a couple of seconds, I'd be asked rudely why I was staring. But the love of parents and their treatment of you, especially through those wonder teen years, determines what we grow up to be.

There were times I had misgivings, moments when I would question God as to why I'd been chosen for birth into a conservative family . . . a family which wasn't sure I would excel at what I had undertaken. It's sad that parents, even today, are happy when their children secure management and engineering degrees, but rarely encourage a child in the pursuit of art, dance or music.

I'm in my early thirties now, but people often take me to be older. Yes, I matured much faster than others because I experienced so much, so young. Destiny ordained that I learn young.

Kailash Kher
(As told to Anurita Rathore)

So, What's New?

Like a circle, life has a way of coming round. The same things that used to irk me, bother me or shame me about myself as a teenager are the things I'm downright grateful for today.

I hated the way my name was spelt. The name itself is common enough, but the spelling was, to a teenaged me, an oddity, difficult to explain to strangers, needing frequent repetition.

Today, working in a world where I'm only recognised by my name in print, it's an invaluable asset.

As a teenager, I hated my big hips. They made me run slower than everyone else in my class, ruined the effect of any outfit I wanted to wear—in fact, didn't allow me much choice of clothes at all—and made me an easy butt of jokes (pun intended).

Today, having birthed two healthy children through normal deliveries and carried them for years on these wide saddles, I look at my hips with respect. They may not look great, but they do their job well. Like many successful people I know. As a teen, I hated my hair. It was curly and either stuck out around my head like a frizzy halo, or fell all over my face, poking my eyes. *Totally* not with it.

Today, I can style my hair any way I want. I can colour,

curl or do absolutely nothing, and still not have to worry about hair health: I'm blessed with resilient locks, says the hairdresser.

As a teen, I hated myself for being soft and gooey and touchy-feely, the odd one out in my practical, unsentimental family. I cried during romantic movies and kept a pretty girly diary under my pillow, complete with heart-shaped stickers and motivational quotes pencilled in with love. I broke down when I was teased. I even wrote poems, for God's sake. How much more of a sissy could anyone be?

Today, my emotions are my strength. My poetry started me off on a highly fulfilling career; my journals give others inspiration; my sensitivity helps me reach out to others in pain; my sentimentality helps me *feel* life and not just live it. And my tears? They still pop out at the least excuse. But they cleanse me, heal me, release me when my jug fills over; moderate my reactions to the outside world and my inner battles. They are a direct line to and from my soul.

As a teenager, I used to hate my circumstances. We lived in Abu Dhabi then, after having spent almost a decade in Dubai when I was a child. I hated being a second-class resident of a foreign land. I hated my shortness in comparison to the strapping Caucasians and Arabs. I hated not having the fair skin of my Lebanese neighbours (white skin was too distant a fantasy) and the grace of my Pakistani friends. I hated being an Indian, was looked down on for being one. I couldn't wait to grow up and get blonde highlights and blue contact lenses.

Today, I've learnt—the hard way—to love my country and I've understood how cultures and races work. I've learnt to hold my head up high because I belong to a brainy, hardworking and progressive nation. I've learnt to appreciate the melanin in my skin because it protects me from cancer. My short stature does not bother me any more because my personality makes up for it. (I did try out the highlights and lenses for a while, though. It was fun. But eventually, I made peace with the default me.)

Frankly, as a teenager, I hated the person I was, the whole package. I thought I'd gotten a raw deal.

Today, I know I'm blessed. Simply because I've learnt to count my blessings.

So maybe that's how life is—you come back where you started from. You trace the same steps, meet the same people, do the same things, touch the same feelings. But you do it the other way around. And suddenly, there it is, the ring, the O, the halo. Complete, whole, plump and fulfilled. You've come full circle—you've accomplished what you were meant to. And there's not a single thing you'd change about it.

Aekta

There's Always a First Time

To take the first step
To learn the first word
To unlatch a cage
And free a lovebird

To scrape an elbow
To stumble and fall
To dream in deep slumber
To see a waterfall

To hide behind a tree
To watch a shooting star
To feed a hungry kitten
To lick clean a jelly jar

To discover the hidden ego
To nurse a broken heart
To try and climb with balance
First time on a cart

To fall in love
In hope of nothing to gain
There's always a first time
And then another again.

Sharmishtha Bhattacharjee

2

ON GROWING UP

'I am the highest Brahman . . . ever-shining, unborn, one alone, imperishable, stainless, all-pervading, and nondual—that am I, and I am forever released.'

—Adi Shankaracharya

Music to Help You Grow

There must be thousands of music-lovers all over India, each of whom thinks that he or she alone knows what a unique vocalist Begum Akhtar was. Her numerous admirers find a splendid articulation of their own unspoken angst in her singing. Such music redeems even as it spans the enormous distance between the wild joy of love and the inescapable loneliness of the human situation. With her perfect emission, her open vowels and her unique capability to articulate each phrase in its entirety without breaking the flow of the notes, Begum Akhtar remains an inspiration to all younger music lovers.

But strangely, in her context, one rarely hears the usual question applied to celebrities: what was Begum Akhtar nee Akhtari Bai Faizabadi really like?

When my siblings and I were in our teens in the '50s and early '60s, her stature as a major Indian singer was somewhat obscured by the then common bias against professional female singers. The all-male gallery of illustrious ustads and pandits alone was considered by the cognoscenti to be the authentic representatives of the various gharanas, and their pronouncements on the ragas were the accepted benchmark for all renderings of classical music.

Despite the fact that in their earliest days many of the

ustads were sheltered from abject penury by well-heeled professional singing women, to them a woman who came from a long line of professional singing women, was doubly removed from the highest rungs of our classical heritage: once as a woman and then again, as a member of a family of performing female artistes.

When news came that Akhtari Bai Faizabadi had married a barrister and chosen to leave singing and go in purdah as Begum Akhtar, there were many who sniggered openly.

Fortunately, Begum Akhtar chose to come back to the world of music before the self-imposed isolation destroyed her, or her marriage, or both. In the historical context, her marriage to Abbasi Saheb is quite understandable. When a talented and financially independent female artiste is made to feel insecure emotionally (which is often the case), she may begin to see herself as an aberration. So she usually looks to marry a man who, she thinks, has the gravitas she was being denied in a man's world. Thus a Meena Kumari married Kamal Amrohi, a Gauhar Jan married Seth Chandulal Shah and a Carla Bruni marries a Sarkozi. Of course, their considerable talents hardly ever stand to gain much from the association. It is mostly the male partner who gains fame (and also money) by association. But strangely, the women's brave refusal of stardom and fame draws less approbation than the men's decision to marry them.

And then, suddenly, one day, Begum Akhtar was gone. She died of a massive heart attack at an All-India Radio concert. I remember being told of her sudden death as I was dusting my mother's bookshelves. I still remember the moment and the titles of the books facing me with a stunned clarity usually reserved for a sudden death in the family, or the assassination of a world leader. It was certainly one of the most anguished moments in the already dramatic experience of adolescence.

Today, markets may grow and shrink or multiply, audiences are targeted through multimedia, but Begum Akhtar's music remains a perennial. Whether you play an old 78 RPM disc or download her music from the Web, you can taste the searing honesty and realism of her mind through her notes. And it still spans the entire gamut of human feelings that feed a female's awareness of her sexuality.

Begum Akhtar's wonderfully creative years happened to coincide with the years when India was waking up to the beauty of her own classical heritage and the rare creativity of many hitherto disempowered groups. For that reason, her music, like my late mother Shivani's writings (they were good friends) has a rare moral cutting edge and a communicability that transcends time and space. Both these talented women also exposed through their art the neediness, the terrible pull of physical desires and the terrible grief that comes with self-denial to Indian women. Perhaps that was why my mother—a lonely itinerant, loved her music so. And we young ones in turn loved her.

'Listen to her whenever you can,' she said to me, 'so one day you can tell your children you actually heard Begum Akhtar sing live'.

Mrinal Pande

All Grown Up

In 1998 I was about eighteen years old. I used to go for tuition in accounts in the evenings after college. I am an extrovert and never short of words at any time. So after class, when my friend Rishabh and I got talking about our futures, we didn't realise we'd been having a conversation for close to two hours on the main road. It was 9.30 at night.

My dad got worried and came looking for me. He saw us standing on the road engrossed in talk. My dad is really strict and my brother and I are terrified of incurring his wrath. So the minute I saw my dad, I was gripped by fear. I was mentally prepared for a showdown right in front of Rishabh. Instead, my dad smiled at me and said, 'Let's go home. It's really late.' I was relieved that he hadn't embarrassed me in front of a friend but suspected I was in for it once we got home.

To my pleasant surprise, all he did then was sit me down and say: 'Listen, I have no problems with your friendship with other boys and I have implicit trust in you. But, there is a time and place for everything. You can invite your friends home or you can visit them yourself all you want. I just don't want complete strangers seeing you talking to guys on the street and coming to the wrong conclusion. And, for your own safety, please make sure you don't stay out so late at night.'

I thought of what someone had rightly said: 'Treat people as if they were what they ought to be, and you'll help them to become what they are capable of being.' Perhaps Dad realised that he ought to get things off his chest without losing his cool, as he began to understand that I was at a sensitive age. It was heartening to hear him say that he had confidence in me. Under the circumstances, he could have drawn his own conclusions from the lateness of the hour and the company he saw me in, and disciplined me as he always did. I felt happy to hear him speak so calmly and explain his views to me, as if my feelings mattered. I felt he respected me and treated me like an adult that day. That is what every teenager secretly wants.

As a teenager, you are in the midst of developing your own individuality, and an ego in addition. At that point, if my dad had shouted at me, I would have been emotionally scarred for life with the memory of being humiliated in the presence of a fellow student, and it would have spoiled our already delicate relationship.

That day provided a revelation. It transformed my attitude towards my dad and I felt proud of the faith he placed in me. Since then I have made it a point to ensure that I do not breach the trust of my parents in any way. I always inform them of my whereabouts, the friends I'm meeting, and important decisions I plan to take. I even told my father about the occasion I bunked classes in college and went to a movie instead!

Janani Rajagopal

Fact & Fiction

I have always been a loner, lost in my own little utopia. And when one is growing up, that can pose quite a problem, though looking at things now, at twenty-three, those problems seem trivial.

Born to extremely protective parents and being a single child, my movements outside home were always restricted. To add to that my dad was on the move most of my life and Mom and I had to move with him. The result was obvious. I never really made friends because I was never really crowd-loving. To top it all off, I am not very easy to understand. It takes time to figure me out.

Close friends for me were fictitious characters. I went with the flow. Most of the time, I had nobody to talk to when I wanted, and the lack of siblings only added to my misery. I learnt to handle all my problems myself and gradually created a little world that was mine, peopled by creatures of my imagination. I narrated stories to myself, I wrote and I talked to myself. People felt I was abnormal. Slowly, I started thinking that too! Needless to say, in my world, I was the hero. I was the saviour. Maybe that was my way of combating the feeling of being an absolute loser. It was something akin to Calvin's alter ego. But it wasn't that pronounced.

Life wore on and at every stage I found myself distinctly

different from kids my age. I was lost in the maze of a serious identity crisis. Nothing in life seemed permanent except my own little world. Time and again I went back to it to seek solace. It became a part of me. Sometimes the pain and loneliness seemed unbearable. I was as clueless as I could be. Lost, unconfident and strange; three words summed me up quite well. It seems unbelievable now but I was on the extreme of being an introvert.

Then it happened. My writing brought me accolades. I won my first essay writing competition. It seemed too good to be true . . . not just to me but also to the people who knew me. If there was a major turning point in my life, it was that. People who didn't even know I existed started befriending me. It's strange how a little success can change a lot of things in life.

Today, I write for a living. Lots of things have happened in life. Nice and not so nice. But the thing that has stayed is the fact that writing helped me let things out. I have found my vent. And for those who're undergoing a similar problem in life . . . don't worry, you will find your vent very soon.

Soumyarka Gupta

How My Father Taught Me Non-Violence

I was sixteen years old and living with my parents at the institute my grandfather had founded eighteen miles outside of Durban, South Africa, in the middle of the sugar plantations. We were deep in the country and had no neighbours, so my two sisters and I would always look forward to going to town to visit friends or go to the movies.

One day, my father asked me to drive him to town for an all-day conference, and I jumped at the chance. Since I was going to town, my mother gave me a list of groceries she needed and, since I had all day in town, my father ask me to take care of several pending chores, such as getting the car serviced. When I dropped my father off that morning, he said, 'I will meet you here at 5 p.m., and we will go home together.'

After hurriedly completing my chores, I went straight to the nearest movie theatre. I got so engrossed in a John Wayne double-feature that I forgot the time. It was 5.30 before I remembered. By the time I ran to the garage and got the car and hurried to where my father was waiting for me, it was almost 6. He anxiously asked me, 'Why were you late?' I was so ashamed of telling him I was watching a John Wayne Western movie that I said, 'The car wasn't ready, so I had to wait,' not realising that he had already called the garage. When he caught me in the lie, he said: 'There's something wrong in the way I brought you up that didn't give you the confidence to tell me the truth. In order to figure out where I went wrong with you, I'm going to walk home eighteen miles and think about it.'

So, dressed in his suit and dress shoes, he began to walk home in the dark on mostly unpaved, unlit roads. I couldn't leave him, so for five-and-a-half hours I drove behind him, watching my father go through this agony for a stupid lie that I uttered.

I decided then and there that I was never going to lie again. I often think about that episode and wonder, if he had punished me the way we punish our children, whether I would have learned a lesson at all. I don't think so. I would have suffered the punishment and gone on doing the same thing. But this single non-violent action was so powerful that it is still as if it happened yesterday. That is the power of non-violence.

Arun Gandhi

In a Lighter Vein

I was probably ten when I first vented the full fury of my temper. I had been ticked off by my mother for not eating my vegetables—or something equally trivial—when I went temporarily berserk. I think the tantrum resulted in a few broken knick-knacks and my mother at her absolute wits' end deciding on a suitable punishment for me. I can't for the life of me fathom how someone so tiny (I've always been on the smaller side) could have so much pent-up anger.

I think this first outburst was what got the ball rolling. By the time I was in my teens the situation had gone from bad to worse. The provocation would be infinitesimal but the outcome, colossal. I would treat the smallest jibe, the silliest joke, even the most innocuous comment as a vengeful attack. The person most often at the receiving end of my anger would be my sister. Being a little over five years older than me, her sense of humour had the edge of maturity to it, which I, often unable to take in the right vein, would mistake for sarcasm. Even now, so many years later, I can't bring myself to understand why I suffered from such low self-confidence; why the silliest thing would have me up in arms.

By the time I finished school I had successfully created a humourless image for myself, though, sadly, I remained good at cracking jokes against others. It was around this time that my sister moved to the US. With her away, I was quite lost. There was no one to poke fun at me, no one to get mad at. My parents were already used to my sulks, so there was no point in provoking either of them into a yelling duel. I remember coming back from classes sometimes and asking myself why I had wasted so much time fighting with my sister. I remember missing her immensely.

I guess this was when I taught myself to sit back and relax. Not to get wound up by what people said, laugh at myself once in a while and just be more fun around others. I think my family noticed the change in my outlook sooner than I did. Family dinners became more fun without me refusing to eat because someone had maybe laughed at how I held my fork. My friends and cousins found it easy to have fun at my expense without the threat of losing contact with me for the rest of our lives.

When my sister moved back to India a year and a half later it was under strained circumstances. She had been through a personal upheaval and had changed quite a bit. While she'd been away I had resigned myself to the fact that things would never be the same, so when she returned I was actually overjoyed, even though she was going through a horrid time. But it was then that I decided to change my take on life. To have fun in the moment, to forget about ruing and cribbing, and to appreciate everything I had.

It's not like I don't have arguments anymore or that I don't sulk every now and then. I still do. But the instances are few and far between and their intensity has abated. I think I'm a much better person today simply because I've learnt to see the humour when someone has a go at me.

Ayesha Sindhu

It's My Happy Heart You Hear

Even as a baby, I was hyperactive. Elders tell me I was restless, inquisitive and more than two handsful! I would boldly explore all forbidden nooks and crannies, treat appliances as edibles (while protesting vehemently in refusal of good food!), jump on couches, and just run amok in general. I was, on the whole, mischievous. But whenever a song or a jingle played somewhere, I would leave my mischief for the moment and listen in rapt wonder.

Boyhood saw me as a typical 'rough and tough' boy, who loved crashing Hot-wheels, deploying all my G.I. Joes into fierce, raging battles, and having mock fights with soft toys. Even in school, all my games and past-times involved action and fighting. Though focus and concentration were problem areas, I was a good student. But I detested and despised the music and dance class. I thought that music was for fops, and for people who could do nothing more productive with their time. I disliked the music teacher and would never be able to sing to her satisfaction. Mainly because my voice, at that time, was always hoarse and croaky, due to my excessive shouting while playing games. I liked dancing though, simply because I could kick other boys, step on their toes and then pretend it was a mistake.

My parents, in their efforts to help me become a 'complete

individual', made sure that my evenings were devoted to various coaching classes—one of which was classical music. Being active was fine with me, but sitting down to learn classical music made me squirm. Learning the harmonium and the 'saptak' began to feel 'uncool'. Taking a cue from naughty children in books and movies who drove away tutor after tutor, I would find novel excuses to end the services of many a dedicated teacher. Some were allowed to stick around if they could be bullied into not expecting me to learn, and allow me to play the fool. Thus, I ended up wasting a lot of time and my parents' money, pretending to learn music, but actually gaining nothing.

At the threshold of teenage, I moved from the cocooned atmosphere at home to the enticing environs of a residential school. I say enticing, because I was thrilled at the prospect of living amongst friends and peers, where no one would govern my life and tell me what to do, and I could choose my own spare-time activities, sports, etc.

Thus, in my new school too, I disregarded all creative activities, especially music. I studiously avoided the intimidating head of music, fearing disgrace. I decided to engage myself in physical activities and sports. But I soon learnt that while I was celebrated for game skills amongst lesser peers back home, the boarding school was teeming with better players and athletes. It took me less than the first term to realise that I would never be able to make the mark, even less leave my mark, in the field of sports.

It was when I was going through a period of dejection, and harbouring doubts about my ability to ever accomplish anything of consequence, that our school started auditions and practising sessions for the annual 'Founder's Day' celebrations. Ever hopeful, I tried to land myself a role in the play which was to be enacted in front of guests and parents. But of course, with seasoned seniors around, I was just reduced to a spot boy. Then, I decided to finally shed all my prejudices and fears, and to give an audition for the choir in music production. To my utmost delight, I was short-listed!

Sometime during choir practice, a realisation dawned on me and caught me by some surprise. First, I discovered that the head of music was actually a genial genius. Secondly, he thought I had potential and talent, and best of all, I was really enjoying singing! These thoughts kept me buoyant for quite some time and opened for me an avenue where I could dream to excel and redeem myself in my opinion. Well, the final day dawned, and I proudly presented the music catalogue and choir credits to my parents. My name was in print! Well, *somewhere* in the sea of print, but it was there for all to see!

After that, I knew that music was one field in which I could leave my mark. I took it up as my spare-time activity, and chose it as my craft as well. I represented my house in the inter-house music competition, and my school in the Founder's Day productions and concerts in Delhi and Dubai. I was actually getting opportunities to sing solo, and people complimented me on my voice and vocal ability. I couldn't believe that! I was really enjoying my life in school now.

Even though my interest in and respect for the field arose as a result of the respect I got from it, somehow that didn't seem like the only reason for my extreme pleasure. I realised that music struck a chord inside of me, and that it had always been playing deep down there. I would probably have understood that earlier, had I not denied and suppressed my inclinations, thinking it was 'uncool'. So it came to be that, because I 'allowed' myself to enjoy classical vocal music, I became much better at performing it.

The confidence and success I got from singing, now started reflecting in my other endeavours as well. I was popular, therefore happier; happier, therefore more patient, and because I had inner satisfaction, I could focus better on other things too. This focus has made me better at academics and enabled me to make my mark in other creative fields such as writing, public speaking, acting, etc. I feel I can study better with music playing, and I have grades to prove my point. My concentration has increased. All the restlessness, which was in my being since birth, has turned to peace. I have a heightened sense of humour and a supreme sense of well-being. It's as if I am in tune with myself and the world around me is in harmonious sync.

You should never close your mind to an idea. Keep your options open and you *will* go beyond your horizons. All you need to do is 'allow' yourself to soar. Now, whether it is math or art, I always allow myself the thought: 'It's a wonderful experience, I like it, and I am going to be really good at it.'

Yashvardhan Jain

Not This, That. Not That, This

'What do you mean, you wish you were older? There's nothing great about being old.'

'I didn't say old, I said older.'

'How old are you anyway?'

'I'm fifteen.'

'Wow. I'd give anything to be fifteen.'

'How old are you?'

'You never ask someone their age.'

'You just did.'

'Well, I'm older than you.'

'So?'

'So, it's not impolite if I ask you.'

'Says who?'

'Says me.'

'All you grown-ups say the same thing.'

'How old do you think I am?'

'You look thirty.'

'You guessed right.'

'You're just saying that.'

'Why do teenagers always a have problem with everything? If I didn't tell you my age, you'd have a problem. When I say you've guessed right, you still have a problem.'

'See, that's the problem with adults. They think we have a

problem with everything. We just want reasonable explanations, that's all.'

'When you want them, you should have some of your own too.'

'What?'

'Explanations.'

'Why should I have to explain myself to *anybody*?'

'How can *you* expect an explanation from anyone?'

'I am entitled to one.'

'That's what you think.'

'That's what you think I think. I think you think wrong.'

'I think you think too much of yourself.'

'I so do not. I just happen to know I'm right.'

The train they were on sped on through the evening landscape as the sun spilt gold outside the window.

'So, what's your problem?'

'I wish I could just snap my fingers and find myself instantly older.'

'I wish the same. Just snap my fingers and be fifteen again. But why do you want to be older?'

'I want to be free. I want to live alone.'

'Why would you want to do that to yourself?'

'You're saying that because you get to stay alone. What can possibly be wrong with staying alone? Come home when you want, do what you want, dress how you want, watch what you want.'

'No tea when you wake up, no dinner waiting when you come home hungry. Add cooking to that list, will you? Not to mention washing clothes. And the occasional utensils too. And yes, remembering to pay bills, buying grocery, buying household essentials, cleaning toilets. If you want a maid to do all those things, you have to pay her.'

'You have to do all that?'

'Of course. You have a mom to do all that for you. You're lucky.'

'I hate my mom.'

'Really?'

'No, I mean, I love her, but you know, I hate her. She keeps telling me I can't do or have most things because I'm too young. I should wait till I get older.'

'It's better than having a girlfriend telling you things. Remember, even as a man, there's always someone who's going to be telling you dos and don'ts. What sort of things did your mother forbid you from doing, by the way?'

'Having a girlfriend, first and foremost.'

'Oh, you can have mine. I'd love to be single again, happiest with my cricket bat or video game.'

'She says I'm too young to do stuff too.'

'If the stuff that pumps your blood to predictable destinations is what you're referring to, that lasts for a few minutes, boy. The rest is a punishment. You have to wait for her, pick her up, wait for her while she shops, listen to her, be sweet, compassionate, thoughtful, buy her gifts, treat her, compliment her, praise her—and drop her back.'

'Why do you have to treat her? I thought both people paid.'

'Most feminists disappear when the cheque comes.'

'Okay, forget girlfriends. I'd get a cell phone.'

'Man, I'd give anything to be without one again. You can't meet anyone without at least eight missed calls to interrupt you, you can't catch a nap at home, you're always traceable, you are always in touch, you have no privacy, you have people harassing you constantly with offers, you have silly 'forwards' disturbing you. It never ends, man.'

'Well, I'd get to drink.'

'Hmmm ... that's great, if you like headaches and hangovers. Or blabbering things. Or having a numb nervous system. Or having your face feel like sandpaper. Or not remembering anything the next day.'

'I'd get to work, you know. Have my own money, buy my own stuff.'

'I'd love to be carefree again, man. No boss. No deadline. No uniform. No expectations. No obligations. No fake relations. No meetings. No travelling. No traffic. No presentations. No tensions. Summer vacations. Diwali vacations. Christmas vacations. Why do you want to spend your money if you can spend somebody else's? Parents' money is the best thing in the world. I'd spend that over mine, any day. No guilt, no second thoughts, no budgeting, no being broke. Self-earned money is over-rated. And it's always too little.'

'I'd love not to go to college, being asked to study and being compared to my sister.'

'College is better than office or work! You have proxy. You can bunk. You don't have a to-do list. Your day is a series of coincidences, not chores. You can loaf around. You're not compared to an idiot just because she has better assets. You're not being compared *by* an idiot just because he has more grey hair.'

'I'd love to travel. Adults get to travel. And have no deadlines, either.'

'You surely must love to check in hours before the flight and sit twiddling your thumbs, or fight with and over-pay auto and cab drivers, eat bad airline and railway food, adjust to different climates or time zones, pay for water, sleep in a new bed every night, live out of a suitcase, eh?'

The train had come to a halt. It was the last stop. The thirty-year-old was stretching his limbs while the fifteen-year-old watched.

'You know, you're probably right. Being an adult is not such a great thing.'

'It isn't. You get introduced to your knees.'

'I can see that. And your back too.'

'Yes. The grass is always greener on the other side. But it's just as hard to cut.'

They parted ways.

And that's how it passed. 'It' being teenage. Passed wishing for everything else, little realising, all you'd ever want the rest of your life was yours then.

Teenage. It's what happens to you when you're busy wishing for other things.

Omkar Sane

The Boy Who Taught Me

The night had gone to sleep. There was tranquil silence all around. As I sat near the window of my tiny living room, turning the dog-eared pages of a book I had read countless times before, I heard a sound from my bedroom. What was Nitin, my fourteen-year-old domestic help, doing at two in the night when he was supposed to leave for school merely four hours later? I left my antiquated wooden chair, stood up uneasily, and sauntered towards the room.

Inside the room, the table lamp emanated a gentle glow, its light being as much—or as little—as that of a candle during a power cut. The fan was rotating lazily, and Nitin stared at it from time to time while holding the English language textbook in his two rather tiny hands. An English-Marathi dictionary was placed on his lap, and he seemed to be making an effort to construct a sentence in English independently.

So immersed in his objective was he that he didn't see me standing about three feet away. 'I wanted to, no, no, I want to . . .' he mumbled while scribbling a few words with his cheap ink pen. Having studied in the Marathi medium in his village at Latur, the town in Maharashtra that made major news when it was devastated by an earthquake, Nitin's English was very poor when he first came to Pune, where I stayed. Within a few months, however, he could write simple English pretty well. The lad's hard work had yielded results and, what's more, he wasn't satisfied with what he had learnt. 'I need to know a lot more,' he used to acknowledge in clumsy English, his lips spread in a happy grin.

Time flew. Nitin finished his schooling and moved on to college where, at eighteen, he took up political science so that he could become a lawyer. Enamoured by the conviction that working hard would make him a distinct somebody and allow him to help his poor family, his sincerity at studies made me acutely recall my own inability to concentrate when I was his age.

Not only had he developed a passion for Hollywood films, he also used to sit and analyse the story with me once a film ended. He loved the Hugh Grant-Julia Roberts starrer *Notting Hill*, and once told me that the romance between the characters of Grant and Roberts was 'very realistic, although that doesn't seem to be the case'. I remember smiling at him without saying a word. I thought I understood the contradiction really well.

It was only a few days later that I came home and saw him sitting quietly, reading a Marathi newspaper, while his luggage lay nearby.

'Is anything wrong at home, Nitin? Why have you packed your bags? Do you need to go urgently?' I rattled off the three questions at one go while reaching for my wallet.

'I want to go home,' he replied. 'Can you give me money? I will send it back to you once I reach my village.'

'Why do you want to send it? You can give it to me when you come back. Anything seriously wrong?' Once again, I spoke rapidly. Something was seriously wrong indeed, and I needed to know what it was as soon as possible.

'I won't return from my village,' he said in a tone that was both soft and determined. 'I want to teach English to young boys so that they won't have problems getting admission to English medium primary schools in the city.'

'But what of your degree, your ambition to become a lawyer?' That I had been taken aback revealed itself in the way I spoke.

'Nothing really,' he said. 'I will finish my college from Latur and get a job. But I will help many youngsters do well in life. That matters a lot more.'

I said nothing, and just smiled. Slowly, I opened my wallet, took out a few hundred-rupee notes, and handed over the money to him. Nitin looked at me, took the money, murmured a 'thank you', and touched my feet. Then he picked up his bags, walked towards the door, and left my house, the weight of his luggage a heavy burden he seemed happy to bear.

That was the last time I met him. But, somewhere in his village, I am sure he is teaching children how to write correct English which he, as a five-year-old, never could. How I wish I had learnt a lesson in selflessness while he lived in my house for a few years. But then, I had never understood little Nitin at all.

Biswadeep Ghosh

The Year I Turned Macho

It was my mother's idea. Marching me off on my fifteenth birthday to a local supermarket to seek part-time work. Although I didn't realise it at the time, this had probably been as hard for her as it was unwelcome to me.

'He's a withdrawn little lad, isn't he?' her friends had long observed. My tough uncles, hard-bitten highlanders to a man, would dismiss me less generously as 'a wee English pansy'.

'He's delicate,' my mother would insist, ensuring that my weak chest was well wrapped whenever I ventured out, and that I was routinely excused rough games at school. I suppose now, looking back, I was pretty wet. I liked solitary hobbies: model-making, drawing, listening to music. I found the world outside my bedroom rough, depressingly masculine and unsympathetic. School certainly confirmed this suspicion. My contemporaries there were burly, brawling and sporty. Everything I envied and despised in equal measure.

'It'll make a man of you,' my mother assured me as she left me at the door of the supermarket.

'Great,' I mumbled, glumly. 'Happy birthday, me.'

*

And it certainly was a macho environment. Whilst most of the staff were female, all the managers were male, and every job that had any claim to professional knowledge—butchery, accounts, delicatessen—were the preserve of men, all of whom seemed to me horribly confident in their masculinity, preening themselves, speaking in deep voices and strutting about before the studiously unimpressed check-out operators and shelf-fillers. These were real men, who arrived at work on motorbikes, dressed in faded denim and leather; who drank and smoked, and shook their heads in pity and disbelief at the bright yellow cardigan my Mum had knitted me specially for my new job.

Backdoor Man. That was my job. To receive deliveries, unload lorries, crush up used boxes, watch over the bins and large hoppers of rubbish, and guard the rear entrance to the store. The manager had warned me on the first day to expect to be challenged in my new role. It happened almost immediately. The area director, a tall, angry man with a south London accent, came striding up to the large sliding door and rang the bell. 'Let me in,' he demanded through the little window that allowed me to check callers when the door was locked. 'Now, sonny.'

'I'm sorry, sir,' I shouted back. 'I'm afraid I can't.'

'Don't call me sir,' he snarled. 'I'm not a bleedin' teacher an' you're not a schoolboy. Now open the @£$*& door.'

'I'm sorry . . .'

And so it went on for what seemed like an age. He got ever more angry, I got ever more scared. Then, just when it seemed like he would kick the door in and tear me limb from limb, he stopped, nodded and said, 'Well done, lad. Keep up the good work. Now let me through.'

Now, wet I may have been, but stupid I was not. I shook my head. I was starting to enjoy this.

'Look,' he sighed, exasperated. 'It's over. You passed the test. I'm not walking all the way round to the front. Now open the door or I'll fire you.'

I didn't. He did. My mother was bemused, horrified and impressed in equal measure. The manager, who hated the area director with a passion, found the whole thing quite amusing and I was quietly reinstated a week later.

*

Among the various deliveries and collections I had to handle, by far the most unpleasant was the bone lorry. A malodorous old vehicle that reeked of decay which, once a fortnight, picked up the offcuts and general detritus from the butchery. Its driver was a surly, forbidding character who seemed to hate the world. One day, in the midst of a heavy storm, I watched him struggle to haul sacks of bone and fat up onto the lorry, drenched and alone, so I went out and, in silence, helped.

From that day on, he took to arriving around midday, and inviting me to share his lunch. He had recently come out of prison. Had a lot of money stashed away, he said, but was keeping his head down, working at the poorest paid job he could find for six months to ensure his recently divorced wife was not entitled to any alimony. He regaled me with ghastly tales of life behind bars and the brutal fights in pubs which had put him there, proudly showing me various knife and broken-bottle scars he'd sustained, and generally scared the living daylights out of me. Once, as we sat in the sun outside the back door, him talking and me eating my sandwich in nervous silence, the assistant manager looked out and shouted cheerily, 'McCallum, you lazy little git. What do you think this is? A holiday camp? Get back to work.'

My new friend was up and at him in a flash. Eyes blazing, he lifted him clean off his feet with just one hand around his throat. 'Never, *ever*, speak to him like that again, or I'll kill you,' he snarled, his face an inch from that of his terrified victim.

'He's mad,' gasped the assistant manager.

'Yeah,' said the Bone Man with a horrible grin. 'And don't you ever forget it.'

The assistant manager and I watched the Bone Man depart in silence. 'You're fired,' he croaked, as the battered old truck pulled out of the yard.

*

It was around the time of my second reinstatement, which coincided, no doubt coincidentally, with the date when the Bone Man was next due to call, when I first spotted the old man in the flat cap. He was pencil-thin, his bony chin dusted with white stubble, and he rode an ancient bicycle with a beautifully made wooden box secured behind the saddle. Slowly, with movements careful and delicate, he dismounted, propped the bike against the backdoor and began to rummage through the dustbins, drawing out discarded foodstuff.

'That's all rotten,' I called out to him. 'Bad. Gone off.'

He looked up, grinned toothlessly, and waved some wilted greenery at me. 'For my sheekeen. For my Wobbits,' he replied in a heavy Polish accent. 'Good.'

I told him that he shouldn't go through the bins, but he took no notice. Every time he came I told him the same thing. He just ignored me, promising that for Christmas he would give the manager a chicken in appreciation. I told the manager about it. He shrugged. 'He's not doing any harm,' he said. 'Forget it.'

December. The store was brightly decorated for the festive season and heaving with frenzied customers. Deliveries were twice, then three times their usual level and we were still running short. Amid this mayhem, the old man in the flat cap knocked at the door. 'I have manager's sheekeen,' he beamed, beckoning me out. Proudly, he opened the wooden box on his bike, and there, sure enough, was a chicken. Fullyfeathered, beady-eyed and very much alive. Nervously, I carried it in through the back door and settled it into an empty cardboard box. I found some packing material to make it more comfortable, and went off to find the manager.

He rubbed his hands together, highly pleased, when I told him I had the promised chicken for him. 'Fresh?' he asked enthusiastically.

'Oh, it's certainly fresh,' I assured him.

'Bloody hell!' he cried when he opened the box. He closed the lid down quickly. 'You'd better . . . you know . . .'

'What?' I asked with a sinking feeling.

'You know, wring its neck.'

I went pale, and shook my head.

'It's part of a backdoor man's duties,' he said.

'I don't think so,' I replied.

'Well, I do. And if that . . . thing isn't dead and ready for me to take home tonight, you're . . .'

'I know,' I sighed. 'Fired.'

*

There was no way I was going to do the deed. But where was the problem? Here I was in one of the most macho environments, surrounded by tough guys who wouldn't think twice before dispatching the poor creature. I first tried the greengrocery manager. A true countryman, wise in the ways of the land and a rich source of folklore and rural wisdom.

'Ever killed a chicken?' I asked him, innocently.

He chuckled at the naivety of the question. 'I had a small holding. Poultry, pigs, a few sheep. A cow. What do you think? Second nature to me, son.'

'Could you do this one for me?' I asked, opening the box.

He paled visibly. 'Well,' he began, 'normally yes, but . . . I've twisted my wrist. Sprained it. Yes, just yesterday. Otherwise, no problem. Sorry.'

The butchery. Why hadn't I thought to go there first? The head butcher, a wizened ex-soldier with a fearsome temper and an individualistic approach to first aid—any apprentice who accidentally cut himself, as often happened, wasn't sent to hospital for stitches. Oh, no. Bloody sawdust off the butchery floor, pressed onto the wound and tied tightly with a greasy lambscloth. There was a real man. He'd do the job.

'Ever wrung a neck?'

'Ha!' he roared. 'When I used to be dropped behind enemy lines I'd wring a sentry's neck, just like that . . .' His strong hands made ghastly movements before my face. 'They'd drop with hardly a sound. Just that death rattle in their throats . . .'

'Could you do that to this chicken?'

'Blimey,' he murmured, recoiling from the poor creature I offered up to him.

'Health and safety.' He said suddenly. 'More than my job's worth, killing that here. Not licensed for slaughter, see? They'd shut this place down soon as look at you if they ever found out . . .'

And so it went on. Every one of these hard men quailed at the prospect. I sat with my new friend (I'd secretly named him Charlie) on my lap at the back door and contemplated another dismissal when the bone lorry clattered into the yard.

I told my terrifying friend about my problem. He shook his head in wonder, not at my inadequacy, for by helping him that one wet day, I'd become one of his people, and as such could do no wrong. No, his scorn fell on my colleagues and their feeble masculinity. He swept Charlie up in his scarred and tattooed arms, assured me he'd do nicely on his table on Christmas day, wished me a happy Christmas and went on his way. The manager was relieved to see the back of both chicken and Bone Man and I kept my job.

Early in January, the Bone Man was back. 'How was the chicken?' I asked him.

He looked strangely uncomfortable. 'Kept him,' he grunted, avoiding my eye.

'I thought you said you lived in a flat,' I couldn't help observing.

'Yeah, well, I'm out all day. He's company for the goldfish.'

I learnt a lot about being a man that year.

Dawood Ali McCallum

Your Own Jigsaw Puzzle

Jia was the storybook rich princess, already sexy at fourteen. In Class IX, I was squint-eyed and, invariably, a hideous pimple would sprout on the tip of my large nose exactly when there was the chance of running into that class XI boy I had a crush on. I was good at studies, a favourite with the teachers and had a loyal set of friends, but at that time, all that paled before Jia's stirring performances in school plays, her pert singing voice and chipper dancing skills. She was desirable and seductive. Every boy in school was crazy about her. Even though I have changed her name here, everyone from those years at school will know who I'm talking about.

We wouldn't have become friends had she not failed her class VIII exams. I had never known anyone so poor at studies that they would have to stay in the same class for another whole year! I was snooty and scoffing. But there she was, silky hip-length hair tied in snaking plaits, diamond nose-pin shining and a smile that made you feel she was happy to be with you. I had two other close—*tight!*—friends, and somehow Jia pirouetted her way into our closed circle, bringing a cheeky lightheadedness to our pursuits—jiggling earrings, lipstick shades in red, pointy high heels, and sassy yellow pants with the polka-dotted panties showing up above. She nicknamed me 'Squinty', much to the disgust of my two pals, but Jia thought it was cute and intimate and loving.

We started gang-girling—hanging out, copying her lipstick application and slick dance steps clumsily in front of the enormous dressing table in her room with the wall-to-wall red carpeting and a burgundy velvet bedspread. It was a sprawling house and she even had her own dressing room. Her bathroom window looked out on to the bathroom of the adjacent house and she was in love with the boy there—a young man really. Because both sets of parents would have had objections if they knew, the boy and she had a signal system. He would put out his shaving kit when he was home and she would place the loo money plant on the sill; then they would be sure the other would pick up the phone when either called. It was so romantic.

My life, on the other hand, was tortured. In a joint family, we kids slept on divans in the living room. My mom was a lovely but suffering woman, her bright, laughing warmth shining forth despite the hard time my father gave her. My brothers and I would skulk around when he was home, hoping no fracas would explode that day, shrinking ourselves to keep out of the way. We never went on a single holiday or anywhere, to movies or shops or out to eat. I never knew any 'happy family' time, that lighthearted, loving banter between parents and kids, of the kind I saw my friends experiencing. We knew he was wrong but we were too ashamed to tell anyone and too scared to do anything. I lost myself in books, in lives that seemed magical and worth chasing, and others so tragic they made mine seem more fortunate. In an extreme way, I identified with Anne Frank and dreamed of the book I would write, like her, before I, unlike her, wilfully died.

Jia had a car and a driver to herself when only a few of us even had a family car. She was out a lot, buying cosmetics and costume jewellery at posh shops, getting her hair trimmed by micro-inches and meeting her boyfriend for secret trysts.

She was the lead in all the school plays and even choreographed a few of the dance sequences; when she sang a full-throated song on the school stage, even the most truculent boy fell quiet and listened. Her family was big and bustling, with many brothers, their wives and kids. Her life seemed a dream compared with mine.

Or so it appeared.

Slowly, the curtains parted.

In Class X we had our board exams and got re-admitted into the next class. Jia said her father didn't think she should continue studying. We were horrified. Her father was an orthodox businessman. I had never met him, strangely enough, but his brooding shadowy presence darkened evenings at her house and was even more frightening than the open heartlessness of mine. He thought girls should get married and tend the hearth. When we went to persuade him to let her come to school, he looked the other way, pursed his lips and merely nodded—or shook his head, I can't remember because I was so tense. We spoke to her mother and then in a few days, Jia said it was all right.

Meanwhile, she and I had gotten closer—she lived only a ten-minute drive away—and, following me, she had started reading a lot. I'd tell her to not be a bimbette all the time, and study: Only a moron could fail a state exam in a country where half the schools didn't even have proper teachers. Finally, she did, ending up with a first division in the board exams two years later—the first girl in her clan to get that, she said. It was clear to everyone that the right place for her would have been to go to drama school—we even heard a rumour that the top school in the country was ready to give her admission without the usual procedure. But she joined a home science course where they taught cooking, nutrition, grooming, designing clothes and stuff like that—the so-called essentials to becoming a good housewife. Her father had come to know about her love affair and threatened to kill himself if she followed her heart. A few months later she was married off to a rich man abroad.

It was all like in the movies. Scripted, directed, canned, screened—with no space to follow a giddy choice or change the plot. Perhaps, like in many movies, she has had a happy ending, if only because she had the gift of dancing to any kind of music life played.

Back then, in Class IX, I would have swapped my life with hers any day. Somewhere on the way, I realised that whatever I had, it was a better deal. It was an incomplete jigsaw and the pieces that I had often seemed to suggest an unfair game, but the challenge they posed forced a hesitant courage in me to juggle them around and build the picture I wanted.

My knees have trembled from fear and hurt, I have made mistakes, I have wept and screamed silently, I've wanted to kill myself or someone else, but that picture—a simple joyful water colour—has always stayed on my mind's wall. At different times and from different angles, its images change and its pigments are a swirl, but it always says the same thing: Life is about being happy, and sharing and giving happiness. It's about locking hurt away in a box and leaving it to self-combust. It's about stretching the skin tight over wounds. It's about shining in the night like a star, so people point to you—and make a wish.

Cheat the jigsaw. Be creative with its missing pieces. Chase happiness like your life depends on it. The colours and shapes of your future are in your head and no one can snatch them away from you.

Vatsala Kaul Banerjee

Your Smile in New York

I felt the chill of the wind on my cheeks, and pulled my jacket snugly around my neck. My eyes zigzagged over the heads of the crowd, hoping to find the face of the person I was waiting for. As I stood there on the corner of New York's busiest street, I reached into my pocket and pulled out a worn piece of paper. I opened it and double-checked my scribble: 'Broadway and W.35th Street.'

The wind whistled mischievously as it sucked up small plastic bags and newspapers from the kerb and carried them through the air. I stood and observed a little boy holding tightly on to his mother's hand. He gazed upwards with curious eyes at the objects in flight. Before he saw where they were headed, he felt the yank of his mother's hand and dutifully followed her.

It had been thirty minutes already and Vicky was nowhere to be found. But what if I had misheard him on the phone? What if he had actually said 34th street, or even 33rd, or 32nd? Here I was, waiting on the corner of Broadway, in the cold, observing people as they passed me in a rush, and I wasn't even sure of where I was supposed to be.

It was moments like this that brought my insecurities to a head, making me wonder how I was ever going to make it. Little things like not understanding someone properly and making quick assumptions, only to discover later how wrong I had been, made me feel so incompetent.

I had been born with a severe hearing-impairment, the first in my family. My parents had held me close to them, breathing hard in shock, as the doctor told them the news. After three years of saying one-syllable words, staring blankly into their faces as they talked to me, and not answering when they'd call for me, it was finally understood. Mummy and Papa tried their best to provide me with the most normal life I could have; they also tried to shield me from noticing that I was different.

As I grew older, I noticed.

Differences began surfacing between my siblings and me. I wondered why I could never hear the waves crash against the rocks on the beach while my sisters would jump and squeal with excitement. Their faces would brighten as they listened, their eyes focussed. Phone calls used to come regularly for them, but I realised that none came for me. I would question them incessantly on why I was the only one who had to wear a hearing-aid. I thought it was normal to make up nonsense lyrics to sing to any song I heard, but when my brother sang along, it was somehow different, exactly in tune.

As I leaned against the streetlight pole on Broadway, all the frustrations I'd felt during my teens, the days I lived and breathed self-consciousness, came flooding back. The hot, sticky, sunny days in school, when I would enviously watch my friends flick their ponytails while I left my long hair down—to conceal my hearing-aid. Wallowing in self-pity as I sat alone in my room during get-togethers my siblings would throw. I didn't like how I couldn't follow conversations in big groups of people so I preferred to stay away. Even with close friends, there were always moments of fast-paced repartees and humour that I couldn't participate in.

Nevertheless, I never failed to laugh along, masking the uncertainty I felt inside.

I sighed as I glanced up from my sneakers, wondering where Vicky could possibly be. I shifted my weight to the other side and watched as people gathered on the corner, waiting to cross the street. As the 'WALK' sign flashed green, women in business suits and men in jeans and T-shirts, with construction hats on, began to cross Broadway. As the massive crowd ebbed, I saw a lone woman hesitating.

Dressed in a lavender dress with tiny white and purple flowers, and a wide-brimmed straw hat with a purple ribbon, a mulatto woman was standing on the kerb holding a walking stick in her hand. As she moved one white sandal hesitantly in front of her, it occurred to me that the woman was blind.

Glancing at the people who pushed past her without a second thought, I felt ashamed for the amount of insensitivity in the world. I ran to the woman, linked my arm through her stiff arm until it relaxed in dependence and trust, and led her across the busy street. She held onto her straw hat with the other hand while she latched on firmly to me, with the walking stick dangling awkwardly. Bringing her safely to the other kerb, I withdrew my arm shyly and brought my eyes to her face.

There, waiting for me, was the biggest smile I had ever received. It shone of beauty and goodness and most of all, gratitude. Her eyes were empty and lifeless, but her smile made up for it. The woman bowed her head and whispered '*Thank you*' to a face she would never see in this lifetime. But that did not stop her from expressing her feelings to a stranger. I was touched beyond words, and I smiled back. She wasn't able to see that, but I knew she had felt it. As Helen Keller once said, 'T*he best and most beautiful things in the world cannot be seen or even touched—they must be felt with the heart.*'

I watched her depart on her own and fought the urge to follow her and make sure she would get to her destination safely. Looking at her with admiration, I became conscious of how lucky I was. I couldn't for the life of me imagine walking around New York City blindfolded, and here was this courageous woman who refused to let her disability stop her from living the life she deserved to live. I turned my back and crossed the street again, dodging a car because I didn't hear the warning horn. As I found my spot again on the corner of Broadway and W.35th Street, I found Vicky waiting. There was a look of apology on his face as he prepared for my typical scolding but I just smiled at him. I was grateful when he smiled back . . . because I was able to see him smile.

Meeting that woman was a stroke of fate. Talk about being in the right place at the right time! Maybe it was God's way of telling me that no matter how bad I thought my situation was, there are always things left to appreciate. Always.

Rachana Mirpuri

I watched her travel on her own and fought the urge to follow her and make sure she would get to her destination safely. Looking at her with admiration, I became conscious of how lucky I was. I consented for the life of a blind person walking around New York City blindfolded, and here was this courageous woman who refused to let her disability stop her from living the life she deserved to live. I turned my back and crossed the street again, doubting it, or because I didn't hear the warning horn. As I found my spot again on the corner of Broadway and W. 29th Street, I found Vicky waiting. There was a look of apology on his face as he prepared to give me a typical scolding but I just smiled at him. I was grateful. He smiled back, because I was able to see him smile.

Meeting that woman was a stroke of fate. Talk about being in the right place at the right time! Maybe it was God's way of telling me that no matter how bad I thought my situation was, there are always things left to appreciate. Always.

Radhika Anupam

3

IN THE CLASSROOM

'But the idea that I should be a teacher and a researcher of some sort did not vary over the years.'

—Amartya Sen

A Complete Individual

I turn twenty-seven this September, and if people were to ask me what I regret the most in my life so far, I would say I regret that I scored such high marks in school and college. I regret that I secured a state-level rank in my Boards, I regret that I was in the top ten ranks in engineering college, I regret that, through my childhood and teenage years, all I thought about was studying.

As teenagers, most of us are very mechanical in our approach to studies: we go through school with the dream of getting into a good college; we study well in college with the aim of securing a seat in a great professional college . . . All we need to do is study, the rest is already predetermined for most of us. Somewhere along the way, one's individuality is lost. The person becomes what society wants her to be, rather then what she could have developed herself into.

It is very easy to blame this on someone else—in retrospect. Parents become the easiest targets; they are the ones who want us to study all the time, who want us to obtain high marks in every exam, who want us to build great careers. But are they really to be blamed? I don't think so; certainly not in all cases, and most definitely not in mine. Of course my parents told me to study, but they never told me not to do other things. So it is nobody else but me who is solely responsible for the decisions I took, things I did and the things I didn't.

So if someone asks me what I read as a teenager, I can only say, 'My textbooks. As I discovered the world of books as a grown up, I realised what an idiot I'd been to have missed out on so much at an age where it could have helped me the most. Reading for pleasure was totally alien to me; no one ever told me what I was missing, and how good the world of books could be for me to grow as an individual. I wish I had spent time reading rather than watching mindless films, or wasting time watching any programme that aired on television.

I wish I had developed a hobby; there had been so many choices. I was interested in painting, and how wonderful it would have been to be able to spend a weekend away from the busy study schedule in this activity. Perhaps I should have tried to learn a musical instrument. Or a sport.

Today's concept of a strong independent individual irks me. As a teenager, I never cared for other people; I believed I did not need anyone else. I thought that if I wasted time with friends, I would not have enough time to be 'successful'. So I did not spend time understanding people, developing friendships, building relationships. And if success is what I thought it was, I am successful—I do make money, I do have a lovely job. It's sad that I've only now realised that success is not just about money, not just about a career. It's also about having people around to share it. So I do regret that I did not invest time in friendships, in relationships. Trust me, you don't want to end up as a person who has to think three times about how you are going to spend your weekends.

So go get yourself a good book, start doing things that interest you, try to develop a hobby, play a sport. And most importantly, try to develop friendships that last a lifetime. That's what will make you a complete individual.

Rambler

Chrysalis

Till the seventh grade I was one of the backbenchers. There was nothing good about us. We did not pay attention during lessons, did poorly in the extra-curriculars and bunked games. The teachers had given up on us, never picking any of us to answer questions. And of course we never volunteered. Our knowledge on the subjects at hand was limited to exam days when we'd cram just enough to pass.

I remember vividly the day I received my report for the seventh grade. My class strength was 51 and I stood 40th . . . 11th from the bottom! Three of my gang had flunked altogether. All three were sobbing and didn't know how they would face their parents at home. I remember, more than fearing their wrath, it was the hurt that their moms would feel that was the chief cause of their distress. One of them looked up at me and said, 'Not to mention the treatment that waits us at the hands of the seventh graders.' It was common knowledge that the failures almost always stuck to each other. No one associated with them, neither our present class who made it to the eighth, nor the present seventh who came in from the sixth. A chill ran through my bones at their plight. I was aware of how narrowly I had missed that situation myself.

At assembly on the first day of the new academic year, all

the three sections of eighth-graders were asked to stay back. Names were called out and we were reshuffled. I found myself in section 'B' while the lone friend who had managed promotion with me was in section 'C'.

In class I found myself in the second row, next to a newcomer. By lunch break we had become friends. During the break three other girls who'd been uprooted, much as I had, gravitated towards us. Within a week we had formed our five-some. None of them were backbenchers. I was the odd one out in that group, as all the others were rank-holders and had been so since the first grade. And just like that, without portent, without thought, without my really putting in an effort, my world changed!

My focus, my values, areas of interest, priorities, even the way I looked at myself, changed. My topics of conversation shifted radically, from ridiculing teachers and laughing at poems by Shelley (because they seemed incomprehensible), I began discussing concepts, ideas, interpretations, postulations, exponents with them. From cramming to secure a passing grade, I launched into understanding the course material at its very core. From thinking at every moment, 'How long do I need to do this for?' I began to thoroughly enjoy the information presented and came up with creative examples myself. We quizzed each other, competed to solve mathematical problems, patted each other on the back for merits gained, discussed what we'd read in the newspapers, debated, jammed . . . and, of course, shared our tiffin with each other.

There is one incident in particular that will be etched in my memory forever. We had set ourselves to learn the generic names of chemicals, long before our chemistry teacher had assigned us the task. One day, the chemistry teacher announced a surprise oral quiz: on the generic names of chemicals. We five dominated that quiz! And at the end of it, I stood first.

I never slid back to my old self. I worked hard, concentrated on my lessons, and yes, had loads of fun too. When I got my first term results, I had stood sixth in the section. We went on to participate in inter-school competitions and gave every activity on the school campus a shot. I even remember auditioning for vocal music although I am not even a bathroom singer . . . well, that is the amount of confidence I gained.

So from being an 'I don't have it' to 'not bright enough' to 'no one cares' to 'I must become invisible', I turned into an 'I can', 'I am intelligent' and 'I matter'! All this because I found myself with a new set of friends who believed in excelling. Their halo pulled me in and I rediscovered myself.

Company matters!

Raksha Bharadia

Grades Don't Define You

I studied in a prestigious CBSE school in Kerala during the 1980s–'90s. The ranking system for examinations—monthly, quarterly, half-yearly and annual—was put to an end while I was in the fourth grade. Other schools in the region continued with the ranking system and the families of the students in these schools continued with their quarrels over their children's respective performances.

These ranking systems place a heavy weight on students, especially those weak in studies, and the ensuing competition—arising from fear of reprimand from teachers and parents—leaves most students with little option other than copying during examinations.

Mercifully, my case was different. 'It's not the high scores which count, but how much knowledge one acquires,' my father used to remind me often. My marks had come down dramatically when I reached the fifth grade, for reasons unknown to me. Till then I'd been scoring full marks in subjects like mathematics and Hindi. I would wake up at 5 am every day, study till 7 am, have a bath, eat breakfast, and get dropped off along with my brother Roop to school. During free sessions in school, I preferred to read my lessons rather than chatting with the others. Back home by 4.30, I studied for at least three hours—sometimes five—depending on the portions to be covered.

There were six subjects, and examinations every month, and the results would appear in progress cards which the parents had to sign. My parents took every opportunity to applaud my work, whether I'd scored well or not. When I didn't, they'd say, 'It's okay, you can do better next time.' 'Good' students scored at least 70 per cent marks. My score was around 60 per cent and sometimes, even less.

When the results of the Class X Board examination were announced, I was devastated because I didn't make the 72 per cent I thought I would. I knew, again, that my parents wouldn't scold me for that. They soothed me with the words, 'There will be a way out.' And I did get admission to college in the science group (with mathematics).

When I opted for the AMIE Section A non-diploma stream from the Institution of Engineers, Kolkata, everyone warned me I wouldn't manage studying on my own. 'You'll never pass a single paper without help from experienced minds,' they said. I proved them wrong, passing in six papers. I chose the multiple computer courses too and later, changed my stream. Gradually, my scores improved.

Distance learning and courses at private institutes probably helped me gain freedom to learn without being dependent on a teacher. I fared well, graduated in computer applications and acquired multiple diplomas in software engineering and programming. I made sure to score between 70 to 90 per cent once into learning computers. 'Move ahead,' I kept telling myself. 'Do your best. Success will be yours one day.' I knew a day would come when I would shine in my chosen field.

Several years passed. I moved to writing for publications, although I had no degree in journalism. Today, in our twenties, both Roop and I have good careers and we have those values our parents taught us. My friends who went on to study professional courses—mainly engineering and medicine—and did further studies abroad, wound up with jobs that fetched them several thousand a month. Some others are still doing their research. But, these people have a hitch. They work under a boss.

I, at the same time, improved my language, got rid of my fear of writing English essays, moved ahead to write features, interview celebrities and have my name in several publications, including international ones. I have the freedom to choose the topics I want to write on, whom I wish to write for, and when to take a holiday. Roop completed his B.Tech, got a PG diploma in industrial automation, joined my father's business, and freelances as a photographer for publications in India and abroad.

My parents were right. Scores don't mean much once you grow up.

Resmi Jaimon

It's All About the CV

It was the night before the interview for the literary society coordinator that I found out that non-core team members could also apply. I was left frazzled because one of my classmates—who had no reason to hate me—had told me that I wouldn't qualify for the interview because I hadn't volunteered to be a core team member. (Carelessness on my behalf.)

Since I had worked as a junior executive for the society earlier, I asked my senior executive if I could apply. She told me to go ahead. So at 3.30 in the morning, I was scanning lists of potential guest lecturers, workshops, writers, authors and publishers who could come to talk to the society in the coming year. I did not want to be caught ignorant if I was asked whom I was considering inviting for a certain event. My intuition told me I would get selected. I had worked on my agenda, and liked what I had come up with. I was really enthusiastic about working on the core team—there would be so much to change and do.

Ten-thirty the next morning found me outside the interviewer's office. I was the first to be called. My friend, Ankita, had told me to stress my agenda—it was my only card, she'd said, because I hadn't been as active as the other candidates in the society's events.

I walked in and brightly wished the teacher a good morning. She responded coolly and asked me to take a seat. 'Well, Arpita, give me three good reasons why I should select you?'

To tell the truth, I was quite unprepared for this. I had expected to be asked about my agenda. This question demanded that I hold forth, and yet be modest at the same time.

'Well, I think it's a great society, but we need to be more vigilant when it comes to exploring opportunity,' I managed. 'There are so many opportunities out there for budding writers that never come to light, simply because they are not publicised enough. For example, I learnt of some creative writing contests in the UK which are open to all students, yet so many people would be unaware of this option. As a coordinator, I would make sure that I gather and highlight as much information about such opportunities as possible so more people get a chance to do something they like.'

Phew. One down, two to go. That didn't sound so bad, after all.

'Can't you do that as a member? When you see such an opportunity—can't you say, "Hey, this sounds good, let me tell the executives about this"? Why should I make you a coordinator on this basis alone?'

I knew people were ripped apart, I just never thought it would be me. *Me*!

'Your second reason?'

'As clichéd as it sounds—I am very committed towards making this society a more active and lively organisation. I think it has enormous potential—and I am motivated to run the extra mile when it is required.'

A slight sneer.

'How active have you been? How many creative writing contests have you entered?'

'Two,' I mumbled.

'Come again?' I could hear the contempt drip.

I winced . . . took a deep breath. 'Two contests.'

'Aha.'

She looked at me with scorn. As if I had no business being here. Out of the corner of my eye, I could see one of the executives mouth to another, 'Why is she being so wicked?'

'And . . . err . . . the third reason?'

I paused. My mind gave up on me at the very moment I was expected to be smart, quick, witty and urbane.

'Erm, I'm really passionate about English, and creative writing . . .'

Realising the utter stupidity of what I was saying, I trailed off into embarrassed silence.

'Yes, yes, you're repeating yourself. Please send the next girl in.'

'Thank you, Ma'am,' I muttered, even though I didn't mean it.

I walked out feeling like a moron. I'd forgotten to mention I'd won both of the creative writing contests I'd entered, and been a junior executive in first year. I'd forgotten to tell her I had experience. I'd forgotten to tell her I'd been selected for the poetry workshop. I hadn't told her I had organisational abilities. Why had I left all that out in an interview?

I wanted the earth to swallow me up. One of my friends was acing interviews and getting selected by organisations like Citigroup. Another friend was applying to Oxford, with a brilliant CV. Yet another friend was invited to perform overseas. And I, with all my potential, had done nothing of substance.

It's painful accepting that you screwed up. But I guess that regret is a catalyst to project a better image of myself. I try to appear brilliant, talented and creative—and perhaps I am all those things—but without exploring any of the opportunities that I've got, I'll go nowhere fast.

I also realised that every little choice I make makes a huge difference to my future. If I had tried, I could have been more actively involved in the society—and worked beforehand for the position I wanted. But I chose not to. And so I must live with the consequences.

I can't dismiss this lightly, saying it doesn't really matter. It does. And because it does matter, it has made me sit up and actively analyze each choice I make.

Sometimes, having it easy isn't always the best thing. Failure, regret and guilt may be unpleasant—but they deepen your experience more than success can. It's fine when you're the one who always 'makes it', 'pulls it off' and 'aces it'. It's hard having to accept the fact that you weren't good enough—and need to try harder.

I made a promise to myself that day: the next time I walk into a job interview, I shall have a CV full of relevant accomplishments. And three good reasons why I should be hired.

Arpita Bohra

Minus Three Plus One

When I was twelve years old, I had the perfect school life. I got good grades and had not one, but two great best friends. The three of us were never apart; we sat at the same table, ate, talked, played and even went to parties together. And because we were so happy just being a trio, we thought that whoever tried to force us to be with other kids was just jealous of our friendship. I had known Chintal for over six years and Devashree for three. Chintal was plump, out-going and loved challenges. Devashree on the other hand was quite the opposite, skinny, shy and artistic. As for me, well, I guess I was kind of in-between. We all had our weaknesses, sure, but together we were unbeatable.

It all changed when Chintal's mother wanted her to change schools. Half of me thought I would never survive our being parted, but the other half thought, 'Why not wait and see how school *is* without her?' However, nothing was final since it was Chintal's mother who wanted the change, while Chintal herself preferred to stay. While things didn't change drastically over the next few months—we still did all our usual stuff—I found my restlessness growing with every passing day. Some time towards the end of the school year, Chintal came up to Devashree and me and said that her mother had left the decision to her . . . she asked us what she should do.

A friend of mine was banking on my opinion to make a huge decision. I searched hard for the right thing to say, but found myself as hopelessly confused as Chintal. For the first time, an awkward silence ensued between the three of us. Devashree broke the silence by asking Chintal to stay. She agreed. The three of us were happy for the rest of the day.

The next day we discussed the topic again, but this time Devashree said that perhaps it would be better for Chintal if she went. I didn't know how to respond to this and so I simply nodded my head. The next few days I was in a world of my own. Slowly, the realisation hit me that Chintal was leaving the school for certain. On the last day of school, the three of us wept on each other's shoulders. It was hard to let go of each other's hands.

Finally, the summer vacations came and we met up a lot and watched many movies together. It was as if the whole school-leaving episode had not happened at all. We were still the same and doing the same things that we had always done: we had sleepovers, went for lunches, and things seemed as if they hadn't changed a bit. However, I guess things were bad for Chintal as I still had one best friend to count on while she had to go through a whole new set of friends and class teachers. Changing schools is, after all, one of the toughest things in a teen's life.

Little did I know that more was in store for me! One afternoon during those same vacations, I received a call from Devashree saying she too would be leaving as her elder brother had secured bad marks and her parents blamed the school for that. This time I didn't shed a tear, as I was still in summer holiday mood and I thought it was a joke. After another week, when Devashree didn't call to tell me that it was indeed a joke, I rang her up. Her mother came on the line, only to confirm my fears. I was in total shock. In less than six months, two of my favourite people in the world were going away.

I tried to look on the bright side: not all was lost. I still had one more friend left in school—Kshitisha. She wasn't 'one of us' but she was still someone I considered a close friend.

On the first day of school, I was in a daze. When I entered the building I felt a wave of panic, I couldn't find any of my classmates and I didn't know who my teacher was. I had no idea what to do, I had no one to go too, I was lost. I regretted asking my mother to stay at home and not come to drop me off. I walked in, anyway, hoping to find the other girls from my class. I didn't see any of them, but they saw me and came running towards me, comforting me by saying stuff like they would stay by me and how sad it was that both my close friends had gone away together. I was touched by their thoughtfulness. After a few minutes of this, Kshitisha entered, and I was with her the entire day. Over the next few weeks, there weren't any new girls, only some new boys. I was with Kshitisha the entire time.

Just when I thought that we weren't going to get any new girls in our class, along came Catherine. And we really hit it off. I was so happy. I had two new best friends, Kshitisha and Catherine. Things went along smoothly for a while. And then it turned out that Kshitisha had to change schools as well. I had now lost three friends in less than a year. It was down to Catherine and me. I started spending more time with her and we soon had our set of firsts: we had our first sleepover, first set of secrets and so on. In less than a month we became the closest of friends.

Now I am thirteen. When my two best friends had to leave school, followed by a third, I had thought that my school life was over and that there was never going to be anything great to look forward to. But then Catherine came along and, instead of losing three friends, I gained one more. All my friends are close to me and each is special in her own way. I think it's true that at times we are so afraid of what we are going to lose that we do not give a fair chance to what we might gain instead. God really does keep those windows open.

Aishwarya Bharadia

Only in Your Dreams

'Open the door, sweetheart, here's dinner.' It was my mother, holding a plate of warm food.

'Careful, don't step on my papers,' I said to her, without taking my eyes off my textbook, as she carefully tip-toed into my room and proceeded on what was now her daily obstacle course . . . stepping deftly over piles of books, newspapers, current affairs magazines and various items of stationery. After making a small clearing on my study table, which reflected the chaos of my room, she asked me to eat and get some sleep.

'Not now, Ma. I have to finish this test paper, update my scrapbook, learn new words and then solve a set of Data Interpretation papers. I'll go to bed after that. You go ahead and catch some sleep instead.'

I was chasing my dream: to get admission to the prestigious Indian Institute of Management, Ahmedabad. For me there was no second choice. It was IIM Ahmedabad or nothing. Not even the other IIMs. It was a dream, but I was slogging to turn it into reality. I was a fourth-year student of electronics and communications engineering, studying for my college exams, yes, but more intent on cracking the CAT.

IIM-A. I focussed on nothing but my goal and I knew that commitment and single-minded dedication were the only way to get there. My parents were my biggest support. Dad would stay awake while I studied, and Mum would come nudge me awake and coax me into bed if I happened to doze off on the study table.

One September morning started off on the same note as all my other mornings. It was going to be just another hectic day. My alarm reminded me that it was time to go to college. I mentally ran through my day's timetable . . . college, lectures, home, nap, Quant paper, Data sufficiency test, tutorials. My day was set. I closed my books, put them aside and tried to get up from my chair.

Instead . . . I fell down. I felt immense pain waist downwards; there was what seemed a heavy rush of blood to my head and then . . . nothing. I couldn't move.

Mum heard the thud and rushed into my room. She lifted me up and I realised something was terribly wrong. She thought I had fallen off the chair in my sleep. I told her I was in pain and couldn't sit. She held me close and comforted me, saying it was probably just a muscle pull. But I was terrified. Something did not feel right.

I didn't go to college, and slept instead. After a long nap I felt better. That evening I went for a walk with Dad and we discussed the forthcoming exams. After we returned, I felt fresh and decided to study. I sat on my chair, set the timer for two hours and started solving a test paper. Mum called me just as the timer went off and asked me to take a break. I tried to get up, but . . .

The pain was back. I felt the tears stream down my face as the agony became unbearable. I was rushed to Dr Ajay Seth, a renowned orthopaedician. He took x-rays and we waited for the reports.

I stood the entire time, as the simple act of sitting felt like torture. The pain was excruciating, but truthfully I was more worried about my exams, which were only two months away. My tutorial mock tests were also around the corner. The doctor said the problem was my tailbone. It was slowly wearing away and there was also a small crack in it triggering the paralyzing effect. 'Prolonged and continuous periods in one place often cause this. She needs complete bed rest for two months . . .'

He gave me a list of dos and don'ts, lots of medicines and a warning that neglect could require surgery to correct. I requested him not to give me sedatives as I wouldn't be able to study under their effect. Unfortunately, they were a must. My morale shattered, I wept. Mom had tears in her eyes, too. I had to stop going to college and soon lagged behind in my semester studies. I couldn't even lie down on my back and read because of the pain. Life just seemed to be spiralling downwards.

It was in those moments of dark despair that my friends, like angels, rallied round me. We held combined study sessions, discussing the MBA coaching sessions in great detail. I would prop myself up on cushions and study for small periods of time. The sedatives made me sleepy, but dreams of IIM, Ahmedabad used to rouse me.

On Dusshera, Mom held my hand and helped me walk to the Kali temple. I could see the tears she tried to hide. Seeing me in this condition must have been hard for her, but she knew I was a fighter. My mentors at the MBA tutorials made special arrangements for me to take my mock tests.

Things were progressing, slowly but surely. I still had the same goal; only the approach was different. I believed in myself. More than that, my parents believed in me. Finally, D-day arrived. The CAT exams! They went well, except for the fact that the pain surfaced at irregular intervals. But, I wasn't going to let that stop me. Being able to take the tests meant everything to me.

Judgement day. The CAT results were declared and I was

offered admission by four of the IIMs . . . just not IIM-A. Everybody was happy except me. I felt my world crumbling away. I decided if I couldn't go to IIM-A, I wouldn't go anywhere else. My parents went along with my decision. Time passed. In the glow of my parents' love and my friends' support, I shook off my feelings of hopelessness. I was still dejected about IIM-A and not yet completely rid of the backache, but in a way that helped. A fire raged within me; I yearned for my lost zeal. I steered myself towards a new goal and started taking my semester studies seriously. My best friend slaved to help me cope with the portion of the syllabus that I had missed.

The final exams came and went. The results were also out. And . . . I had topped the university! I was a gold medallist. I floated on cloud nine as my friends rejoiced and my parents cried with relief and pride. Time flew and one fine day I got a call from one of the biggest IT companies in the world. And here I am now, working in the firm's business development team, sitting in my cubicle and writing this tale of mine. I have fully recovered from that torturous back pain, but more than that, I have overcome the mental agony.

I still dream, because it's important to. You just need faith, passion and sincere dedication, along with the blessings of God and your loved ones to make them come true.

But there's another thing. You sometimes need to let go of a dream. That's okay, because another one comes in its place and you need to embrace it with the same fervour.

Dreams can be larger than life. But then again, some can become your life.

Ekta Bhandari

Reaching Out

Booming economy, nuclear power, ancient civilisation, job outsourcing, good food and weeklong weddings! These are some of the words and phrases that come to mind when one thinks of India. But then again, the words poverty, corruption, illiteracy and disparity define my reality too.

Though I have had a privileged childhood—formative years at home in India with an indulgent family, and high school years at a liberal residential school in the US—it is the lack of opportunity for the majority of India's students that concerns me deeply.

I was seventeen and full of youthful aspirations when, towards the end of my 11th grade at George School, my mother shared with me over the phone her concern for another teenage student. He was the son of a housekeeper, whose family would have to incur a heavy debt to fund his college education, as borrowing from private lenders at an interest rate of 100 per cent seemed their only option to fulfil their son's academic aspirations. This would push the family into a vicious cycle of debt—propelling poverty for generations.

How was an economically disadvantaged student to break out of that cycle?

This was the defining moment in my life.

I had taken much of my life and its opportunities for granted—a comfortable home, good food to eat, great friends and quality education. That was my scripting.

My world view changed the moment I understood that education—that fundamental right of all citizens—was not so fundamental after all. That disparity in education levels due to socio-economic hurdles was a harsh reality in even progressive 21st-century India: the world of my future.

It was the last three days before the summer holidays. Mom and I drafted an appeal to the George School community for students and staff to contribute towards this student's fees so he could go to college. The response was absolutely fantastic and unimagined. Everyone came forth with contributions from $1 upwards and within a short time of three days we had $500! This was adequate to fund his first year at college, and it started us thinking about a sustainable, long-term solution to such situations.

The realisation hit home and has stayed with me since. India is plagued by good intentions that lack action. Our numbers tend to overwhelm us and most of us tend to take the route of 'Nothing will change'. Sure enough, nothing does.

A desire to be part of positive change—to lead by action—and the overwhelming response to the appeal at George School is what inspired my friend Meredith Zoltick and I to start a formal high school initiative called 'Reaching Out', to fund education for socio-economically disadvantaged students in India.

With the motto of 'Empowering through Education', Reaching Out aims to partner with public and private institutions to facilitate the education of motivated students whose socio-economic conditions limit their educational prospects. Reaching Out scholars are motivated to do their best in academics and create a ripple effect of 'giving forward'—continuing the gesture—in their respective communities.

Reaching Out funds the scholarship programme through various fund-raisers that tap into the kindness of those who are fortunate enough to avail of good education. Since 2006, it has raised more than Rs 10 lakh, and currently sponsors eight students.

Reaching Out has given me an invaluable lesson in life: to 'walk the talk'.

And that yes, things can change if we make them. As Gandhiji said, 'Be the change you want to see in the world.'

Kahan Chandrani

Cinderella Lives On

She was the new girl in her posh all-girls' school. Gawky; unsophisticated; perpetually ill at ease among her more worldly classmates.

For thirteen years she'd loved watching the children's movies screened biannually at her local community centre. It was only after moving to the big city that she learned people had things called televisions and could watch sitcoms at home every day. The other girls laughed at her because she had never heard of *I Love Lucy* or *Top of the Pops*. They wondered which burrow she had been hiding in when she admitted she'd never seen a Bollywood movie. And they thought her a freak for not caring which sexy actress the current heartthrob was dating.

As a matter of fact, she didn't know what dating involved. To her, boys were the people she raced bicycles with, not creatures she gossiped about. While her classmates had been experimenting with make-up and clothes, she'd been climbing guava trees, chasing dragonflies, and reading books—not the fashionable Mills & Boon romances, but outdated stuff like Jane Austen, Arthur Conan Doyle and P.G. Wodehouse.

She was the school freak, and she knew it. Her classmates teased her because one or the other managed to beat her in all subjects except geography, science and mathematics. Her teachers loved her, but she hated herself for being different. She thought she could win her classmates over by doing better then them in class, but the better she did, the more she was teased and the more she was teased, the more she withdrew into herself. That was her only defense—erecting a protective barrier of shyness around her. Stuttering when she spoke at all.

She was a swift runner, and everyone wanted her on their team, but they selected her so grudgingly, she felt she had to burst her lungs in gratitude to them for bestowing that mark of approval on her. Her paintings were good, but never good enough to be pinned on the classroom board. Her needlework was neat, but never as good as the professionally-done embroidery her classmates turned in. No matter how hard she tried, she was never good enough, and she knew herself for the inferior creature that she was.

They were putting up *Cinderella* that year. When the class was told that they would all have to be on stage, she resigned herself to the part of the footman who carried the glass shoe from house to house. Her classmates, however, had other plans for her.

'We need to find just one Ugly Sister,' said one cruelly. 'I-if o-one h-has a s-st-tutt-tter, we d-don't t-need the-the o-other.'

But she knew that her skills were inadequate to enact even that part.

Like all the others, she was forced to audition for the title role. She could empathise with the girl who was forced to become the perennial misfit, and amidst general twittering, read Cinderella's lines in her scared, faltering manner.

*

She was the perfect Cinderella, and when she smiled at the Prince while he bestowed a kiss on the hand she proffered him, she brought the house down. The red velvet curtain swung open and closed seven times while she came back for encores.

She was a star.

Her stammer was a thing of the past.

Natasha Ramarathnam

The Astute Teacher

Rev. Father Gill was a Spanish priest in our school whose simplicity and sternness stunned the students. I had noticed two other things about him. One, he would vehemently protest whenever someone called him Spanish; he'd proudly say he was a Basque . . . although that didn't mean anything to us then. Two, his powers of observation were acute.

My father was a cop. We four kids were forced to study in the Gujarati medium of instruction, though our school was renowned to be one of the best English-medium schools. We hankered to be with our close buddies in the English medium stream, and slowly ended up mastering English much faster than our classmates.

The disparity was so huge that by the time I was in the 8th standard, while my classmates were struggling with basics, grappling with sentences like 'Rama, open the door' or 'Sita, close the window', I was already reading P.G. Wodehouse and Charles Dickens at home.

The torture a child has to undergo in such a situation cannot be described; it has to be experienced to be understood. So it was inevitable that within a week Rev. Gill caught me daydreaming and drawing cartoons while he taught the basics of English grammar.

'Why aren't you paying any attention?' he asked me like an

unsmiling executioner. I shivered and replied that was because I already knew whatever he was teaching. So he asked me some basic questions and I replied successfully.

'Where did you learn English?' he asked me more gently.

'At home, Father. I've been reading the *Times Of India* since I was twelve.'

I stood there, worried sick, and he kept smiling absent-mindedly at me for what seemed like an eternity.

'Okay,' he said, after pondering for some minutes. 'Don't come to my class from tomorrow.' I was about to break down when he surprised me by saying, 'I want you to go to the school library and start reading *Robinson Crusoe* by Daniel Defoe. Every kid loves it. And remember, I will ask you questions on it, so don't rush through it, study it.'

That 'punishment' was a turning point in my reading career.

None of my classmates were interested in English literature, but I grew addicted to it. I always scored such high marks in English every year, there was a gap of thirty marks between what I'd scored and what the next student had.

When the school chose me on Teachers' Day to be sent to teach a higher class in the English medium stream, I cried. This had never happened before and, according to the teachers, was never repeated.

The astute Father Gill had his own weird punishments, but his thinking was crystal-clear. I remember him fondly.

Max Babi

The Eleventh Hour

The phone in my house jangled with a disquieting urgency. It was Ankur, my best friend, with whom I'd spent a good part of the class XII academic year studying movies and girls: subjects we found a lot more appealing than the ones we were taught at Bhavan's Public School, Vadodara.

'Just two days left for the chemistry paper, *yaar*,' he hollered. 'How're you placed on organic?'

'Not very good,' I said, 'I haven't even started revising yet.' There were no secrets between us.

'*Same* here!' He sounded almost jubilant. 'Do you really think we've a chance of clearing chemistry this year?'

I felt my insides turn to jelly as the seriousness of the situation sank in. We had barely scraped through chemistry in the mid-term exams.

Our problem was not with the subject or its teacher. What we detested was organic chemistry, the esoteric branch which dealt with compounds of carbon. Adopting the typical defence mechanism that seventeen-year-olds do, we had conveniently avoided studying it with any thoroughness that make-or-break year. Friedrich Kekule might have discovered the structure of the benzene ring through a serendipitous dream and won accolades for it, but for us he and his cronies had only left behind the stuff of our nightmares. With 40 per cent of the chemistry syllabus looking like a Black Hole two days before the Board exam, the two of us were staring at the tonsils of failure.

Not long after that wake-up call from Ankur, we were on my scooter, heading towards the residence of the only man on earth who could save us, Mr Ganesh, our chemistry teacher. It was 8.30 in the evening.

In school, Ganesh Sir was best known for two things: his 100 per cent command over his subject and his 0 per cent tolerance for lethargy. On more than one occasion, Ankur and I had been at the receiving end of severe admonishments for neglecting his subject. Now, as we approached his home, I felt my heartbeat rising to a crescendo, and my forehead feeling damp, even with the wind blowing in my face. Ankur, too, was uncharacteristically quiet.

As I pressed the doorbell, the rattle of plates and spoons from inside told us that we had arrived at the wrong time. Even more wrong because we were there seeking full amnesty and an undeserved bail-out package.

The door was opened by Ganesh Sir himself. His prominent nose and bushy whiskers, that we had often poked fun at behind his narrow back, now represented hope and deliverance. The spare-built man was dressed in a spotless white kurta, quite becoming a person of his formidable intellect. Standing there before him, we felt tiny.

It was Ankur who said, 'Sir, we need some help in organic chemistry.'

'Sure. Which chapter?' Ganesh Sir asked, prepared to clear our doubts on the doorstep itself.

Ankur gave me a 'your turn, buddy' look and stepped back.

I found words deserting me as I stammered, 'The . . . the entire organic chemistry, sir.'

Did the pedagogue's eyes turn red and his face black? Did

his ears start smoking and his nostrils flaming? Did his indignant outburst cause pots and pans in his house to fall off their shelves with a clamour like beakers and test-tubes sometimes did in his lab with more destructive effect?

No. Nothing of the sort happened. I think I saw an eyebrow go up but I cannot be completely sure of that either. What I do remember are his words that are etched in my memory due to the utter disbelief they evoked in me at that time.

'Right . . . come in. I'll finish my dinner and join you.' That's all Ganesh Sir had to say after we had practically admitted to treating with contempt the subject that was his very life.

In twenty minutes, he joined us in his study. What happened in the next twenty hours was an academic miracle. Starting with the very definition of the term 'organic chemistry', our teacher started packing inside our minds the course material of an entire year, knowing fully well that he only had a few hours to do it. The night was long and dark but Ganesh Sir guided us through the vast jungle of molecular structures, chemical formulae and tongue-twisting nomenclatures of carbon compounds. He taught us mnemonics with which we could slay the monster of memory loss and he showed us how to identify the booby-traps of simple-looking questions carrying heavy marks. He offered us insights into the relative weightings placed on different portions of the textbook so that we could expend our desperately short time on the most important sections. The next day, after a two-hour break during which we scurried back home for a wash and breakfast, the two of us were back at Ganesh Sir's place. This time he gave us mock tests and problems.

Something remarkable was happening here. Under Ganesh Sir's focused and exclusive guidance, Ankur and I were actually grasping the most arcane subject we'd come across that year. Soon both of us felt something rising like bread in the oven of our pounding hearts. *It was confidence* ... confidence that perhaps we would not secure a distinction in the paper but that we would surely pass the exam.

The next day, we came out of the examination hall smiling. Two months later the results were out. I had scored an astonishing 82 per cent in chemistry! Combined with my performance in the other subjects, it was enough to get me a seat in computer engineering in a reputed college. Ankur didn't do badly either. He secured admission in a degree course in pharmacy.

'Now you're stuck with chemistry for the rest of your life, my friend,' I taunted him.

'Ha! The subject doesn't scare me anymore,' Ankur brushed off my jibe. 'It can be conquered in a night!'

By going beyond his call of duty that night many moons ago, Ganesh Sir not only rescued me from failure in that crucial exam but also from a life that in all possibility would have been permanently bedevilled by low self-confidence and poor self-esteem.

Sandeep Shete

The 'It' Girl

I was always 'the fat kid' in class. I never really noticed my weight in school until a classmate pointed out my paunch to the other girls in the changing room after P.E. class. I was hurt, but that never really motivated me to do anything. I was too busy being misunderstood by the world at large—and writing poetry about it.

After I finished my 10th standard, I was desperate to change schools, even though mine had just started a plus-two (standards 11 and 12) programme. I wanted to get away from all the bad memories, the taunts and jibes. I wanted to start afresh.

I so loathed myself, I even wanted a personality makeover. I joined an all-girls' school and I became what I was not . . . enthusiastic, bubbly, flirtatious. Traits that were so not mine, only adopted. And I must say, I did attract the attention of the it-crowd and soon I was part of the gang. I was short and stout, but I was still 'in'! My cup brimmed over in those days.

Acquiring a new personality required dumping some of the old. I didn't only stop my angsty writing, I stopped writing all together. I emotionally shut my mom out of my life and I wanted absolutely nothing to do with my kid brother. I looked down upon the 'uncool' and 'unpopular' girls who studied the same subjects as I did and only kept the company of the 'famous' and 'fabulous'.

How I hate those tags! But hey, back then, I was riding the popularity wave and nothing could bring me down.

How wrong I was. Waves do come crashing down and that's what happened to me. My happiness as well as my popularity was short-lived.

What happened was typical teenage girl stuff . . . catfights, accusations and the blame game. There was a huge misunderstanding between me and somebody else. I was accused of backbiting. I didn't try to defend myself, because I was partly at fault, but not totally. There were others to point fingers at in the whole sordid mess, but I kept quiet, because I truly believed in the diktat, 'Never rat on your friends'.

But they were the same friends who made me out to be the 'bad' girl. Overnight, from fat but fabulous, I went to fat and freaky. I went back to being an introvert, something that I was once good at being. Out came my notebooks and my angst-ridden words. I wrote poem after poem, short story after story. I spent more time with my mom, but I never unburdened myself to her, because I wanted to spare her, her child's pain. My brother and I talked, went to the movies and grew really close. And the girls I used to look down upon became my new friends and companions. They welcomed me into their midst, unquestioningly and with open arms, and for that I will be ever grateful to them. They made the remainder of my stay in school bearable. One girl from that group became my best friend . . . someone who I am close to even today. And I found others who made themselves a home in my heart.

I still wish I had done some things differently.

Today, I wish I had stood up for myself. I lost a friend I truly, *truly* cared for and she just ended up thinking the worst of me. Not just that, many people were left with a poor impression of me, which probably wouldn't have been the case had I stood up for myself and my natural character.

Today, even after over a decade, I miss that particular friend of mine who believed that I could say such things about her. I hate that she thinks so lowly of me . . . if she does think of me at all. Because, truth be told, I still care for her and wish she knew that.

The point of my story is this . . . if your integrity is at stake, fight for it.

If you are about to lose a friend, fight for him or her.

Don't wake up every day of your life for the next ten, twenty, thirty years, saying, 'If only . . .'

And above all, be true to who you are. There will always be people who love you.

Baisali Chatterjee Dutt

To Be Words-worthy

I learnt in my formative years that it isn't funny learning English. I was thirteen then, in class VI, and we had shifted to a new senior school. What we had left behind was a sandpit, easy-to-tackle bullies without acne, and teachers who probably cared a bit too much.

We were uncomfortable, perhaps even distressed, when we arrived. The campus was huge, the older students looked mean, and the textbooks seemed grossly overweight. Besides, we were told there would now be exams and no more of those class tests where we would get stars and smiley faces. And I knew then how everything would depend on the amount of that terrible red ink on my answer sheets, and circles over my earnestly ambiguous answers.

It was our big shift. My younger brother and I would come back from school, have our glasses of milk, watch *Small Wonder* and *The Wonder Years* on TV and head out to cycle around the colony. Sometimes, our grandfather would choose either to tell us a story or take us forcibly out on walks (if we behaved we would get an ice cream; if we didn't, we ended up with a haircut).

There was something I particularly dreaded about school. At the end of every academic year, the teacher in English would call out a few familiar names, and mine would be one of them. We were then to attend a separate class for all of the following year, as students of Remedial English.

So I was embarrassed. Embarrassed when I heard my name repeated twice, every syllable clear, and I had this terrible feeling that everyone in that class was smirking at me in a knowing way.

I don't think I was dyslexic. I remember being tested for that once, but the academic who had come to conduct the check dismissed any sign of that. I had to struggle to keep up with the work, though. The teachers were kind and empathetic. But I was worried about my English. I had grown up reading the right books—by writers such as Enid Blyton and Roald Dahl— why didn't it work for me? I was having a lot of trouble speaking straight lines, and my writing was a messy soup of mistakes.

I learnt to like the Remedial English class sometime in the middle of the term: we had a wonderful course and a wonderful teacher. The students in this class were a lot more honest, at least with themselves. They knew they had a problem. I would wind up with extra homework, but it was in a joyful mood that I would rush after each class to meet my friends, worried that I had been forgotten in those forty-five minutes.

But all the same, when I went to a boarding school in Ajmer, there to spend the last five years of my student life, I was relieved that there weren't any special classes for English there.

I had other issues to worry about, however. A few of my classmates took a dislike to me—which meant I was cornered and cursed. There was exhaustion resulting from the activity-filled days which led me several times to the school hospital. There was perpetual hunger and I was introduced to homesickness.

I thought of all this as I stood one evening facing 300-odd

students at an English elocution competition. I was a bit nervous under the tall, yellow lamp, and somewhere in the middle of the poem by Robert Frost, I forgot my lines. Someone started to laugh.

Many moons fast-forwarded from that night, I stumbled upon some courage to write, inspired by my father's favourite music. He had a wonderful collection of cassettes and when I was home in the holidays, I would spend hours listening to singers like Bob Dylan, Leonard Cohen, Neil Diamond and Jim Morrison.

I was fascinated by their lyrics, their fresh ideas. They seemed so twisted, so incorrect—so cool. And I began to scribble my very own. I was seventeen, and I felt poetry was for those who couldn't write long and difficult lines.

One day, I left my book of poems on my English teacher's desk. He was definitely one of the best we had. I waited for him to say something to me at the end of the class. He mumbled something then that I didn't hear. I headed for the next class down the corridor, wondering why he hadn't returned my book.

Later that day, I met a senior and a friend on the basketball court. His English class usually came after mine. I had just begun to tell him that I had committed a grave sin by revealing my writing to an adult, when my friend stopped me. He said the teacher had spent half the English period discussing my poetry.

Jairaj Singh

Win-Win

Even thinking about that day brings out goose bumps on my skin.

It was 1996 and I was giving my Standard X Board exams. The school topper Maheshwari, popularly known as Mahu, called me to check out what time I was going to meet her at the bus stop, because we had planned to go together to St Anthony's School in Chembur, the centre allotted to us for our exam.

I informed Mahu that my dad had taken off from work to drop me to the exam centre and that she should reach the bus stop by 9.15 am, so we could pick her up from there. Just before I disconnected the call, I happened to ask, 'Do you remember which genus the water hyacinth belongs to? I was reading through last year's Science-II paper, and it had posed the question. I couldn't recall the answer. Do you remember having read it in our Science-II text book?'

I could sense she was flummoxed. After pausing for few seconds, she said, 'What's wrong with you? We're not yet done with the Science-I paper. Are you already preparing for tomorrow's exam?'

'What???' I remember screaming back. 'This isn't a good time to joke, Mahu! We're writing the Science-II paper today, *not Science-I*.'

Listening to me declare the matter so confidently, Mahu was in a dilemma herself. Strangely, she accepted that if one of was wrong, it had to be her and not me.

That boosted my confidence. I checked my time table which confirmed that we were indeed to write our Science-II paper that day, and headed towards the bus stop to comfort the inconsolable Mahu.

When I reached the bus stop I realised Mahu was so distraught that she had summoned her mother for help. But in a matter of seconds, their roles were reversed. Mahu's mom started crying bitterly while Mahu got on with the comforting act.

They hesitantly got into the car and I could see that Mahu's mom was still hysterical. 'What are you going to do now?' she reprimanded Mahu. 'After goofing up so royally how are you ever going to top the class?' Saying so, she slapped Mahu hard.

My dad, who was witnessing all this in his rearview, now looked back and said, 'Relax. It's not the end of the world. I don't understand why people attach such importance to these Board exams. Please don't freak out. She's barely fifteen, already stooping under the pressure of exams, and now reeling with this shock.'

Hearing my dad speak, Mahu's mom tried to bring about some semblance of calm on her face, although I knew that was not the way she felt inside.

We reached the centre. Suddenly, what I saw around me filled me with dread. I recognised the cover of the books that seemed to be glaring back at me from everywhere. All the students were deeply immersed in their copies of the Science-I textbook, held well up against their faces.

I realised that not everyone could be wrong, though I secretly wished they were. I saw Mahu's mom's cheer up instantly, and Mahu, on her part, clapped her hands with joy.

My own head was reeling. 'I'm not giving the exam,' I told my dad, tears filling my eyes.

Mahu's mom wasn't about to lose an opportunity. 'I'm so sorry for you, Mr Nair,' she shot at him. 'Now, try telling yourself that it's not the end of the world.'

'Well, it really isn't!' my dad retorted.

'It really isn't a big deal for *your* daughter,' she replied. '*She* isn't expected to top the class like Mahu, is she?' One had to have a heart of stone to have said what she did then. My tears now flowed uncontrollably and formed stains as they rolled off my cheeks and onto my clothes.

My dad ignored her, turned to me and said, 'There's nothing to worry about, Baby. Just relax and write the paper like the outcome doesn't matter to you. We know well that you've been studying hard all through the year. If you clear your exams, we'll be happy for you. But even if you don't, trust me, we'll be proud that you had the courage to make an attempt. And believe me, either way, nothing's going to change for you. Neither your mother's love for you nor my faith in your capabilities. I want you to know that there's much more to life than clearing the Standard X Board exams.'

'Besides,' he continued, 'we'd enrolled you into school a year earlier than you ought to have joined. So, you see, it's a win-win situation for us.' Trying hard to bring a smile to my face in that bleak moment, he said, 'Give it your best shot, darling, and remember that you have nothing to lose.'

I went in and not only gave the exam but also went on to secure the highest marks in the Science-I paper, partly because of my rigorous preparation well before the exams, and undoubtedly, owing to my dad's assurance that the outcome wasn't going to change anything for me.

My joy knew no bounds when I saw my marks. And what multiplied the experience by almost a thousand times was the priceless look that I witnessed on Mahu's mom's face, when the results were publicly declared.

Divya Nair Hinge

4

ON REBELLION

'Age considers, youth ventures.'

—Rabindranath Tagore

An Answer to a Question

I Just Want You to Let Me Be

It all started the day you proclaimed
That I was big now, I must be tamed.
So you declared: follow the rules every day
Be smart, be nice, be good all the way,
It's rude, that's what you grown-ups say,
That I never ever behave in the right way?
Manners is what I need to cultivate,
And why do I turn everything into a debate?
It's rude when I talk in between,
Or if I don't say hello when I'm seen.
It's rude if I question why
The many rules you bind me by.
It's rude if I say no, or roll my eyes,
I become ill-mannered in a trice.
I'm selfish if I say I want my peace.
I want your comparisons to cease
What others do, that's what you measure me by.
I'm so difficult, that's what you say and sigh
What I did finish, that's what you've never seen
Why can't you be like them? That's how it's always been!
Who removed all the fun

Out of the work that is to be done?
Why is it always a race?
Does it really matter—that first place?
Look into my world, see my pain
See me struggling to break the chain
The strong shackles in which you bind me
I want to be free, can't you see?
Let me make my mistakes
It's only my pride at stake
Let me stumble and fall
I want to do it myself, that's all.
The outer masks you make me wear,
Away from my face, I want to tear.
Why are there so many rules?
If we don't follow, are we fools?
Free to live my life, that's what I want
In my own way, without any taunts.
I want to be free, to be me,
I just want you to let me be . . .

A Better You

This is my answer to you
It's something you always knew:
Rules will always be a part
Of making sure you get the right start
It's how we grew up too
Sometimes hating it all the way through.
Every phase brings a change
To help us prepare for the next stage
It doesn't really matter, that first place,
What matters is your effort in that race,
To reach that goal in sight
Have you put up enough of a fight?
Look at the traffic on the street

A few guidelines they do meet
Without rules, what would the world be
A mess, don't you agree?
Everybody would get away
Nothing would be black or white, only grey.
It is to make sure you don't stumble so hard
So hard that you cannot get up at all.
Too much is too bad, I agree,
But a few are very necessary, don't you see?
Rules are just to make sure you are safe
Till you reach that certain age
The age when you can decide
The difference between wrong and right.
It can still be fun
All the tasks that need to be done
Together let's change, a few rules for me,
A few rules for you, together let's see
A future that's bright and new
A future that's you!

Suma Rao

Angst with Pimples

A Buddhist poet once said that as one grows older, one grows stupider. I attributed this claim to bitter cynicism, but now I'm not so sure.

You see, I'm a teenager. Mine is the stage of life that is full of learning, confusion and acne. But the infamous 'teenage' is something else too. It is a catalyst. I don't know if it's the raging hormones, or the complete isolation that teenagers seem to feel, but something happens to us. Something triggers us to do something lots of people seem to have forgotten how to do—question.

Till the happy age of twelve, we are told a lot of things, and this is how our foundation as a human being is built. Then, if we are unlucky, at the age of thirteen, we begin to question everything that we have been taught. You distraught parents and teachers like to call this the naturally 'rebellious nature' of teenagers, but actually it is just us trying to understand things that have been taken for granted for so long. Matters such as death, ethics and the purpose of life might be what that drug-abusing, tattoo-covered, apparently 'lost' son or daughter of yours is actually thinking about. I know I am.

To me, grades, getting a job or making money seem the least of our problems. What about dying? Why spend all our lives trying to 'secure a good future' when actually all our futures are quite similar? What about the difference between good and bad? Everyone knows that what we consider good or bad is only what we've been conditioned to believe through our upbringing, so why should anyone still cling like leeches to obsolete views and archaic opinions—on the glory of nationhood, the sanctity of tradition—that are neither absolute nor relevant. What about countries at war? What about religions and the riots they cause? Why isn't everyone worried about these things? Does everyone just want to keep living in complacence, only to die one day, not knowing anything more than what they were taught by others? Think about it—we begin dying the moment we are born. Time is short—too short to worry about policies and possession.

The teenage years are probably be the most tormented time of one's life, but given a choice between confused teenager and habituated grown-up, the pimples don't seem half as bad.

Kabeer Kathpalia

Bad Boy Joy

I despised the likes of Joy—a typical product of the emerging punk culture in college campuses in the late '80s—who spent all his time in shallow pursuits, drinking, smoking, partying, skirt-chasing, getting into fights, driving outrageously and, of course, blowing up *'baap ka paisa'*.

Joy was my batchmate during post-graduation. He evinced no genuine interest in pursuing the course for reasons of career. It was probably just a ploy to get his parents to extend his irresponsible and reckless life as a student by another year.

I was, myself, a 'good student', balancing academics with numerous extra-curricular activities and wholesome fun. Naturally, I was scathingly judgemental about Joy and made no attempt to consider him anything but worthless.

One day, I had to team up with Joy to complete a task. We set out on Joy's scooter, already short of time. Negotiating the late morning traffic, we rounded a corner and almost ran into a beggar lying dangerously sprawled by the side of the road. Joy showed good reflexes and we managed to miss the beggar by a hair's breadth.

The next instant Joy had stopped the scooter. 'What are you doing?' I asked him. 'We haven't hit him!'

But Joy had already alighted from the scooter. 'I know that, but someone else could. Let's shift him to the side.'

I was caught between the urge to do the humane thing, and the revulsion I felt at touching someone so filthy. 'But we're already late,' I said hesitantly.

'What's wrong with you?' Joy shouted. 'It'll take just a minute.' He beckoned me to hurry.

I walked to the prostrate body, queasy about touching the matted hair, the grimy limbs and clothes, breathing the foul odour emanating from it. And then, as I stood over him, I noticed that one of the man's legs was rotting with gangrene, infested with maggots. I almost threw up and drew back involuntarily.

'C'mon, what's the matter?' Joy said urgently.

'His leg has gangrene,' I managed to say.

Joy looked down for a moment, then said, 'Okay, you hold his head, I'll take the legs.'

I nodded weakly and together we shifted the miserable human being. All I felt, thereafter, was the overwhelming urge to wash my hands again and again with soap and disinfectant.

It was only later, in the light of introspection, that I saw the disturbing contrast between my none-too-heroic actions, and the instinctive compassion of Joy, the 'bad' boy.

From where did the humanity of the flippant Joy spring? What was it that prompted him to lead a shallow, self-indulgent life on the one hand, and respond to human suffering so readily on the other? And what was it in my nature, that for all my so-called goodness, I shirked from applying it where it was needed most? Was it upbringing or was it religion? I was a Hindu from a middle class family, Joy an upper middle class Christian.

Doubt gnawed at me for days! Not that I had suddenly developed any false illusions about Joy because of the incident, but my illusions about myself were suddenly under scrutiny!

Eventually, I came to the conclusion that Joy's life would perhaps always be essentially frivolous, with momentary sparks of meaningfulness because of some spontaneous acts of kindness.

As for me, I realised reluctantly that I would probably go through life as a nice person in a sanitised sense, but would remain incapable of compassionate acts that really mattered. I wasn't sure which life held less worth.

It's over fifteen years since that incident. I was basically right about my nature—but I have also surprised myself randomly, by actually doing a few things that could qualify as humane deeds. And I suspect if it hadn't been for Joy that day, I would never have given in to these stray impulses of compassion over the years.

I have no idea where Joy is or what he is up to. But I sometimes wonder whether I was right about him too.

Salil Desai

Dark Victory

In college, I skipped classes but always did well enough in the exams so nobody bothered me. The skipping became legitimate because I had the resourcefulness to get permission to attend various extra-curricular activities. I was too busy totting up 'things I've done' and 'people I've met' to bother about whether I was truly acquainted with the people I interacted with. I was in a hurry to become 'a winner'.

One day, in this course of things, I must have met Devi. I say, 'must have' because I don't remember when. She was in my class but since I was not there often enough I probably hadn't noticed her. She was also perhaps a bit too traditional for my taste. Then she started attending inter-collegiate competitions and began commuting to those events with me. She was smart enough, but it was the extreme effort she put into her academics and extra-curricular activities that made her shine.

I forgot to mention that Devi had a problem with walking because she had lost a leg to cancer while still in school. While the illness was under control, she needed help at doing some of the things that were mere routine for me.

When she increasingly and sometimes, a bit irritatingly, asked for help from us, I didn't appreciate the courage she'd required to do that. She'd undergone physical and mental pain. She'd realised that life was too short to do all the things you wanted. And she had understood the necessity of interdependence between people, but I was so blinkered by my need to be rebellious and unconventional, I recognised none of that.

We left college and she made it to the top higher education institute while I got into the second-best. She continued to focus and learnt to live away from the security of her home and family. I continued my search for elusive glory and was determined to forget the fundamentals of what my family was about. Devi and I kept in touch through a network of acquaintances sporadically, so I learned that she had got a good job after graduating and was living on her own in a completely new and bewildering city even for people like me who were fully physically equipped. I lived in the same city, had got a great job and was doing well superficially but inside I continued to be confused about where I was going.

A few years later I heard Devi had died. I felt bad at that time, wishing I had met up with her sometimes, that I had been more patient with her requests, that I had spent more time understanding her approach to life. Then I forgot and went on with my own.

Almost twenty years after we left college, I suddenly remembered Devi and reflected how different our lives had been. I'd had an unfettered, healthy childhood protected by a privileged family. She had suffered through a major illness and some monetary issues. She knew that her time was short while I had not even thought of death. She had intelligence and honed it by sheer hard work but I chose to dilute mine in the pursuit of teenage frivolities. I chose not to listen to my well-wishers because they never seemed to say what I wanted to hear but she learned by asking everyone to talk to her.

If I could go back to my teenage days, I would choose to

know Devi better and emulate her in some ways—in her focus, her ability to stretch her capabilities, and her real winning spirit.

Anonymous

Down the Road

The circle inspector stared at us angrily. He looked at me and asked haughtily, in Telugu, 'Where the hell do you live?' When I mentioned the locality, he said, 'Ah—just the place infested with goons.' He pointed to my silver wrist band and added, 'And you are not very far from getting to be a bloody loser.'

At the time of this incident, I was a sixteen-year-old studying electronics engineering at the Government Polytechnic. Each day, we travelled to college in a special bus which was a circus on wheels. Students would be hanging out of the bus doors and windows and would create such a riot, you would think we were heading to a picnic or a political rally. Any passerby would be promptly greeted with catcalls and names and hooting. And if the bus drove past a young lady or another busful of young girls, they were met with blood-curdling shrieks. Mostly, it was annoying behaviour, and implied contempt of others, but youthful exuberance often crosses bounds.

One fateful morning, when our bus passed a young woman and her father in a car, the students who were hanging out of the bus let out such a scream that the father and daughter were shaken and it took a few minutes for them to recover. The livid father overtook the bus and promptly informed the traffic police at the next junction. A bunch of cops quickly stopped the bus and asked all of us to walk into the police station. I'd been somewhere inside the bus, chatting away, completely unaware of the unfolding situation. Once I was told what was happening, I quickly told the cops that there was no need for the entire busload to be detained for the fault of a few students. I volunteered, along with a few others, to go into the police station and reason with the higher officials.

Those days, students were on a high, just after the Mandal Commission and such tectonic events. But this Inspector didn't care about that much. All he was looking at was an angry father and his teary daughter and we were going to have to apologise. I spoke in English and pacified the cops, pleading that we were students and wouldn't get government jobs if we had a crime registered in our names. They were gracious and let us go with a warning. The inspector took our names and addresses and threatened to haul us up at the next instance of trouble.

Some of us went on to become famous for rescuing others from trouble. I was not sure whether I was daring or foolhardy but I hadn't learnt my lessons yet. I got into more trouble with student politics. Once, a political rival group tried to hurt me badly. For months I carried a Rampuri—a barber's knife—to protect myself in case of an assault. I was tormented in my heart because I am a friendly guy by nature but the vortex of student politics had a violent side to it. I was a rebel at home, struggling with my studies and I hated my life. My parents, who were largely ignorant of my exploits outside the home, were struggling with their own problems.

At this point, I had a defining experience. Through an entirely different set of friends, I went to a youth camp and found inspiration. I discovered that my rebellion was a manifestation of an inner restlessness. Only if I found inner peace, would I be able to tackle the more visible issues that were troubling me. The story of Daniel in the Bible influenced me profoundly. Daniel was a rebel, too. He rebelled against the highest authority in the land of Babylon because he found a cause larger than his life.

I needed a cause too, that was larger than me and my circumstances. I made a decision that day to embark on such a path as had faith, hope and love. I needed something to live for and something to die for.

Through a painful and long journey, I was able to turn my life around. Through a series of second chances, I moved away from violence and resolved my rebellion. I started giving back to society right away. For years, I have joined hands to help young people find answers to their own pressing problems. Whether it was at a suicide prevention centre in Hyderabad or a sports organisation in Bangalore, whether it was communication workshops we had organised or in family circles, I was now guiding young people through counselling in the area of careers and relationships. We organised rock concerts to rally against drugs—I know that's ironic, but music is too powerful a tool to ignore to reach young people.

I am a recipient of graceful, forgiving opportunities. I always insist that young people be given second chances.

Sunil Robert

Healing

Under musty layers of murky time
There lie trembling secrets kept
From hearts close to mine.

A shadowy illusion existing in reality
A painful scar, a symbol of insanity.

What do I tell you about me?
Perhaps I should just let it be
Maybe I shouldn't reveal
What I've tried to forget was real.

Me. A child of seven. A dark room.
A furious father.
An avalanche of guilt, fear and pain leaves me reeling.
Slapafterslapafterslapafterslapafter ... slap ... after ...
slap ... after slap ... after slap.
'You're bad' slap 'You're wrong' slap 'You're wicked'
Was what you screamed at me.

You drummed my invisible sins into my senseless head.
You never wanted to beat me, was what you said.
But God said I was bad (because I woke up late, didn't
make my bed)

And God told you to beat me, to paint me black and red.
Wasn't that what you said?

And after you were gone, I'd curl up in a corner
And wail and wail and wail.
You took away the God I believed in
You left me no reason to pray.
Taking all my chances at magic away
Stealing my colours, leaving me with grey.

You told me the God I loved and talked to inside my head
Had given you orders to hurt me, to beat me till I bled.
Whom do I believe in now, whom can I beg for hope instead?
Whom do I pray to protect me, before I go to bed?

Fear. Extreme fear. Forget ideals. Cower in a corner.
Beg for mercy, beseeching you to be kind. I swear I'll be good!
A whiplash of smarting pain.
A seeping crimson stain.

Tears hurt me more.
Outside, the wound heals
Inside, it grows into my being.

Later, I grew up and read
Books that God sent me, instead
Of listening to the lies you tell.
And I break the seven-year spell.
And throw coins, sending lost wishes
Into my childhood's enchanted well.

I question your motives
No longer am I the kid who believes she's bad.
I am
A survivor, a child matured by the pain she's had.

My eyes aren't blurry any more,
And when I look at you I see
A grown-up kid who was beaten like me
Still smarting, hurting, bruised from an old beating,
Through my pain, seeking your healing, venting.

I am a grown-up kid, with colourful band-aids on her cuts,
Healing
I vow
To batter this eternal legacy of hurt
To soothe it with peace
To still it with love
My kids will know my God, not yours.

Crystal

His Heartstrings

Today the world knows me as Pandit Vishwa Mohan Bhatt, creator of the Mohan veena, winner of a Grammy award. What it does not know is that at sixteen, I had an experience that changed and shaped my beliefs for all time.

Born into a family of musicians, I inherited *sur, lay* and *taal* in my blood. I grew up to the sound of music. I trained early in vocal music and then tried my hand at the violin. When I was about ten, I took a liking to the sitar, trained in it and played it for about three years.

A German lady came to stay with us to learn music from my father, and it was then that the guitar entered our household, and so began my tete-a-tete with this beautiful instrument. My attraction towards it was all-consuming and I found it difficult to concentrate on anything other than the guitar. I saw this as a sign from God and decided that it was going to be my life henceforth.

I was aware of the repercussions that this love would have. I belonged to a family where the sitar, vocals or classical violin were practised. The guitar, though respected, was still looked upon as something foreign to our culture, our heritage. A few members of my family asked me whether I was sure of what I was doing. They did not want any one of us to waste precious hours trying out something so alien. But my mother and father supported me in my endeavour and encouraged me to follow my heart's desire.

I decided to modify the Western instrument and make it suitable for playing pure and pristine Indian classical music. I was keen to bring out from it the nuances of pure Indian traditional sound.

By the time I was sixteen, I had already spent two exclusive years with the guitar. We lived in Jaipur then and had close family friends, the Mathurs. Great lovers and patrons of music, they regularly organised musical evenings with a small gathering of connoisseurs at their place. My brother, sister and nephews were already performing artistes by then. One evening, I stated that I too would like to perform.

The first comment I received was that I would need to work very hard to make a mark with the new instrument. One of the gathering said, 'If it were the sitar, you would have been in league with your brother and sister with the two years that you spent on it, but this instrument needs more.' Someone else said, 'Listen for yourself, the sitar's sound is like a flowing stream. Your instrument lacks that depth.' Yet another said, 'Hear your brother play the violin; his sur and taal are so beautiful. What are you doing with this instrument?'

I was depressed and cried the entire night. I had just given two years of my life to the instrument. From a musician's point of view it was not much and I could easily have switched over and taken up something which was more in tune—literally—with my family. But I was sure that there was no other instrument for me but the guitar.

Along with that, I had another belief: this was the instrument that would become my face to the world. Even then I was sure I was going to make it big . . . very big. The next morning, I vowed to myself to prove all of them wrong, I would work hard and change their opinion of me and of my passion.

That was the turning point of my life. Since that day I doubled my *riyaaz* and practised for about ten hours a day. Along with that I also studied other aspects of the guitar. What really is the instrument, how is it made, what goes behind the sound that emerges from it?

In my mind I was clear what I wanted. I would establish this instrument on the musical scene so firmly that people would say yes . . . it has the depth of any other. I wanted to incorporate the speciality, technique and sound of every instrument into mine. I wanted to merge and produce a new sound, a new concept. I wanted to invent something which gave the sound and tune of the Western guitar but could be handled like an Indian veena.

I also knew that not only was the sound that my instrument produced important, but the story of my music too. It must express my vision; what I want to say through the instrument must come out without me spelling it out. Do I want to tell a story of romance, or of devotion? Is my music about harmony or the pure love of a mother for her child? Can I truly express myself through my music?

I knew I had to gain knowledge, deep knowledge, remember the dos and don'ts of raagas, and then create. I knew what I had to do and I knew how to do it. I knew that it would take hard work, time, single-minded focus, relentless pursuit, but I also knew that there was nothing else that I would rather do all my life.

I just followed my heart's passion and here I am . . .

Vishwa Mohan Bhatt
As told to Amita Dalal

Love, Actually

Like every little girl you know, I love my mom and dad. I am secure in the knowledge that they too love and value my sister and me dearly.

I have always thought my mother to be a very special person. She is bright and smart and has supported me in everything I do. Every time we were given a project in school, she would give me ideas for it, and my teachers would heap praise on me when I submitted it. I soon became a star student and in my heart I knew that it was my mom's encouragement and guidance which helped me to do so well. Dad is fantastic as well, but since he has very long working hours, it's Mom who's around for us most of the time.

As I grew up and entered my pre-teens, I began to get into arguments with my mom regularly. I would take too long in the bathroom—something she hated—and block her out by turning on the volume on my iPod. Our daily arguments turned into full-fledged fights and the day would often end with one or other of us crying, and my sulking in my room. I was having problems in school as well. Some of my friends had moved on to other groups of friends and I was feeling isolated. I took out all my anger on my mother. I found fault with everything she did and misinterpreted whatever she said. It was almost as if she was my worst enemy.

It's not as if I felt good after those outbursts. On the contrary, I was miserable, but I was unable to control my behaviour.

One day I was especially mean to my mom and said all sorts of nasty things to her, although I knew in my heart that what I was saying was wrong. I saw her in tears and still ranted on. I then rushed off to school in a huff.

When I reached school I realised that I had left a very important assignment at home. It was the last day of its submission and not submitting it on that day would mean that I would lose my grade and my chance at a scholarship. I spent the first period agonising over my loss. Just then, the school receptionist walked in and handed a package to my class teacher. She looked at it and said that my assignment had just come in from home and that there was a note for me as well. I looked at the note. It just said, 'I love you always, Mom.'

It was a long wait till 2 o'clock, when I went home. When I saw my mother, I hugged her wordlessly. She held me tight. There was no need to say anything.

Divisha Mehta

Remembering a Room and an Age

It was perhaps the room, the classroom at the farthest corner of the top floor, that seemed disconnected from normal school activity. Or perhaps, it was my age, thirteen years, an unlucky number for some, but also the threshold between innocence and experience. Or perhaps I just needed to teach myself a lesson.

About a hundred students of St Anthony's High School had gathered on the second day of Father Ivo Fernandez's seminar on the religious communities that populate the world and the need for them to live in harmony. As representatives of our school, we were expected to be on our best behaviour for the visit of the guest lecturer.

My friends and I were the first to arrive in the dingy room. Some of us occupied ourselves looking out of the windows for the others and some drummed impatiently on their desks. Being the studious kind, I went to the blackboard and started reading the notes of the previous day, written by Father Fernandez. Nonchalantly, I rubbed out an alphabet from the blackboard and the act urged me to continue doing so further. In no time I was joined by my two friends, discretely rubbing out alphabets from the blackboard, freeing the language of its syntax, grammar and even meaning. Soon, 'Hindus' became 'in us', 'Islam' became 'Is am', 'the' became 'he', and so on. Every word could be read individually but together they were an Esperanto of meaninglessness.

I found it funny that all the students gathered at the blackboard could instantly recall the notes of the previous day, but when they tried to read them now, they could only laugh at the sea of words.

Father Fernandez, when he came in, did not laugh. He stared at the blackboard for a long time as if to extract some meaning out of the chaos. Then he turned around and asked the class, 'Who did this?' The class was silent. He started to ask each student in turn whether he was the one to spoil the notes on the blackboard. All answered in the negative, including my two accomplices. When it was my turn to answer, I stood up, bowed my head and confessed to what I had done.

When I recall the incident after all these years, I think I did the right thing. I preferred being a prankster in front of everyone than being dishonest in my own eyes. Even though, being an ambassador of the school, my act breached discipline, lying about it would have been a greater misdemeanour. What opinion would Father Fernandez have formed of my school, if he had not found out the culprit? But these were not the thoughts I had when I stood up to acknowledge my guilt.

Father Fernandez asked, 'Shall I call Father Peter, the prefect, and ask him to cane you?'

He continued, 'Shall I ask the headmaster, Father Regi, to call your parents?'

I was silent and resigned to my fate.

He raised his voice, 'What should I do?'

The whole class had its eyes on me.

Then Father Fernandez changed his tone and said, 'It would have been easy for you to choose to lie and deny the charge. Yet you stood up for the truth. I shall ask that you be made president of the class. You deserve to be.'

That day I found out how difficult it is to lie to a person who is willing to believe me! I also believe people, even more now, and find people, especially teenagers, finding it difficult to lie to me.

But what made me play a prank so unusual to my nature? Perhaps it was the room. Or, perhaps, it was the age. But what a timely one it was.

Amit Shankar Saha

Ruben

With three cars, five maids and a nice big bungalow in the heart of Chennai in the 1980s, we were well off, you could say, and very conservative. I remember Ruben, the manservant. We loved Ruben. He was short, dark, bald, skinny, had a moustache like Veerappan and smiled like the perfect Colgate model. He groomed the garden, drove the cars for us, helped the women of the house in the kitchen and managed to find time to pluck us mangoes from the tree in the backyard. He would treat us to playing with the numerous stray animals he'd bring home. He once tried catching a rat and it bit his thumb so badly that his thumb actually split in two—the '80s version of Hrithik's thumb. Needless to say, at ages five and six, my sister and I found him fascinating. He lived in the slums in Chennai but went home only to sleep, returning by 4.30 in the morning to resume his routine. I never thought of him as a servant.

I turned sixteen and I became the typical hot-headed teenager eager to try out new things. Part of my new and improved lifestyle was a boy, John, an engineering student. He was rebellious and lived life on the edge. He pursued me like I was gold, on beach trips, at the movies, at coffee shops and at the malls. The pressure began building between us. We wanted to . . . kiss. One night I asked him to pick me up from a friend's place, because it was late, and drop me home. He'd been asleep but at my invitation at 2 a.m., his hormones got the better of him. He scurried to my friend's house and I left with him, lying to my friend's mother that he was my brother. Standard procedure. Before we knew it, we were in the corner of the private lane to my house. It was 4 a.m. and conveniently dark, so there we found ourselves kissing away to glory.

Then it happened—Ruben, making his way back to our house, saw us: John with his hands where they shouldn't have been and me in a position I would have never wanted Ruben to see me in.

Not Ruben of all people. This man was my grandmother's favourite; he'd raised my mom, aunt, my sister and I. And here he was, a witness to this embarrassing situation, watching us doing something no one in my house would approve of. My mind was already running a series of chain reactions. Ruben was going to tell on me to the family, and he would do it to score some brownie points. He would of course add masala to the account so that my grandmom would give him hush money to keep him from talking to the neighbours' servants. Oh my God, if he told the servants, that would be like broadcasting it on BBC.

I pushed John away from me, smiled apologetically at Ruben and begged him not to let on. I still don't know if he understood what I meant. The look he gave me was stoic; he neither smiled, nor looked angry, nor embarrassed. He just moved on quietly. All I could then think of was my freedom, my precious freedom that I would lose from the first rays of the morning sun. I was sure once Ruben had spilled his story there would be no more nights out, parties, phone calls, or new clothes. I cursed Ruben with all my breath for walking in on my private moment, spoiling my first kiss and worse, perhaps ruining my social life forever.

I bid a fast and sad goodbye to John, knowing that I would probably never see him again. I reached home ten minutes after Ruben and was prepared for the women of the house to be standing at the door with knives. I entered the hallway, but no one was there. I wondered if Ruben was narrating the juicy details right then in the kitchen. I dashed to the kitchen, but my grandmom stood there cooking and greeted me with her usual sarcastic 'welcome to the guest house' speech. I found my mom in the backyard plucking flowers and my aunt watching morning *satsang* on TV.

Everyone went about their lives. No one was told about the incident.

I went on with my life and Ruben went along with his. I did start avoiding him because whenever I saw him, the embarrassing memory of what happened would hit me like a flashback. Years passed. I finished my post-graduation at Mudra Institute in Ahmedabad and returned to Chennai. Not finding Ruben at the house, I inquired casually after him. My grandmom told me that he had been drinking and was suffering from multiple-organ failure. He didn't have much time.

Suddenly I wanted to meet Ruben and apologise for all the misgivings and suspicions I had heaped on him for years. But the next day, news came that Ruben had passed away.

I was shocked and mourned for hours. That day, I realised the immense value of what he had done for me and my family. He showed me that love does not have to be slotted as romantic and filial—it can just be wanting the best for another, without any expectations in return. I never got the chance to meet Ruben to thank him but I think of him and his love every day.

Priya Krishnan

Rude is Crude

I'm the kind of teenager who always has a story, a joke or a wisecrack for every occasion. That's me, and I have a lot of friends.

A girl in my class—let's call her Anita—was quite the opposite. For some reason, she had friends in the senior classes, but nearly nobody in our ninth standard could stand her. Including me.

The funny thing is, Anita used to be a pretty good friend of mine. She even went around with my best friend—let's call him Gaurav—but things soured between them and so our friendship suffered in the bargain. She then bad-mouthed my friend behind his back. To get back at her, we started taunting and teasing her . . . not behind her back, oh no, but right to her face! So she would cry on her senior friends' shoulders and ask them for advice. All the tears and sob stories only served to irritate us further, and made us merciless when ridiculing her. The scary thing is, we later learnt, she even talked a couple of times about committing suicide.

Anita probably wasn't the best judge of character. Four girls from our class made a show of interest in her. One of them, Rita, was a friend of mine and I knew her to be genuine, but the other three were only interested in material for gossip. They used her stories against her; they would sit together, rip her to bits and laugh.

One wretched day, I found myself flicking Anita's bra strap. She sat in front of me in class and I was just trying to get her attention, because I needed to borrow a pencil. I had no intention of humiliating her.

Well, thanks to that, I was in a foul temper. Gaurav and I were walking around the playground during the break when we got into a spat with Anita and her so-called friends. Rita was also with them. I called them all a bunch of hypocrites and we had a huge shouting match; Gaurav and me against Anita and the others. Suddenly, Rita threw water on me, and something in me just snapped; I was full of red-hot rage. Before I realised what I was doing, I pushed her really hard and she fell down.

When I saw the shock on their faces, I knew that I was going to be in trouble. I managed to last through the rest of the day and hurried home. I didn't tell my mom anything, but my head was reeling with shame.

The next day, I convinced my mom that I wasn't feeling well enough for school and so she let me be. I went through the whole day feeling queasy and jittery.

The call came the following day. My mother and I had been summoned to the principal's office. When we got to school, she went into the principal's room alone. I was called in later. My mother listened, livid, as the principal narrated the incidents again in front of me . . . including the unfortunate one involving Anita.

My mom looked at me, totally zapped. 'You pulled her bra strap? Are you crazy?'

I tried to protest, 'It was an accident.'

But she wasn't interested. She was fuming.

I was suspended from school for being a 'bad influence'. I was crushed. I started studying at home. My friends helped me get through it all by getting my homework and filling me in on what had happened in class. They were furious with the girls who had complained against me.

After two weeks I was allowed back in school. But I didn't get put back on the bus route so my mom had had to put her entire day on hold just to drop me off to school and pick me up for the following two weeks. It was only after I sincerely apologised to the principal that I was pardoned and allowed back on the bus.

Then all those girls, one by one, came and said 'sorry' to me (even though it was my fault . . .). And everything was normal again.

The two weeks at home gave me a lot of time to think and made me change my perspective on a few things. No one had intended to get me suspended. Not at all. It had been entirely my fault. That's why I found it easy to talk to all the girls again.

Also, I learnt that being sassy can get you into trouble. That jokes and wisecracks don't always help in a sticky situation. That a devil-may-care attitude is a turn-off for teachers. That an untucked school shirt does not mean you're cool, it means you're a fool. That bad manners brand you. That we go to school not just to learn how to read and write or about science and the world we live in. We're also there to learn how to become better human beings.

Nikhil Sundar

Smoke

If you smell smoke in her hair,
Will you think of swept-up leaves burning
Sending blue spires into the morning sky?

Or will you remember
An evening walk along the seawall
When she bought peanuts
And stood in the thin smoke
While she paid for them, and then
Walked on, crunching, and sometimes
Offered a few to you in her hand
As to a horse, and you longed, longed
To kiss her palm, and could only inhale
The smell of the smoke in her hair
As you walked, because of a by-law
That says you may not kiss, may not sit
Facing the sea, may not hold hands
May only walk together, and eat peanuts
Slowly, one, or even half at a time
To make them, and this moment
Last a little longer.

Jane Bhandari

'So, What is Your Son Up To?'

'But of course—engineering!' used to be my parents' prompt response for anyone enquiring about my future plan during school days. The decision was a no-brainer of sorts. Ever since childhood, I boasted an excellent academic performance which, by default, meant I was cut out either for medicine or engineering. No questions asked. A childhood spent within the triangular confines of home, school and tuitions created a narrow vision, never allowing me to see what I was heading towards, having no clue about what I was missing out on.

Since the very beginning, I was party to the plan and my nod only strengthened my parents' aspirations to see their only son as an engineer. Around them were ample examples of kids securing admission into technical institutes, their first step towards a bright, secured future. Little did they know that my junior college, my two-year stopover before engineering, would lead me a different direction.

Travelling to a south Mumbai college from far-flung suburbs meant stepping into a new world altogether. The transition exposed me to alien ideas and perspectives. Seeing the college offer so many different subjects, I realised there was more to academics than circuit diagrams and mathematical expressions. The inquisitive side of me raised his antenna. 'After all, it's not like I will move away from my original plan. But learning something new will never harm me, right?' was how I excused my explorations of a tabooed world.

But exploring alternative routes is possible only when you are, at least roughly, aware of your destination. The more I looked outside, the more it demanded me to look within and answer one basic question—what do I enjoy doing? The self-discovery was wonderfully surprising, like a baby who discovers that his hands can hold and legs can be used to take him around. The biggest revelation was that I loved doing things that I hadn't been able to do all my life. Having spent most of my time within the confines of my home, I now wanted to travel. Because my evenings were wholly dedicated to academics, I now wanted to meet more people. Having lived a painfully structured life, a nine-to-five job was the last thing I wanted. With self-discovery came a rebellious strength. By the process of omission, I zeroed down on pursuing what I believed would provide me all the above—media. And that's where the trouble began.

When the twelfth standard results were out, I discovered that my PCM (Physics, Chemistry, Math) score was a whooping ninety-eight per cent. My parents were ecstatic since my score would guarantee a red-carpet entry to the topmost engineering colleges. But out of the blue, I announced that I wouldn't be pursuing engineering. I didn't beat around the bush, just told them upfront, in the least possible words. Rightly so, they couldn't understand where I was coming from. I was bombarded with questions.

Their lack of support was discouraging, yet I stuck to my decision. I expected them to stand by me, but didn't complain when they didn't. What made matters worse were some nosey aunties who declared how I was on full gear to spoil a supposedly bright career. 'Who goes for media in spite of scoring so well? Why don't you tell him anything?' was their incessant argument. The concern was fake, but their words riled my already concerned parents even more. The matter took time to cool down with intermittent comparisons between me and the 'good' kids who did what they were 'asked' to do.

Having secured admission in a mass media course, I set out on a different journey. The everyday comparisons made me insecure and I used the same insecurities to work harder. I was hell bent to prove all those wrong who declared that I was a fool to follow my heart. The next three years were a mix of fun and struggle. Fun, because I basked under the satisfaction of doing what *I* wanted. Struggle, because jumping into a creative field from a science background required immense reconditioning of the mind.

Juggling internships with academics helped me network with various publications. And by God's grace, I bagged a job in one of the better-known newspapers months before I graduated. And yes, with a salary more than what an average engineer, passing out from an average institute, was paid at that time. My parents' fleeting disapproval for my choice was put to rest the day I got my first salary. Money changed their perspective, not because it benefited them in any way, but because they were happy for me.

However, my parents haven't stopped dreaming. Earlier, they were keen to see me as an engineer. Today, they want to see me settled, with a big mansion, a car, an even better salary and yes, happily married. But I have my plans as well. Some dreams of theirs might fit in, some might not. It's a constant tug of war, and years down the line, we have learned to have our fun with it. Today, when the same annoyingly nosey aunty asks my mom what I am up to, she says proudly, 'My son is a journalist!'

Vikas Hotwani

The Name Board

Somebody said it couldn't be done,
But he with a chuckle replied
That 'maybe it couldn't', but he would be one
Who wouldn't say so till he'd tried.
Somebody scoffed: 'Oh, you'll never do that;
At least no one we know has done it';
But he took off his coat and he took off his hat,
And the first thing we knew he'd begun it.
With a lift of his chin and a bit of a grin,
Without any doubting or quiddit,
He started to sing as he tackled the thing
That couldn't be done, and he did it.

—Edgar Guest

I had enrolled for my chartered accountant course with lots of enthusiasm. The course is known as one of the toughest exams in India and my father (a chartered accountant!) added to the tension by stating that he didn't personally know anyone who had completed the course in his or her first attempt—other than himself and his good friend, Rajesh. I decided that I wanted to be the next in this list of first-attempt successes.

But this was easier said than done. The course lived up to its reputation—it was very difficult, and I needed all the help and encouragement I could get. My parents did a great job on that count. However, I needed more and more emotional support for the entire five years. I turned to the popular self-help books and learned about positivism. I changed my attitude and replaced my fears with optimism. I dreamt of my success and made hypothetical mark statements proclaiming my success. I kept looking at these mark statements every day and felt enthused with confidence and joy. I started to study well, focussed on my goals, and my performance soared. So, I decided to take my positivism plans a little further.

I created my own name board proclaiming in bold letters '*ARCHANA B.Com., A.C.A.*' I hung it on the door of my room. Looking at it every day made me happy and hopeful. Then, one day, my father announced that his friend, Rajesh, was coming home for dinner. My mother embarked on elaborate preparations and a feast was made ready. Rajesh was a childhood friend of my father. They had played together, studied together and worked together. They had a lot in common but differed vastly in character. While my father was patient, simple and polite, Rajesh was short-tempered, shrewd and had a vicious tongue. Neither did he care about what he said in public nor did he worry about how his words could hurt another. Little did I know that I was to be his next victim.

After he came home that day and all of us had had a cozy chat, my mother invited him to the dining hall. As he walked towards the room, he passed my room and stood still, staring at my nameplate.

'You're doing your CA, right?' he asked.

'Yes!' I replied.

'Aren't you a bit over-confident? What makes you think

you can clear the exam? I know of zillions who never completed it in their entire life!' I was speechless with anger hearing his words. In spite of my flashing eyes, he continued, 'Don't waste time in making name boards. You can use that time in studying another chapter!'

My parents did not come to my defence. They continued to remain the gracious Indian hosts they were. That dinner was a sober affair for me. I clenched my fists beneath the table to avoid bashing our guest or something else. Halfway through the meal, I got up, excused myself saying I had a headache and retired to my room. I did not come out again till he left the house.

That night, I was so upset that I could hardly sleep. In the middle of the night, I crept near that name board and touched those two letters, 'C.A.'. Maybe I was acting in over-confidence . . . Had I mixed up optimism with hubris? Had I been rash?

My hands slowly went up to remove the board. Suddenly, I stopped. What was I doing? Why would I remove my hope . . . my dream . . .? No, I was not proud or arrogant—it was he who was so! Why would I listen to the words of a pompous buffoon and take away a reiteration of my dreams and goals? No way, I decided, and went to sleep peacefully. Now, years later, that name board still hangs on my wall. Now it is not a dream or a hope—it's a reality!

Archana Sarat

Why?

Here's the story of a young Indian boy
It's the truth, the whole truth and no lie
He decided one day
To do an MBA
And everyone asked him, 'Why?'

The friends with whom he was rooming,
Said, 'If you really want your career zooming,
Try for IIM-A
Why the US of A?
When the economy in India is booming!'

His parents were quite happy with his choice
But Mom in her worried mother's voice
Felt it natural to express
A very slight distress

'Why not nearer home, like most other boys?'

His parents' wishes he always heeded
But global experience and exposure he needed
So one day he sat
And took the GMAT
Thus the MBA process was well seeded!

The long essays that he had to write
Kept him busy till late in the night;
Articulation of vision
Rewording and revision
And voila! He had just got it right!

Each school had its own quirks, and fussed
Different questions and topics were discussed
But soon he was done
'Cos common to each one
Were 'Why MBA?', 'Why now?' and 'Why us?'

His lengthy tryst with questions continued
When by the Darden School of Business he was interviewed
There was no hesitation
Just the realisation
That by now all answers for 'Why' were imbued.

(For the following poetry, I beg pardon)
Soon life starts resembling a rose garden
With bright cherry trees
And busy bumble bees
For he finds out he has been admitted to Darden!

At last he goes up to his boss
Who is juggling with figures of margins gross
And tells him, 'This is
My one month's notice'
To which the boss for words is at a loss.

'Why, oh why do this to your career?
You're eligible for a promotion, my dear;
Heed my advice
And take up this nice
Long-term on-site opportunity for a year.'

To this our young friend then replies
'I've had it up to here with the Whys!
Maybe then and now
I'd like a little How
Even a Who, What, Where or When would be nice!'

Roshan Shanker

5

ON ADDICTION

'You may ascribe to the universal delusion that that you can avoid pain and only have pleasure in this life—but that is utterly impossible.'

—The Mahabharata

Never Again

It was way back in 1988, and if you thought drug users were not rampant in India back then, think again. Many engineering colleges, too, had more than their fair share. I know because I was there, in BITS, Pilani.

My friends were decent guys and girls from diverse backgrounds, with impeccable academic records. Although we were from different parts of India and were studying different subjects, we became very close.

Our favourite meeting place was Connaught for delicious yummies such as Midnight Beauties (milkshakes with ice cream), dosas or Maggi cooked with butter, peas and chunks of paneer. We would sit on the cane chairs, spend hours sipping chai or cold drinks and we would bond. Even our study trips to the library saw us trooping in together. This camaraderie was a vital support system . . . it helped keep us sane in the face of the intense pressure to excel.

As I said, it wasn't all serious business. There were fun times too, when we would go to movies, take part in music nights or in our college festival, Oasis. We were one big happy family.

The reason I'm rambling is to show you that drugs, in whatever form, mild or hard, can creep into your life anytime, anywhere, from anyone.

The incident I want to share took place during the Holi festival of 1988. My gang and I had a truly fantastic day . . . complete with dousing each other with wet colours and dunking each other in a dirty pond nearby.

One of our friends, Chhotu, produced a box of laddoos but he wouldn't give me any. 'No, not for you,' he said. 'They contain bhang.'

Everybody in India knows about bhang and the notorious use of the intoxicant during Holi—made even more appealing thanks to many Bollywood song-and-dance sequences. 'It'll be fun to try,' I grinned.

'Boss, you have play practice after this. You'll be a zombie,' Chhotu tried to warn me.

He was right. I was taking part in a hilarious Hindi play, *Premnagar ki Dagar*. While the play was a comedy, theatre was very serious business in Pilani and the director was known to be a perfectionist.

But I was in no mood to listen to the voice of reason. 'Don't worry about play practice, I have enough control. Nothing can wreck that,' and so saying, I downed a laddoo and ran away laughing. Chhotu looked concerned, but I had bravado written all over me. Bravado, mind you, not bravery.

After the revelry, my friend Neena silently escorted me back to our hostel. I was fine till, suddenly, a lightheaded feeling took over. I felt like I was floating. I managed a bath somehow, put on fresh clothes and ran to my bicycle.

Neena wanted to escort me to the auditorium where we practised but I wouldn't hear of it. I felt strangely happy and kept singing the same two lines of a song stuck in my head, over and over and over again. Once I'd got to the auditorium, I parked my cycle and went in to greet my merry band of thespians.

The evening went by in a blur. I know I was extraordinarily focused, but I felt like a robot, pretending to smile, walking on air and following the director's commands with extra care. Practice seemed to go on forever when in fact it had been cut short because of Holi. When would the effect of the bhang wear off? And if something as simple as bhang could do this to me, what would be the influence of something more hard-core?

When it was over, I heaved a sigh of relief, I was so intensely tired. How would I head back to hostel? I needed help but we didn't have cell phones then so I couldn't call up my friends.

I looked around and instinctively made my decision. The director. I would ask him.

He was chatting with the backstage crew when I interrupted. 'Can I talk to you please?'

'Sure.' He was always courteous.

'Can you please accompany me back to Meera Bhawan?' There must have been a sense of desperation in my voice because he didn't hesitate for a second. 'Absolutely,' he said, waved everyone goodbye and escorted me out of the auditorium.

I fumbled around for my key, looked around for my bike, couldn't find it and felt I was losing my hold on things. I nearly wept as I looked at Nidheesh, and shrugged my shoulders.

'Look again,' his tone was kind.

His gentle tone had the sobering effect of water splashed on my face. I found my cycle, unlocked it and we started trudging back, me pushing the bike.

'I had bhang,' I blurted out. No preamble, nothing.

There were a lot of people who must have had bhang; it was Holi, after all. In fact there were always some people smoking pot on campus and drinking. I was just never one of them. Nidheesh was silent for a bit, and then finally said he found it unbelievable. I peered at him in a daze, now quite miserable. I confessed in detail the events of the afternoon that had led to my fall from grace.

'You may not know this,' he told me, 'but I handle an anti-drug campaign here in Pilani. What you did may seem harmless, but it's not just about trying some bhang, or weed, or grass. It's about your actions. It's about addiction. You may never do it again—great. Or, on the other hand, once you start, you may think there's no harm in trying something else. Just once. To see what it feels like. To be cool. To fit in. Maybe you're in the right company today, even though your friends were class idiots and need to be told that. But you might be in the wrong company tomorrow. And once the habit starts, it gains a momentum of its own. Addiction—how hard it is to break.'

There was a sense of urgency in his voice. Not anger, but urgency.

'Anu, please understand, addiction claims your very life. We have busted people supplying BITSians with drugs. But those who are addicted find ways anyway. And they find excuses too: they say it helps them to party, to study, to focus, to unwind . . . the list goes on. An addict will always have the means and the excuse.

'Did it ever occur to you that you asked me to walk you back, even though you didn't know me that well? You never once thought that you were in a vulnerable state and that I could easily have taken advantage of you. I'm saying this to scare you, so that you understand the kind of danger you put yourself in today.

'Many people on drugs start them as a lark. But why, when there are so many other harmless fun things to try? Like gliding or cricket or photography. These activities are so much more productive and creative. And infinitely more rewarding.'

I tried to smile through my tears as I fervently promised

that I would never be so foolish again. I meant every word. Never again. Nidheesh gave me the kindest smile as he gripped my shoulders and said, 'I'll watch until you get inside and I hope you remember my lo-o-o-ng lecture. Anu, never again.' Neither of us ever acknowledged this incident afterwards.

And since then, that's the way it has been for me—never again. Every time I see a campaign, 'Do sports, not drugs', or a documentary, a serial or a movie about drug abuse, I recall these words, 'Never again.' My personal motto.

Anuradha Gupta

Safe at Home

About two-and-a-half years ago, I spent a month in hospital because of continuous and frequent vomiting. The doctors were puzzled at the unstoppable abnormality. They could not figure out the cause of my problem.

My parents were extremely worried. Besides sleeping, eating, breathing and taking care of me, all they did was pray—day and night—for my recovery. My sister, too, was anxious. Her days were spent at school but her mind was at the hospital. Even my grandparents, who lived far away, came rushing to Ahmedabad to be by my side.

I was now going through extreme emotional and psychological distress. The only thing I wanted was to get well and go home. What added to the bane was the weakness from a preceding bout of malaria from which I had just recovered.

After a few days, a friend of my father suggested that he consult a child psychologist. At the end of his wits, my father decided to explore this option too.

Now, let me give you some background on my self. Before this long term of ill-health plagued my life, I was actually having relationship problems with friends at school. They'd given me a choice. The choice was either to do what I didn't feel comfortable doing or choose not to be a party to their plans and thus lose my 'friends'. In the end it came down to losing them.

And suddenly I found myself almost friendless and extremely lonely. Though this really hurt me, I couldn't bring myself to share this with my parents. I thought they wouldn't understand.

When I had contracted malaria, I kind of liked the feel of it. I had started enjoying staying at home, watching television and being looked after. I was the centre of attraction for my family, and that was so welcome after those long hours of loneliness at school. I just felt safer and more comfortable at home. After spending about a week at home, because of the malaria, I felt that this was where I truly belonged.

But then one day my comfort zone was threatened. After a check-up, the doctor said that I was fit and ready to rejoin school (or, for me, ready to step into hell again).

They say that the body adapts to a certain kind of behaviour or activity that the mind is undergoing. My subconscious mind wired thoughts around my body, and without my knowing it, my body was trying to find reasons for staying home.

The next morning the frenzy of vomiting began. And I got to stay at home. But I could not stop vomiting and did so five or six times a day. It was awful. No one, including me, had a clue as to what was wrong, since the reports showed no abnormality in the blood or organs. I became physically weak; my mind got tired of this constant attention on the body. I now started pining for my regular life—school, work, games, activities!

Within the third sitting itself, the psychologist figured out my malaise. He explained to me that my behaviour was not out of sorts, given my teen-phase. Had I confided my emotional state to another, perhaps more mature person, at the advent of my problem, it would not have taken such a painful course. He encouraged me to speak to my parents.

I started sharing my problems with them. They suggested ways in which I could stand on my own and yet not offend my friends. I became more extroverted and opened up to my friends as well.

This has changed my life now. I am a different person altogether. I share, talk and discuss feelings instead of bottling them up and ruminating over the same things endlessly.

Teenage is when most of us are confused about our peers, ideals, choices, ambitions, goals, relationships, decision-making abilities, and our capacity to withstand the pressure of academic performance. The trick is to share our fears.

Today, although I wouldn't want to undergo it again, the experience of adolescence gave me more than it took away.

Mehul Mittra

With a Cigarette in My Hand . . .

My story dates back to an age when I was not aware of the meaning of the 'injurious' in the health warnings on cigarette packs.

As a child, I wondered how good an experience smoking could be. Whether lighting up that stick full of neatly packed tobacco would be a mark of manhood and bravery. I was impressed even by the colourful packaging and clever branding.

Nobody in the family smoked. It was only when we had a party or a get-together that my Dad offered cigarettes for the relentless use of one 'Chimney Uncle'. I call him by that name, because he worked on a simple rule: each cigarette on display was destined to live only for a day, so all had to consumed before the party ended. I rather admired his capacity, and I loved making our cigarette box, a marvel of Kashmiri woodcraft in walnut, pop up an endless supply.

In time I began to look for opportunities to open packs of cigarettes to empty them into the automatic popper. Already, the smell of the newly opened cigarettes had begun to give me a kick. I longed to be old and 'mature' enough to smoke.

As they say, moms will be moms. My mother figured out my increasing attraction to cigarettes and saw the future 'Chimney Uncle' in me. What she did after that, totally took me by surprise. You see, she was a child psychologist. She lit a cigarette and gave it to me to smoke. I can distinctly recall how I held the cigarette in my jittery hands, and had my first puff of that delicacy. And what followed was a continuous blast of coughing. I felt as if my throat has been seriously burnt, and that I was choking. I can't even recall where I threw the remaining cigarette away as I dashed off for a glass of water. For a moment I thought my mom to be my biggest enemy, for inflicting this hellish experience on me. But I knew I'd wanted it, needed it.

Ten years from that day, I realise how that incident satiated my curiosity about smoking once and for all, and I have never ever thought of trying a cigarette since.

My beloved Chimney Uncle is no longer around to demonstrate the virtues of smoking. He died of lung cancer a few years back, leaving behind a grieving family.

Prasoon Agarwal

6

ON FAMILY

'Social turmoil is hell, Krishna, for the family, for the destroyers of the family and for the whole society.'

—Bhagavad Gita

My Arithmetic Lessons

The sound of the creaking bicycle rolling on the pebbles of our driveway set my heart beating rapidly. Vikas, our old faithful, went to open the door saying, 'Noor, Vicky babu, your math teacher has arrived, please get ready and come to the dining room. He should not be kept waiting.'

The year was 1975; I was in Class V. My father had settled in the small town of Burla in Orissa. He was a dental surgeon with the state government hospital. He would spend mornings in the hospital and evenings saw him engrossed with his patients in the chamber. But all his spare time he would devote to us, playing not like a father but an opponent, whether kicking a football in the corridor or winning the queen off the carom board.

Ma, his gentle counterpart, provided the serene backdrop to my father's temperament. We were comfortable making impractical demands on her that she would try and meet in a practical manner. Being a pure arts student she was no mathematician—she was our friend.

One evening my brother and I were told that a Mr Debendra Mohanty, chemistry lecturer in B.N. College, would be coaching us in mathematics. Thus begun our private tuitions under the strict vigilance and guidance of Mr Mohanty. As my brother adjusted to this arrangement in an easy manner, it did not take much time for him to be the apple of our math teacher's eye. Excellent grades in the subject saved his ears from being boxed regularly by our teacher. I was not so lucky. My defiant attitude coupled with low marks in math ignited the worst in our tutor and a mutual disrespect grew. He would often say, 'Why can't you be like your brother? Why can't you apply your brains like him?' I would keep quiet, but I would think to myself, 'Teaching needs patience and love and you lack both. Both my ears bear evidence of this deficiency in you.'

A year passed and we were duly promoted to the next class. Physical maturity not only ignited curiosity about the opposite sex but also posed a volley of questions for my mother. Often, I would accuse Ma, 'Why do I get constrained by this monthly bleeding syndrome whereas Vicky enjoys life without going through this ordeal? You lay down a special set of rules for me comprising not only my dress code but also the way I sit or sleep. Why do all my frocks have to have a frill covering my chest?' Belonging to a more puritanical time, she would be visibly embarrassed by my badgering. In reply she would fumble, 'Girls are girls and boys are boys. God has created them with this inherent difference. Once girls begin to mature they are supposed to conduct themselves with dignity.' And that would be the end of our conversation.

As I struggled to cope with these unexpected changes in my life, I found our math teacher behaving more civilly towards me. Displaying uncharacteristic gentleness and patience he would urge me to sit beside him and do my sums. I was overjoyed as my ears were getting a respite at long last and I started to develop an interest in the subject. One evening, as we sat down to our tuition, Sir said, 'Noor, let your brother finish his lessons with me. You may complete your other homework with your Ma. With your exams round the corner I need to devote a little extra time with you alone.'

I readily agreed, as the competitive spirit in the class for the coveted first rank was contagious.

I eagerly waited my turn to sit down for the math tuition. That evening he had given me a test paper to solve. As I struggled through the sums, suddenly I felt his fingers lifting the frill of my frock. I froze as he started kneading my budding breasts. In my young life, this was the first time someone had invaded my privacy. Even though there was no sex education in those days, I knew what he was doing was not only incorrect but immoral. He was taking advantage of my youth and the trust my parents had reposed in him. Repulsed and choking with anger I tried to pry his fingers off but he softly said, 'I see that our small child is maturing. Please allow me to do what I am doing. You can try telling your parents about this but I can assure you that they will not believe you. Good math teachers like me are a rare commodity.'

A hard blow on his hand made him recoil in pain and he withdrew his fingers. Throwing back my chair I rushed to my mother in the kitchen. Incoherently, I blurted, 'Ma, this math Sir is terrible! I shall never take tuitions from him.' Baba and Ma were aware of his habitual boxing of ears but they never interfered with his mode of teaching. My complaints had always been gently brushed aside because they thought he was a good teacher.

In the circumstances, Ma did not realise the enormity of the situation. She continued cooking and said, 'Noor, from day one you have taken a dislike towards this gentleman. Your Baba and I were so relieved to see that both of you were getting on well at last. Please try and adjust to his ill-temper. We shall tell him not to box your ears. Now, be a good girl!' In a wobbly voice I managed, 'Ma please try and understand, this man is not a good human being. He keeps on hitting me. I hate him. Please, Ma, please tell Baba I want this man to be thrown out of the house.' I managed to give all the wrong reasons for ousting the teacher from our house. Perhaps I thought that Ma would guess the truth. But adults seldom guess what a child is trying to communicate. My pleadings fell on deaf ears and I was made to go back and continue my tuition.

The sexual abuse continued for a year and I stopped complaining to my parents. I learned to fight my own war. Retribution from my side took two forms. Firstly, I started to fail in math. It gave me immense pleasure to point out to him the red-inked report card saying, 'Look at the miserable marks I have fetched in your subject. This goes to prove the failure that you are as a math teacher.' But the strategy sometimes backfired as this entailed devoting extra time with the teacher to try and pass the subject. Secondly, I began hitting him back with all my might. More often than not it proved to be futile as physically I was no match for him.

Suddenly, he was transferred to an outstation college. My physical ordeal was over but the aftermath was to be dealt with. I remained weak in math as this subject signified invasion of my privacy by a short, dark and stout man. As a result I could not take up science and had to do my Bachelors and Masters in English. Anything to do with figures gives me jitters even now.

Many years have passed since then. I have been married for almost twenty-five years now and have borne two daughters. My husband, with his love, affection and patience, has nurtured back trust and faith that I had lost as a child. Yet, I enrolled my daughters in an all-girls school and ensured their admission in an all-girls college. And they have never had personal tuitions.

My mature side has forgiven Ma for not understanding my incoherent complaints. With the passage of time I have found answers to many turbulent questions. Today, I realise that in her innocence she could never apprehend such terrible behaviour from a teacher. I should have given her a chance by telling her the truth—Ma would have given me protection as naturally as nature protects its own. The Lord had ordained to teach me a few lessons at the dawn of my life and the most important one was parents are human beings after all with their own share of success and failures, only children put them on a pedestal and expect them to play God. As we evolve and progress let us not forget this and give them their share of understanding and sympathy.

'Noor' is a childhood friend of mine who shared her traumatic math lessons with me. We in fact would make strategic plans of hitting back at the teacher to save her from getting molested. We are still in touch and she confesses that, though the scar of her ordeal remains, her daughters had a normal childhood playing tennis, swimming and planning picnics and hikes instead of fighting a math tutor.

Bipasha Roy

Forgiving Father . . .

My daughter is a daddy's girl.

When she has a bad dream in the middle of the night she cries out for him. When she wakes up every morning, she steps out of her room and calls out to him. She'd rather play with him than with her friends.

When he has to go away for a few days on one of his numerous business trips, she misses him very much. As a little baby, when her father would be away, she'd crawl to the main door every evening, waiting for him to get home. She writes notes to him in his absence and makes knick-knacks for him.

I've read and have been told that girls are always daddy's pets. That I wasn't one made me an exception.

My father . . . never . . . swooped me through the air, cuddled me, hugged me, sang to me, read to me, played with me, helped me with school chores, or spared me unfair comparisons to the toppers in my class, the dutiful cousins who never demanded equality, freedom, time or attention. As a child, I did as I was told. Several nights I cried myself to sleep missing the affection my dad never showed me. Watching my friends whose dads displayed love and warmth made me sad and dejected.

As a teenager, I rebelled. With my sixteen-year-old might,

I fought him.

I disobeyed his every dictum. I learnt to drive a car when he told me not to. I picked up arts as a major in college even though he did not want me to. I refused to study for the Civil Services examination because I wanted to spite him. I did all I could to avoid being in the same room as him.

The problems were compounded when I had to face his 'patriarchal' mindset.

'Don't go out after 6 p.m.' 'Don't chat on the phone.' 'Don't make friends with boys.' 'Don't read novels.' 'Don't listen to music.'

His constant hectoring made me hate him. I'd have quarrels every day and would eventually end up shouting at my mother, whom I adored, for taking 'his side'. I felt lonely and uncared for. I became the black sheep, because I refused to be herded.

I left home after Class XII and lived in a different city for three years. During this phase I grew immensely close to my grandfather, who lived there.

He was so unlike my father. He loved me, cared for me and beamed with pride at every scholastic achievement. For a man hailing from a remote village in Haryana, he was amazingly 'modern' in his outlook. He allowed me to drive his car, pampered me with his love and lavished praise on me.

Because he was ailing, and constantly in and out of hospitals, I was drawn to taking care of him. I became his companion and listened attentively to doctors and their diagnoses. I took care of his medication and diet, peeled fruits for his evening snack, rubbed balm on his forehead to soothe his headache. Soon, doctors started explaining his condition to me, an eighteen-year-old with no background in medicine or science. I would discuss his dosage with doctors, while my relatives stood by and watched.

During his periods of hospitalisation, I would go to college in the morning and rush back straight to the hospital to be by his side. I was determined to nurse him back to health. With his love and care, he brought out the best in me.

I mellowed down, and allowed myself to relax when my father came to see his dad in hospital. After he was discharged, my grandfather spoke to me about his alienation from his children, perhaps noticing something amiss in the manner in which I met my father at the hospital.

He explained that my father could not display his affection or love simply because he had never been hugged or kissed as a child. My grandfather admitted it was too late for him to make amends with him but he was trying to get close to his grandchildren.

He held my hand and said, 'Your father is a good man and a good provider. He did not know how to be a good father, because I did not teach him how to be one. Forgive him. Forgive me.'

That winter morning in February, my grandfather died in his sleep.

For the first time ever, I hugged my father and cried.

Ritu Goyal Harish

I'll Survive

'I'll survive.' I've used this phrase whenever I've been faced with a bad time. But never more fervently till that April night.

I'd gone to a late night show with my friends. My mother was not in town, but I had told my father of my plans. After the movie I drove home, giving no thought to security beyond locking the doors of my car.

When I got to the deserted area leading up to my place, I found a car blocking my way, forcing me to stop. At first, I naively thought I'd got in *their* way, and that they had stopped to admonish me. But then, as soon as I saw that the car didn't have a number plate, I sensed trouble. A boorish guy got out of the car and tried opening my door. Idiotically, I lowered my window to reason with him. This gave him the opportunity to plunge his hand in and force open the door. He pulled me out and assured me he wouldn't do anything as long as I handed over everything I had. Only one guy did the talking while the other kept totally still, not uttering a single word.

When the first man asked me to sit in the car again, a light bulb went on somewhere and I realised that I was in big, *big* trouble. I begged him not to hurt me, but he pushed me roughly to the seat, threatening to stab me with his knife. I decided I'd rather die than be raped. I would put up the fight of my life . . . *I would survive*! With this thought screaming in my head, I became fearless. I don't know where I got the strength from, but I experienced a strange force within me. The survival instinct! I managed to knock the brute by kicking him as hard as I could and then I bit him till I managed to wriggle out of his hands. As soon as I was free, I ran towards my house.

Everything seemed surreal. I screamed my lungs out running for shelter, surprised that the men didn't follow me. The street dogs did, but I didn't mind them as much. I was exasperated by the fact that none of the many workers who lived in the same lane came out to help.

I finally saw a worker's family sleeping outside their hut. When they heard me screaming they switched on their lights and came to my aid. They gave me a glass of water and made me rest for a while. The only thing on my mind was home, and the man willingly dropped me back. On my way back home, I cried tears of joy and relief and I sent a prayer up to God. I had survived!

I used to feel pestered when my parents asked me all those million questions whenever I stepped out of the house . . . 'Where are you going? When will you get back? Who is accompanying you?' Instead of understanding their concern for my safety I believed that they didn't trust me. There are a lot of girls like me who live deluded lives, assuming nothing can ever happen to them and that they are invincible. It's high time they got out of fantasyland. I wouldn't want anyone to go through what I did.

Anonymous

Miracles Follow Faith

I had finally decided to enrol for the chartered accountancy (CA) course. And the day I did, it got tongues wagging. Tongues of cynical relatives and insecure acquaintances.

'Only five per cent of those who enrol pass.'

'You need to be absolutely brilliant to stand a chance.'

'The course is not for everyone.'

But at seventeen, I didn't let these things matter. I was young and raring to go. And go I did. In the summer of 1998, I took the CA foundation exam and sailed through it. Tongues wagged again.

'Oh, the foundation is the easiest. Intermediate will be the real test.'

'Oh, almost everyone passes this exam. It's the next that's tough.'

I didn't care. I was much too excited to care.

The CA course *is* very, very hard. You juggle tutorials, articleship (an internship that is like a 9 to 5 job), weekly tests and, of course, your graduation college studies. A slip in any one can ruin your entire roadmap. But when you're that young, you're motivated to work hard. So that's what we all did.

By November 1999 I was ready to take my intermediate exams—the second level of the CA course. We had study leave of three months from our articleship, at the end of which we took the exams. The study leave was just that—leave to study. There was no time to do anything else but stay within four walls and read your books and solve problems. In January, when the results were out, I discovered I'd got through comfortably. The tongues were back in action, though quieter in comparison.

'Oh, you passed. That's really lucky.'

'So now you have the toughest phase ahead—the finals—let's see you get through that.'

Again, I had nothing to say to them. I was just a little more geared up and a lot more motivated. The final exams were due in May 2001. And so the drill began all over. Soon May came and went and it was time for the results.

I had failed. And miserably. That was the first time in my life I had failed an exam. The tongues had proved their point. For me, the feeling of failure was cushioned by the fact that a lot of my classmates had failed too. And so I kept studying. I took a sum of how and what I'd studied, realised I had done it all wrong and corrected that. I made my second attempt in November 2001. The results were out in January 2002. I had passed in one group; failed in another. The tongues clicked in the we-told-you-so tone.

'Oh well, at least you managed one group.'

'Are you planning to continue or give up? It's tough to give up when you're almost there.'

'Your job prospects can get tougher with every failure.'

This time it mattered. I was disappointed and scared. Disappointed that my hard work had not paid off completely and scared about the uncertainty that hung over my future. The greatest fear was that I didn't know what had gone wrong.

But the one group I passed in was the silver lining. Somewhere in my heart, I knew I was at least capable of tackling the exams. And so the work began all over. Next exams—May 2002. I took them. And I failed.

The tongues got reckless now.

'You should just give up. It's not meant for you.'

'Nobody will give you a job now.'

'Why don't you get married?'

I had hit rock bottom. Things were so bad, they just couldn't get worse. That's what I told myself all the while. I decided to act. A CA firm agreed to give me a job, on one condition. They would not pay me. I took it up.

I also sent in my application to take the re-exam in November 2002 and started studying accordingly. In the meantime, a strong act of faith occurred. My mom, who was herself experiencing a host of emotions, advised me to put in my papers for revaluation. I had brushed her suggestion aside because nobody had ever heard of passing a CA exam on a revaluation. But she persisted and I gave in. On 9 September 2002, an envelope came home which I assumed was the admit card for the next exam. It wasn't. It was a cyclostyled sheet with the names of those who had passed in the revaluation. There were nine names on it and mine was one of them. I was a chartered accountant. That, if you ask me is a miracle, driven by my mom's faith. In two months, I got my dream job in India's largest media house. And today, five years later, the memory of this makes me feel stronger. I know that if I ever face a tough challenge in life, I can overcome it. Because I know that miracles follow faith.

Deepa Venkatraghvan

My Brother Adi

My brother Adi was my other half. I was incomplete without him. So when Adi was diagnosed with osteogenic sarcoma while I was away at summer camp, I hurried home, hoping nothing had really changed.

My brother was his same jolly self, laughing and joked around with me so much that I almost forgot he was fighting a life-threatening disease. Within the next couple of weeks Adi's condition deteriorated and he had to be admitted to hospital. I kept on telling him that he should not let go. 'You're going to make it,' I would assure him every day. But in secret, my parents and I cried.

The doctors told us that he was in immense pain. 'Any other person in his place would surely have let go,' they said.

One evening, when I was sitting in a wing of the hospital by myself, it suddenly occurred to me, why was Adi not letting go? Was it because of me? Was he battling for life, which held nothing out for him except unbearable pain, just for me?

I felt ashamed of myself. How could I have been so selfish? I went to Adi's room, sat down beside him and took his frail hand in mine. 'You know,' I whispered, 'you don't have to go through this because of me. I know life won't be the same without you, but the time I've spent with you is enough to last a lifetime. I hope that God gives you everything that you deserve when you go to Him. You can let go . . . you will always be there in our hearts.'

It was hard saying those words, but I'm glad I said them. My brother was in too much pain to say anything, but he must have heard me. Early the next morning, Adi passed away.

Atasi Ghosh

My Dad, My Hero

The greatest gift I ever had
Came from God; I call him Dad!

—Anonymous

Being the child of a defence officer means you get transferred around a lot. Almost every two to three years my father would get a new posting and that meant leaving your home, school and best friends behind and making new ones. When I was in primary school, it did not seem to matter much, but as I grew up, friends became an important part of my life. I was growing sick and tired of the whole routine of making friends only to leave them behind and repeat the process all over again. That's why, when we were posted to Delhi when I was in Class 7, I made up my mind not to put any effort into looking out for a bunch of fun, like-minded peers. It was difficult enough settling down in a new house as well as a new school, so I felt I didn't need the added pressure of making new friends as well!

There were many girls my age in my colony. But instead of trying to make friends with them, I would just sit in the balcony and watch them laugh and play together . . . and I would miss my old friends terribly!

One evening, after my dad came home from office, he pleaded with me to go out and enjoy myself. I told him I wasn't in the mood. My dad then sat me down and had a heart-to-heart with me.

He asked me if I truly thought it was easy for him to keep adjusting each and every time to his postings too. He explained that a move meant a new place, a new office, new people, new colleagues and new friends for him, too. Not just that, being an amateur golfer, it also meant looking around and finding new golf buddies as well. But then, he told me that while it seemed tough, there was actually something pretty wonderful about the whole process. His trips abroad always meant that he would get to meet new people belonging to different cultures and that it was always an enriching experience. He said, 'You develop your personality by meeting new people and getting to know them. You learn to be adjusting and more accepting of all kinds of people and their quirks and differences. You also become more open-minded and your life is full of wonderful new experiences and wonderful new friends.'

I just wasn't interested in listening to his words, and continued to sulk. So did that discourage my dad? No! Instead, he went one step further and went up to those girls and asked them if I could join them. I was *so* embarrassed. Nevertheless, I did join them. And after playing with those girls that day, I realised that they were all very friendly and very much like my old group of friends! That day, my dad helped me gain self-confidence. And I made some awesome new friends.

Had it not been for my dad's love, patience and 'interference', I would never have met such a great new set of people. And guess what? Those friends are now some of the best I have ever had!!

Nimisha Sinha

Only by Accident

Sometimes things change when you least expect them to. I know now that one can never be sure about anything in life, and I learnt this the hardest way imaginable.

I was out with three of my friends one night and we were driving from one nightclub to another. Because of the thick fog, we didn't notice a stationary truck ahead of us and hit up against it with violence. It was a terrible accident that left me unconscious for over twenty days, during and after which I underwent some major surgeries. I underwent operations for facial reconstruction as I had numerous jaw fractures. Amongst these was one for a cheek implant. This involved bone grafting in my upper palate, skin grafting in my mouth and ear, as well as teeth implants. When I came to, I couldn't accept that something like this had happened to me. How could it? I was the girl who lived life to the fullest, bubbling with enthusiasm and out to prove myself in every way possible. I loved my life and everything and everyone in it. Accidents didn't happen to people like me.

How wrong I was.

I have been told more times than I can count that I am incredibly lucky to be alive. I was brought to the hospital within the 'golden hour' (an hour from the accident, which is the most critical to survival) and looked after by a brilliant team of doctors. The hospital became my second home because I spent some of the longest months of my life there. When I came out of my coma, I was in a daze and I couldn't fathom the severity of it at all. I thought I was there for just a few days, and it couldn't be all that serious.

I guess it hit me the day a doctor came in to show me my face. All the mirrors had been covered in my room so I hadn't been able to see it for a while. When I looked in the mirror I couldn't recognise myself. For someone who preened before every looking glass she passed, who loved to be photographed, it was a rude shock! That's when I realised that this wasn't something small that had happened to me, that I had been injured badly, and that it would take a good long while for me to be all right again. Slowly, the doctors started talking to me, counselling me and explaining what I had to go through in the future as part of my healing. It all seemed too much. And I'd thought I'd be back home in a week!

When I was finally discharged from the hospital, it felt good being back home, but things were just not the same. I was horribly depressed, and would often cry in my parents' arms. I used to wonder bitterly why I had to survive at all if I had to go through so much.

One day, I decided that I had to snap out of it. I was alive, right? I had been given another chance. Gradually, I learnt to take it. I would try to find a silver lining in every seemingly adverse situation. It took me time, but I managed to do it. Whenever people asked me how I was, I would say, 'Physically, better. Mentally, much stronger!'

The accident has thoroughly changed my perspective on many things. Starting with my relationships with people. I now know that there are some truly special people in my life . . . I just didn't see them that way earlier. I also know the value of true friendship. Some of my friends have been exceptionally supportive and have been by my parents' side from day one. They're gems.

At the same time, I was surprised by the reactions of certain people who I'd thought were close to my family and me. Later, I came to a new understanding . . . some people are good at handling difficult situations, some just don't know how to. Some know the right things to say and do, some don't. It's just the way different people are.

Would I have been so understanding and tolerant earlier? No, but today, I am so much more patient. I have become a more serene person and am less talkative than I used to be.

I don't even want to imagine what it must have been like for my parents and my brother. My mother had sat in the ICU and held my hands so that the nurses wouldn't have to tie them up to stop me from yanking my tubes out. My dad had played music I liked on his Ipod while I lay unconscious, in the hope I could hear it. My brother would talk to a semi-conscious me, waiting for a reaction. If I am a positive person today, it is because they were positive for me then.

It's not all over yet. I still have some time to go before I can leave the accident behind me, and sure, I sometimes miss the mad person I was. But there's a lot I have taken away from that incident which I hope will stand me in good stead for my future. Relationships can't be taken for granted. Neither can life.

Meghna Sethy

Pancakes

You know you're the child of an Indian mother when the first thing she asks you on the phone, when you're away from home, is, 'Child, have you had something to eat?'

—Anonymous

'I hate you!' I shouted at my mother the gazillionth time. I had had a particularly horrible row with her. The 'I-wish-I had-my-own-money-so-I-could-leave-home-right-now' sort of row. I was upset at the way my mom never had time to listen to me. When I talked, her eyes would be scanning the room past my shoulder. Sometimes, I would stop mid-sentence just to check if she'd notice. She didn't. I felt like we were worlds apart as people. She was the harried, busy doctor, who felt I was a child too 'mature for my age'. And I grew up feeling a little unloved, and a little resentful.

I stayed up all night after that last fight, crying. The next day, when I had to get up for an early dental appointment, I felt half dead. Mom took me there and back (with me spurning attempts at reconciliation). I sat down on my bed, head in hands, wondering why I had such a strained relationship with my mother.

I tried to think of the most loving thing she'd done for me.

Then a scattered memory came to mind. It was pancake Tuesday, and I was at my neighbour's house, in Ireland. I was watching with wonder and anticipation as my babysitter, Catherine, flipped my pancake in the pan, and added a dash of lemon and sugar as she placed it on my plate. Then, being the strict Brahmin vegetarian I am, I smelt a rat. (Or rather an egg.)

'Catherine, did you put egg in this?'

'Yeah . . . why? Your mom told me you don't have any allergies, right?'

She didn't have time to catch my answer. Before she could stop me, I ran out of her house, and rang the bell of the adjacent house furiously. My mother had come home after a tiring night in the delivery ward, and I, with all the empathy and thoughtlessness of a nine-year-old, ranted at her over how Catherine had made eggy pancakes. I threw a tantrum, right there, on the doorstep.

And then followed something I will never forget. My mother, despite being exhausted, overworked, over-stressed and sleep-deprived, sat me down at the table. She then proceeded to make eggless pancakes for the fuming little brat who happened to be her daughter. And after she had watched me eat, she quietly let me out the door and told me to go back to Catherine for the next few hours because she had to sleep. How did my mom find it in her to cook for me, when she could have easily asked Catherine to handle things, and gone back to sleep? I realised that it was because she wouldn't have been able to sleep knowing I was hungry.

And that realisation was the start of a better relationship with my mother. When I noticed all that she had done for me, unasked, that went unappreciated, I decided to change things. Perhaps she may not be the person I turn to for career advice, boy troubles or poetic discussions. But when it comes to being taken care of and loved without condition—it'll be

Mom I'll turn to. And sometimes, no conversation or advice in the world will be as reassuring as the memory of those pancakes she made for me,

They said 'I love you, and I care' in the quietest way possible.

In my constantly shifting world, that meant security.

Arpita Bohra

Pearls of Wisdom

I heard Mummy getting upset over the phone with the jeweller. It was about a pair of pearl earrings that she had given him to restore a few days back. The jeweller maintained that his peon, Rameshbhai, had delivered them home. Unfortunately, the man was on vacation and could not be contacted to testify to that. But he'd be back in a month. The jeweller assured Mummy he trusted Rameshbhai totally and convinced her to wait for the man's return, when he would give her the name of the person in our household who had taken delivery of the earrings.

The book I'd been reading fell from hands as I scampered off the divan and ran to my room. It had been me! I had answered the door bell. Rameshbhai's wrinkled face had smiled down at me as he asked me how I was and if Mummy was in. I had told him she wouldn't be back till the evening. He had handed over, with his thin, shaking fingers, a tiny saffron-coloured pouch to me and insisted I check that the earrings were inside. He told me to put them away carefully it in my wardrobe and to give them to Mummy when she came home.

I sat on my bed and tried to re-enact in my mind what followed after Rameshbhai gave me the pouch. I remembered the telephone had rung as I closed the door. It had been my friend confirming that she was coming to pick me up. After speaking to her I had gone to my room to get ready. So I must have kept it in my dressing-table drawer. As I ransacked my dressing-table looking for the small saffron pouch, I recalled Geeta, our part-time help, coming into the room to clean it. She had still been on the job when my friend had honked one-two-cha-cha-cha to announce her arrival to pick me up.

My mind started running helter-skelter and it finally settled on Geeta. She did the utensils and cleaning at our place. Since she'd been there when I received the earrings, I concluded that the case of the missing earrings had to be Geeta's handiwork. I went to Mummy, relieved that I had found the culprit, and confessed to receiving the earrings and then losing them. In a small voice I told her that I remembered seeing Geeta around my room at approximately the same time.

Mummy insisted on checking my dressing-table for herself. I was offended. When she didn't find the pouch there, she proceeded to ransack my room—wardrobe, desk, everything. Sixteen-year-olds don't like anyone prying into their things, even—sometimes especially—their mothers. My sense of guilt over the loss was now wholly overwhelmed by irritation at this invasion of my privacy. I told her it *had* to be Geeta.

The earrings were not very expensive but a theft could not be taken lightly. Geeta was summoned and questioned. She vehemently denied she had anything to do with the missing earrings. Her words still reverberate in my ears, 'I may be poor but I am not a thief.'

Mummy told her that it was okay, one can be tempted, she should just put the earrings back and we would forget that the incident ever happened. But the lady did not have the earrings to put them back. She sobbed and kept repeating that she had not taken them.

Mummy didn't feel it was worth getting the police involved. She just told Geeta she could go and to never come back. But for Geeta the matter didn't end there. Within a day the word had got around and Geeta lost all her part-time jobs in our building. Some said she was not to be relied on any more, others branded her as a thief.

About a month later, I happened to pull on a pair of beige trousers that had somehow got stuffed at the back of my cupboard. The pearl earrings sat silently in the right pocket of the corduroys!

I went up to Mummy with the earrings. She was even more embarrassed than I was. I saw tears in her eyes as she said, 'Raksha, I doubted the integrity of a person who had been with us for three years. How can I ask her forgiveness? Can any human being harm another more than I have?'

Mummy did not reprimand me once. When I told her that it was all my fault, she said, 'We've both wronged her and neither of us is more or less guilty. But it's not about us, it's about her. We can't undo what we have done, but we must seek her forgiveness.'

We set out for Geeta's house in the chawl (yes, we knew where she lived).

She was out working. We left word that the earrings had been found and Geeta should come and visit us as soon as possible.

Geeta came the very next day. Mummy said, 'Geeta, it was unfair of us to assume that you had taken the earrings. They have been found in Raksha's trousers. She must have put them there and then forgotten about them.' And then I heard my mother say, 'I am sorry.' I added that I was sorry too.

Geeta did what people like Geeta do. She came back to work for us and behaved as if nothing had happened. Yes, the hurt was visible in her eyes for the first few days, but as time elapsed Geeta became what she had been. The incident was never spoken of again.

Did I forget all about my giddy, teenage carelessness?

No.

Even as I articulate the shameful experience, I know the lessons I learnt then became a part of my core.

Mummy could have put the blame on me but chose not to. She taught me responsibility.

Mummy could have just sweet-talked Geeta into coming back without actually saying she was sorry. She taught me humility.

Geeta could have raved and ranted, could have demanded recompense, yet she chose not to. From her I learnt forbearance and forgiveness.

And of course I learnt that just because someone doesn't own pearl earrings need not mean that she will steal a pair for herself. Being poor does not mean being small. In fact, in all of this there had been only one impoverished mind . . . Mine!

Raksha Bharadia

Security Blanket

Sometimes, love is the best reward a child can receive. Enough to last a life time, actually. I realise this as I run an unending film in my of childhood days. Those idle kisses and rewarding hugs blanketed me in affection as did daily doses of 'Did you eat your apple?' and 'Come on, drink up your Horlicks fast.' What's amazing is, back then, all this seemed quite the 'regular' thing any parent would do. All moms and dads in the world are the same, I would tell myself.

Today, so many years later, I do acknowledge parents are the same. Yes, they all love their children, they care for them, too. But what I also know is their ways are not the same. And, it is these ways that set them apart. Make different individuals of children across the world.

My father would say almost every day, every time he wanted me to assure him I was more *his* than my mother's baby: 'Anurita, *Papa* Baby. Mamma Baby? No, no, no!'

I clearly remember one of those semi-winter afternoons when I was about eleven. My father called me in to look at a photograph from a roll he had just had developed. Me on his lap and his hands enveloping me, it made for an ideal father-daughter picture. Handing me a pen, he said, 'Bebu, write this on the photograph and I'll have it framed.' Papa repeated his crooned love words in the sing-song way he always employed. I smiled at this; my mother did too. We knew it was just loving reassurance he sought. And gave.

Days turned to weeks, months to years. I grew in the comfort of knowing I was important. And special. That photo frame today tells me so, every day.

Getting up in the morning was an exercise I won't forget either. Mamma would want us to be early risers and would energetically begin to wake my sister, brother and me up at 7 am—painfully early, but—with loving words. If she didn't succeed in ten minutes, the words got more encouraging. But if the 'Wake-up'-'*No-please*'-'Please wake up'-'*Let-us-sleep*' exercise extended beyond half an hour, Papa would casually walk past, urging Mamma to let us be. 'After all,' he'd say, 'our children must be tired. They're enjoying their sleep. *Sone do unhe*.' Mamma's reminders (loving *but* constant) and Papa's indulgences (loving *and* constant) ensured one thing: we did sleep a little longer, but the moment we got up, it was a 'Sorry, Mamma, promise we'll get up early tomorrow.' And that would happen when they were having their tea together. A 'Sorry' and a tight hug for both continued to do wonders.

I also remember how the frequency of loving words grew whenever exam days came close. My mother was slightly more particular than other mothers I knew about good grades in school (or so I thought). Something my brother and sister managed well—their names figured in the top five and top twelve respectively. I don't remember getting marks worth boasting about in any subject other than English and social studies. These subjects were normally about writing long answers, you see! And that I was good at. But as the exams drew nearer, my mother articulated study reminders in quick succession. 'Study, and you will grow up to be worthy; don't study and remain just one of the many,' she'd say.

One lazy April evening, my mother said something of this nature and walked towards the other room. My father, sensing my fear (or probably reading my face which clearly said I hadn't studied!), pulled me to him, lovingly placed me on his lap and said, 'Don't worry, Bebu. Even if you fail, the world won't come crashing down. Your father is there for you. You can take your exam again.'

Much as I didn't realise it then, these light, assuring words created a safe world I began to enjoy living in. The comfort that I increasingly drew from my parents and the balance they maintained in indulging us kids created a harmonious equal. One hugged while the other kept a close check. With years I have come to understand one thing: the love and affection that comes in childhood seals the wall against insecurities. The balancing act of parents, with generous doses of love, care and affection, is often the biggest gift. Mine gifted me a secure lifetime. A feeling that lets me believe all is well because I am cared for.

Anurita Rathore

Shake the Rain

My most vivid recollections of past monsoons date back to the summer vacations I used to spend in our ancestral home in Kerala. I was a school kid then, a pain in the neck of my cousin who was just months older than me. In Coimbatore, where I schooled, the monsoons weren't as frequent or powerful, so I wasn't accustomed to the loud claps of thunder that accompanied them in Kerala. It was my cousin who helped me overcome this fear. One day, after the rain had stopped, he took me out into the garden which was overgrown with trees and shrubbery. He made me stand under a small mayflower tree and shook it, gently at first and then with all his might. As the raindrops from the leaves fell on my face, I stood there enjoying the coolness until I was drenched from head to toe. This became a ritual for us and we did it after every monsoon shower. We called it 'shaking the rain'.

As the years went by, visits to Kerala became less frequent and letters home a mere formality. But something pulled me back to my home town and once again I found myself in my grandma's home. It was the time of monsoon celebrations in God's Own Country. The homecoming was warm and pleasant. There was my affectionate grandma, an ever-smiling aunt and uncle, and my now college-going handsome cousin. Everything seemed like the old days except the conceptual barrier that seemed to have formed between my cousin and me. Our interests were so varied that we couldn't engage in even ordinary conversation. I knew that my cousin was trying as hard as I was to break the ice, but somehow our relationship seemed to have frozen in time.

One cool afternoon my cousin and I were walking to the nearby marketplace, both of us trying in vain to bring up a topic that would interest the other. The walk passed in uneasy silence. As we neared the crowded junction, there was a mild clap of thunder followed by more powerful ones. And then, without warning, the drops began to fall on us. We found shelter in a nearby shop and waited for the rain to stop. As I watched the dancing drops, my mind whisked away to those bygone wonderful monsoon days. For a moment I wished I were a kid standing under trees, carefree, just rejoicing in the freshness of the first drops of mango showers.

The rain stopped and people began to come out of their momentary shelters. I looked at my cousin and was surprised to see him smiling at me. Had he know what I'd been dreaming of? Without a word he took my hand in his and pulled me gently to the trees by the sidewalk. When we were under a small mayflower tree he placed my hands on the tree trunk and said: 'Come, let's shake the rain.' As I felt the icy drops on my upturned face, I found a strange new peace.

Maybe it was the power of faith, faith in relationships, faith in each other, or just the powerful bond of shared young memories.

Dhanalakshmi Sashidharan

Skeletons in My Cupboard

I open to the clutter in my wardrobe, to clean it. It is a ritual I follow at the end of every semester, lest the dust on the shelves carry over to the next. On top is the junk of the semester gone by: study material, journals worth countless nights of sleep, photocopies of class notes totting up to Bill Gates's fortune, more xerox copies of books written by geeks (yuck!) and assignments that we copied from the same books. So much for another season of engineering.

The next things to tumble out are the memories. I see memorabilia that act as passports to my past. I come across stories I spun back in fourth grade. I chuckle as I read on: stories with wild names like *Adventure Andromeda*; characters with wilder names like Nutty, Catpole, Grondor, Spidella. Ten is a good age to churn out stories as you have no cognisance of stupid laws of physics that your imagination must obey; you can be as small as you like, travel as fast as you want, and still be normal in the end for a 'happily-ever-after'.

I uncover a small box that holds all the friendship bands I received in tenth grade. It warms my heart to know that such a multitude considered me a friend. I peruse old letters from my friends; I read the cards they sent. We had all promised we'd keep in touch, but soon the hourglass got the better of us. We all grew up and learnt to make excuses for not writing. Now only keepsakes remain.

Next up, something I can swagger about—a letter from Maneka Gandhi. In seventh grade, I wrote to her about local issues involving animals. In her reply, she told me that every movement starts with a single person, and I believed her. I believed that I could change the world alone. I was young. Then I grew up a little more and it dawned upon me that the world changes us more than we change it. Anyone who doesn't walk, talk or think like the world, is viewed as an alien.

Finally, I get to my personal diary. Two recent letters tumble out—one that I wrote to my father a few days before his death, and his unfinished reply. My taciturn father and I shared everything but our emotions. So, after not saying 'I love you' for twenty years I wrote it to him . . . I wanted to build a bridge of letters to the man responsible for my existence. He responded instantly—but he couldn't finish his first and last letter to me. The day he died, I grew up completely and realised: if we love someone, we'd better tell them without reserve.

These are the skeletons in my cupboard: neither shameful nor sad, just a framework of reminders that as we grow up, we lose a lot we need not.

And so, after I've dusted the shelves, I carefully return all those reminders of my childhood and adolescence to where they were. I shut the wardrobe . . . the ritual is complete . . . the cupboard is clean.

Anupama Kondayya

Someone to Watch Over Me

Vikram stared at his notes, aware that time was running out. He was to appear for the final examination of his fifth semester the day after the next, and hard as he studied, he knew tensor analysis was not a concept that he could comprehend, leave alone master.

He had performed well in all courses in the mathematics stream. He had spent the entire semester religiously taking down notes on tensors but had never quite understood tensors beyond the well-known definition: a tensor is an n-dimensional vector.

Vikram ploughed through his notes once again. Every time he looked at a fresh page, the numbers and notations seemed to jump and clamour simultaneously for attention. He looked up to see his room-mate, Hari, studying at his desk. It was small consolation that Hari appeared to be no better off.

Just then he was called to the phone in the hall. Vikram ran there and picked up the phone which had been left off the receiver for him.

'Is this Vikram Menon?' said the voice at the other end. 'Abbas here, from Madras. Sorry to say, your father . . . expired an hour ago.'

He walked slowly back to his room, where he was surprised at the ease with which the words rolled out: 'My father expired this morning. Got to go home.'

'Shit!' Hari said. 'I'm so sorry.'

Vikram sank into his chair, struggling to swallow a lump in his throat that wouldn't go away. 'I have to go home,' he said, but looking at the books and papers strewn over the table, he added, 'but what about the exam?'

He knew that he had to drop everything and rush back to the family. He could always appear for the exam the next year, but that would be a definite setback academically. But Vikram also knew that his father would not have wanted him to miss the test.

Hari took charge. 'Leave for Chennai today. The train leaves Ernakulam at 5.30 in the evening. You'll arrive early tomorrow. You have to return tomorrow evening positively. I'll pick you up at the station the day after tomorrow. We should make it in time for the exam at 9.30.'

Vikram packed some essentials in a small travel bag. He included his notes and a Schaum series text book on tensors. His friends put him on the train, with a return ticket and a packaged meal. 'Remember to study on the train,' Hari told him as the train pulled out.

As the train picked up speed, Vikram felt a familiar throbbing in his head. It was his sinusitis, showing up once again. Good timing, Vikram thought. He leafed through his notes randomly until his eyes ached in the dimly-lit compartment. Vikram closed his book, took an aspirin, and let the tears come, burying his face in the travel bag. Soon, waves of drowsiness overpowered him and he fell asleep.

*

The next evening, Vikram was back on the train. He pulled out the book on tensors and tried to concentrate, while his mind wandered back to the heart-wrenching moments of the funeral when he'd gone through the motions mechanically, before leaving for the railway station as planned. No one tried to stop him nor did he try to explain.

There were twelve hours left for his exam. Vikram riffled the pages of his textbook and saw that there were solved examples after each chapter, in all about 150. The first example proved an easy one to understand, and Vikram went on to the next. The authors had done a beautiful job of pointing the way to the solution in the least number of steps possible. As Vikram found the complexity of the problems increasing, he stopped trying to analyse the logic. He read the solution again and again until he had committed it to memory. At about three in the morning, he succumbed to exhaustion at problem number 116.

*

Hari was waiting for him at the railway station and they sped to the examination hall. There was a hush as Vikram took his seat and was handed the question paper.

Vikram said a silent prayer his father had taught him when Vikram was leaving home for the first time. It was the only one he knew. He then looked at the question paper. The questions danced in front of his eyes, mocking him in his effort to decipher them. Images of his father reading the newspaper on the porch flooded his mind. Vikram shook himself out of his reminiscence and addressed the first question.

The haze broke and light filtered through. The first question was familiar . . . it was solved example number six from the Schaum series book, word for word. Vikram began to write. Question two was a tricky one, but he tracked it down to a solved example from chapter three. Question numbers three, four and five were from chapter five . . .

Vikram did not bother to read the last question completely—it was solved example 115.

There were still ninety minutes to go. Leaving his batchmates still engrossed in the world of tensors, Vikram got up, submitted his answer paper and walked out of the hall and into the garden behind the college.

It was bright outside. Sensing exhaustion for the first time that morning, he sank down on the grass. He recalled the stream of relatives coming over, hugging him and speaking words that never reached his ears. It only seemed like yesterday, when his father's friends used to call up and ask, 'Where is your father? Is Acchan there?'

Now they wanted to know, 'When are they taking the body?'

His Acchan had become just a body.

*

When the marksheets for the fifth semester were released, Vikram was surprised to see that he had scored 84 per cent in tensor analysis. Hari looked over his shoulder and whistled, 'How the hell did you manage . . .?'

Vikram imagined a smile spreading on his father's face as he read the morning paper. Vikram pictured him calling out to Mrs Gomes across the street, 'Mrs Gomes! Vikram has topped again. You know, the boy's very good at maths . . .'

This is not the first miracle that has graced my life. But this is the first miracle which made me look up and discover the others. I believe there is a guardian angel—Acchan—who nudges me on the road to each discovery.

Vinith Aerat

Watch Out for It

I handed over my watch to Somdev, took the ten-rupee note from him, and put it in my pocket. The watch was a designer brand, a work of exquisite craftsmanship, with a Prussian blue dial adorned by massive Roman numerals and set off by a shining metallic bezel, and a golden bracelet. That was the only object of extravagance I possessed. Unfortunately, I had to sell it. I needed the money, you see.

I was studying in the eighth standard then, an average member of the class. I exhibited no special talents but managed to pass all the examinations that were sent my way, was sort of okay at sports, and attended classes regularly.

My parents were worried why I never excelled at anything, but that didn't bother me.

If I had any cause for concern, it was that they never provided me with pocket money.

All my other classmates had theirs. You cannot fathom how it feels in recess when your friends buy goodies like chocolates and all you have is the dull lunch box in your school bag. Sometimes they shared some of their stuff with me, but more out of kindness than friendship.

I raised the issue many times at home, but my parents didn't give in. I was deprived of any form of luxury.

Some of my classmates got ten rupees, some fifteen, some

twenty, a handful. They all knew their arithmetic well. The sum was pooled, divided precisely by the number of school days in the month and spent more expertly than by many a housewife.

The first half of lunch breaks would go in emptying the tiffin box, the next relished in licking the goodies that came out of the day's fund. I munched my shabby meals quietly at my desk. Occasionally, a few rough 'n' toughs would secretly buy themselves a smoke. Such things were as far removed from my experience as a fairy tale.

What was a bigger shame was having girls opening their tiny purses in front of my eyes and taking out those magical coins. To feel inferior to the fairer sex was an idea not acceptable in those days, something my father never understood.

My father had given me the watch on my thirteenth birthday. It cost around Rs 600 and grandly embellished my wrist. But how long could it stave off the daily assaults on my pride? I decided to sell off my wristwatch.

Somdev bought the item. He had his eyes fixed on it for a long time. The contract was simple. The watch would change hands. In return, every month, I earned half his pocket money. To a large extent, the deal was unfair. But both parties were happy to along with it.

The first day I got the money I enjoyed the feel of the ten-rupee note in my pocket, folded into quarters. But it was a short honeymoon. My mother noticed that the watch was missing. When she enquired I told her someone had stolen it. She was very unhappy, my father too. I felt sorry for them. But bigger things were at stake, I thought.

Then I was caught with some coins in my pocket. This time my father went to the school to have a word with our teacher.

Teacher Rosemary spotted the watch inside Somdev's desk. We were both interrogated. Somdev admitted to the crime.

The teacher scolded us and gave the watch to my father.

I returned home from school that day expecting to get heavily caned. How surprised I was when my father did not utter a single word on the topic! At the dinner table he gave me back the watch. 'Your watch,' he said simply.

My mother also mysteriously busied herself with household work.

I went into bed that night with a big question mark haunting my mind.

A week later I asked my mother, 'Why didn't you scold me that day?'

Her reply was in the sweetest words I ever heard in my life. 'Don't you know how much we love you?'

Yes, Mother, I now do.

Bilwadal Roy

7

ON LESSONS LEARNT

'As human beings, our greatness lies not in being able to remake the world—that is the myth of the atomic age—as in being able to remake ourselves.'

—Mahatma Gandhi

A Winner All the Way

I am nineteen years old and have just completed my course in fashion design in Delhi. In the National Institute of Fashion Technology (NIFT), at the end of the course, each student is required to showcase a collection of designs and apparel based on a certain theme. Usually, the ideas are unique and creative, sometimes weird, too. The collections are evaluated on the basis of their attributes in terms of innovation, thematic integrity, as well as execution based on stringent industry standards. A jury, comprising experts from the industry and academicians, tots up the score.

My inspiration was taken from the instinctive styles and details of the semi-rural population of India. Entitled 'Missed India', my entire collection was a dedication to all those rustic models that walk daily, not on the pretentious ramps of fashion, but on the undisguised pavements of our country. I used mainly handcrafted materials, cotton twill tapes, metallic trims and khadi. Basically, it was to complement the common man and woman. From a palette of earth and vibrant pastels, it was to be a mix of the old and the contemporary. Exploring the techniques of deconstruction and reversibility, I had worked quite hard. Since sponsors were difficult to find, I hoped my collection would be affordable. My parents, with similar hopes, also wished it would be wearable.

When my family landed in Delhi for the graduation ceremony, the decision by the external jury had already taken place. I had a hint that they had been impressed with my concept and designs. I secretly told my parents that I hoped I would be rewarded—maybe in the 'Best Men's Wear' category.

But when that award was announced it was not my name that was called out. Through the corner of my eyes I saw the disappointment on my parents' faces. I slowly receded into the background. As the other four awards were given, I kept retreating further and further. And as the name of the recipient of the last award—the Ritu Kumar Best Design Collection—was announced, the world suddenly stood still.

For some time I was shocked into silence. I looked at my parents and saw the same look plastered on their faces. It was a moment none of us can forget. I don't exactly recall our reactions. My dad and my brother probably looked the way any two stunned males would. But the response from the feminine side was instinctive—hands on cheeks, then on the heart, eyes popping with awe, followed by that inevitable gasp of surprise—yes, my mom and I went through the same motions.

My own belief in award systems had been reassured. I had worked hard for this. I surely deserved it. My parents were thrilled when their daughter won the Best Design award from the most prestigious of all the centres. Could they ask for more?

But the human heart, apart from holding the auricles, ventricles, arteries and veins, also encloses loads and loads of hope. So when it was time for the All India NIFT show, in which thirty-seven award-winners from the country's seven centres showcased their collections, it was with a keen sense of expectancy that they sat at the Confluence.

It was a great show. For the fashion-conscious there were zuaves and capes and stove-pipes to feast their eyes on. For the fashion un-conscious (people like my parents), the same apparel merely looked like loose pants with lower crotches, a square piece of cloth with a hole in the centre and slim-fitting pants.

When the awards were being announced all our anticipations rose high. My name was not called out. Yes, that disappointment hurt like a knife, more so for my parents' sake. More than letting down my institution, what pierced me was that I had let down my parents.

I walked back to where they were sitting and quietly joined them, totally disheartened. My mom put her arms around me. Naturally, once again, in the premises of our minds, politics and awards were already walking hand in hand. 'Yours was a better collection, sweetheart,' my parents told me. Yes, mine was indeed a better collection than the one that was awarded. In fact, it was the *best*. What had gone wrong? But one look at the awardee, and her mom, and everything changed. It was their moment. And to be honest, they probably deserved it, just as I had done earlier. But for my mom the creativity on display in the award-winning collection was totally overshadowed by the unique creation of another—her child's.

I pointed out the excited faces of the winners to my mom. 'It doesn't matter, Mummy,' I said. 'Look how happy they are.' She took a deep breath.

'Yes, you're probably right,' she said. 'It must be difficult for any jury to pass a judgement on creativeness. The key probably lies in dissociating oneself totally from the situation and viewing everything like a spectator. I wish I could do that, but I don't think I can. I love you too much!' She hugged me again.

In my mother's eyes, there would always be only one winner. Me. And somehow, losing really did not matter anymore.

Rumana Shanker

Alka Came Out Tops

This took place more than twenty years ago. We were in the second year of college. Young, not so innocent, but most certainly naïve. Life was full and life was good. Classes were interspersed with breaks like picnics, hikes and dance nights. One such break was a picnic to the bird sanctuary at Karnala, on the Mumbai-Goa highway.

We set off early in the morning in an ST bus, some fifty boys and girls. The noise in the bus was deafening, with non-stop songs and hoots of laughter. We had even taken along a dholak. The journey was short and we hardly noticed the time it took.

Alka was one of my classmates—a shy, quiet, unassuming girl, pretty in an understated way. She never joined in the boisterous singing or games, but didn't miss a single picnic either. She was one of the world's followers—or so we thought—and we generally ignored her. But she sat next to me in class, so I did share a word with her now and then.

As we got off the bus, I noticed that in addition to the eats that everybody was carrying, she was also toting a large, black plastic bag—the kind that is usually used for garbage. I asked her about it, but she merely smiled and moved on. I didn't think much of it as I waited for my friends from the hostel to get off the bus.

As we moved into the sanctuary, we looked eagerly around for the birds, but couldn't spot even a crow. There were lots of trees however, and an abundant supply of fresh air—things that our oxygen-starved city-slicker lungs craved for. As my fellow students moved forward, they left a trail of litter behind them. Biscuit wrappers, plastic bottles, wrapping paper, all sorts of rubbish. We saw Alka moving along the fringes of the crowd. She would stoop now and then to pick up the discards and stow them in the plastic bag. She didn't tell anybody to stop throwing the stuff. She didn't deliver any fiery lectures about social duties either. She just went on collecting the litter.

My hostel bunch and I broke off from the main group and found an alcove, where we whipped out cigarettes and lit up eagerly. Relaxing in the shade of the tress and blowing smoke towards the clear sky, we seemed to have achieved our version of nirvana. One of the chaps had also secreted a bottle of beer in his tote bag and this was duly passed around the group of amateur topers. Soon, the bottle was emptied and flung carelessly into the surrounding thicket. Even before the bottle plopped down, Alka was there. She silently picked up the empty, looked around, spotted a crushed cigarette packet and bagged that as well. This was really disconcerting. I stood up and asked her, 'Why are you doing this?'

She smiled and replied, 'Somebody must. Why not me?', and moved on.

I thought she was eccentric, but harmless, and sat down again, but something had gone awry. Our alcove wasn't so snug anymore. I could see, looking at my friends, that they felt the same. We rejoined the main group that was arranging dumb charades. Teams were being formed and while we joined in the fun, I noticed that nobody was throwing litter indiscriminately any more. They quietly sought out Alka and dumped it in her bag. Nobody had been forced to do it. In fact, nobody had been asked to do it either.

I was not the only one who learnt a lesson that day. Only, the import of it didn't sink in at the time. I was too busy having a good time.

Today, when my temples are greying and life has slowed down somewhat, I think back and realise what Alka's lesson was all about.

We keep our homes clean. Why? Because there is a sense of ownership and belonging. Why don't we extend the same argument a little further, beyond the boundaries of our houses? Why should we wait for the municipality or government to do it for us? Why leave a place dirty and then whine about the authorities being lazy or lax or corrupt? The solution is so simple that we overlook it. Don't dirty your surroundings in the first place.

The physical divisions of our world are so numerous. Our neighbourhood, our suburb, our city, our state, our country . . . who made these boundaries? We did. Who can tear them down? We can . . . If we can think of the whole world as our own, what is the problem in our taking care of it? Don't you think we owe it to those who come after us, to leave them something that is beautiful?

To engineer change, you don't need to be a Gandhi or a Hitler. You can do it by just sticking to the basics. Do it yourself. If each one of us does it, sooner or later, the rest will be shamed onto following suit. I can believe that. It's just a matter of time that everybody else will.

That was Alka's lesson. This was the girl we had dismissed as one of the followers.

B.S. Keshav

The Girl in the White Gi

The senior years at school can be heaven or hell, depending on how your classmates see you. But I was in perpetual limbo, as it was difficult for people to pigeonhole me into the convenient and readily available slots—nerdy, sporty, pretty, popular, cool, uncool . . .

I loved reading but never did my homework. I couldn't get the ball over the throwball net but I frequently scored homeruns in baseball. I didn't dress 'hip' but I wasn't the vernacular or 'behenji' type either. And I may not have lived in an Italian marble palace like the rest of my classmates, but I seemed to always have the most unique holidays with my parents.

So, yes, it was really hard for my peers as well as for myself to find the perfect place for me in the general scheme of things.

Which is perhaps why I started to be known as the 'girl who learns karate'. Now, in the new millennium, it may not be such a novel idea for women to practise the martial arts. But in the late '80s and early '90s—even in trendy south Bombay—a female karateka was still something of an aberration.

At seven a.m. each Saturday, I would don my pure white 'gi' (karate uniform), cinching the waist with my coloured belt tied with a special double knot, and enter the school lunch shed which was also my 'dojo' or karate classroom. Unlike other days when I quietly ate my mid-day meal here, on weekends I'd smartly bow to Sensei Sundaresan with loud and clipped 'Os!' issuing from the pit of my stomach and out through my otherwise timid lips. For the next two or three hours, we would go through rigorous warm-up and muscle-toning exercises, practise punches, kicks and blocks and progress towards complicated 'kata' (show moves) and 'kumite' (sparring with a partner). And while concentration is imperative in martial arts, imagine how disturbing and distracting it was for me as a fourteen-year-old—already dealing with everything from the changes taking place in my body and psyche to complex chemical equations in my organic chemistry textbook—to see from the corner of my eye that a bunch of boys from my own grade were watching my karate class while they waited for their football or cricket training to commence!

Far from feeling superior, the way my fellow male karatekas obviously felt as they did their thirty knuckle push-ups in front of an 'audience', I floundered in confusion and felt my heart flutter. After all, among those boys watching us, was also the boy I had a crush on—the senior school heartthrob! Should I try and be as tough as a true blue Perak Okinawa Goju Ryu student so that Sensei would appreciate me in front of him? Or should I toss my hair and come across as a delicate, gentle GIRL so he'd see how feminine I really was? So what if the uniform made me look nice and shapely, I was still screaming 'kiyai' and showering punches and kicks on my sparring partners. My poor, confused adolescent mind seemed sure that a girl who doled out a mean roundhouse kick wasn't exactly the type he'd 'propose' to. Sometimes I'd just pretend I wasn't really there, not making any eye-contact, withdrawing into an imaginary shell that even my

Sensei's 'shootos' didn't seem to rupture.

Thus went my karate sessions all through my early teenage years; being really earnest and focused half the time, and pretending to be invisible the other half, when people came by to watch. I hated it when my classmates called me 'Karate Kid' during the week. I cringed when someone said I should perform a kata for a talent show. I bought the New Kids On The Block posters and wore the bright plastic Madonna-esque earrings that were in style then. I wanted so desperately to be just another regular teenage girl.

Why did I continue when it was clearly such mental torture, you wonder? Well, it was all because of my dad. And the fact that my father was learning karate with me! That he was forty when we started and always the most dedicated student in the class gave me plenty of guilt pangs. After all, just as he'd keep telling me, he wasn't as flexible or as fit as any of us teens were. And yet, he was the one that outshone all of us thanks to his perseverance and painstaking practise. I recall all the weekends when I begged off from going to karate class by faking a fever and he saw through my play acting. The other times, when I cited it being 'that time of the month', he told me, 'Women have become astronauts and you're grumbling about one karate session?' He was the X factor that kept me going. And so we earned our belts—going from white to yellow to orange to green to blue to purple to brown three, brown two and brown one.

It was time for the black belt grading. My dad had been practising for months. To his surprise, not only did I not practise, but I even refused to attend the test and the ceremony. I said that a black belt was only self-congratulatory and that since I already knew the techniques, I didn't need a degree to show off to the world. That day, I disappointed my mum, my Sensei and, especially, my dad.

The years had flown. My dad had completed his black belt

second and third degree. I never really went back to karate except to do the floor exercises as part of my fitness regime. I had lost some of my puppy fat, replaced my glasses with contact lenses and got an all-new glam hairstyle. I was now in junior college and had a busy social schedule. I was quite popular and there was a new confidence in my step. Then one day, as I came out of the Alliance Française, I came face-to-face with him—my high school heartthrob! 'Hey! It's you, the Karate Kid!' he said. The smile on my face quivered ever so slightly as all those old feelings came rushing back. I was that awkward teen in the white gi once again. There was a sinking feeling in my stomach as I thought he would make fun of me any minute now.

The words tumbled out of his mouth in a torrent. I had no lifeline to save me from drowning in them. He said he'd wanted to look me up all these years but didn't know how to approach me. That he'd always had a soft spot for me! That he had admired the fact that I learned karate. That he thought I looked adorable in my white gi. How foolish I'd been, I thought. So determined was I to be an ordinary teenager, that I never realised the worth of being an extraordinary one!

Priya Pathiyan

Hold Your Tongue

'*Aaay*, move your car from there!' shouted the elderly parking attendant as we pulled into a public area. Every time you find a perfectly fine parking spot, a parking attendant makes you move from there to some other spot. Mary, my American girlfriend had just landed in Ahmedabad and I was taking her to lunch straight from the airport.

At nineteen, I was very short-tempered. Combine that with being in a rush, hungry and tired of parking men. I was about to give him a piece of my mind.

'But this is a good parking spot,' I said, getting out of the car.

'Don't teach me my job and park your car where I tell you!' yelled the *jerk*. He was looking to pick a fight—it was very obvious that the man was having a bad day too!

He was five-foot-four-inch, around sixty, had pimples on his face, of dark complexion and was wearing an old ragged khaki pant and a stained white shirt. He looked like the devil incarnate.

It took us almost ten minutes to park the car where wanted us to. Mary said that God was trying to teach me patience.

No one throws a challenge at me and gets away. I was firm in my mind; patient I would be!

I decided to ignore him. He gave us a nasty stare as we

walked away, and continued to yell after us.

Mary remarked giggling, 'Maybe he swallowed a loudspeaker.'

Forty-five minutes later, when we came back and got into our cars, we saw him charging towards us with the same nasty look. 'That's five rupees,' he shot at us. 'First you park in the wrong place and now you are trying to leave without paying?'

I was about to punch him, when I remembered the challenge. I had to show her that I could be calm. Besides, the way I behaved would be one of her first impressions of my country.

The day was particularly hot. I spotted a slushy vendor nearby. I turned to the parking attendant. 'Sir, do you like slushy?'

He said, 'Yes, who doesn't?'

I asked, 'Which is your favourite?'

The *jerk* said, still in his high-pitched angry voice, 'I like the rose flavour and have one every day. Why do you care?'

I walked to the slushy vendor about twenty feet away from the car. The man followed me there out of curiosity. I ordered a rose-flavoured slushy. As it was being made I asked, 'What is your name?'

'Kalyan Shankarlal Patel,' he said, his tone softening a bit.

'So, have you been working here for a while?' I inquired.

'Yes, I have been here for the last five years. After my wife died, I decided to come here so that I would not be lonely. I take care of an entire garage,' he said. A hint of pride made its way into his eyes. I looked around, the 'garage' could hold only up to seven cars. 'Many people leave without paying and then I have to make up for it from my pocket. Sorry to be rude, son'. Kalyan Patel gave me his first smile of the day and he looked beautiful.

'So do you have kids?' I asked.

'Yes, I have one, with whom I stay. I chip in forty rupees

of the sixty that I make every day. He takes care of all the other expenses,' said Kalyan Patel.

'What do you do with the remaining twenty?' I asked.

'Well, son, with ten rupess I buy bird food and feed the pigeons you see over there. With the remaining ten I buy biscuits and give it to the poor.'

The slushy vendor asked, 'Regular or special?' They put vanilla ice cream in the special one. I replied, without hesitation, 'Special!'

Although Mary and I broke up years ago, I am glad she threw that challenge as it has changed the way I view the world. The new and improved 'I' have met several inspiring people because of my changed self.

Amitabh Shah

Lessons in Football

I remember watching my father and brother kicking a ball around and wondering to myself, 'Just what kind of enjoyment do they derive from this mindless sport?' That was two years ago and whenever I think about it, I laugh.

I was really into books and art, and my friends were those who shared my interest; we had nothing in common with the 'sporty types'. Then, some new girls joined our school and whenever they got the slightest opportunity, kicked a ball around the field. My friend Simran's interest was soon aroused. She made friends with these girls and would frequently run off at break-time to join them in running after a ball. And she seemed to be enjoying it immensely! Out of curiosity, I decided to try my hand—or rather, foot—at it too.

As was expected, my first few attempts saw the ball and I at cross-purposes. When I tried hitting it straight, it went left; when I tried left, it went right. But there was something about this game which kept pulling me back for more. Football seemed a challenge that I just *had* to conquer. So I kept playing it every chance I got and soon, found myself totally attached to it.

One day, our school got a letter inviting our soccer team to play for a tournament, the Sintex Cup for an Under-14 girls' team. I was a substitute defender, and I wasn't happy with my position and thought about ways I could improve. I started watching games on television. I learnt all the rules, and with my dad's and brother's help learnt how to kick correctly.

Soon after, during one of the practice sessions, I showed off my newly acquired strength and skills. The whole team was impressed. They let me handle the ball for some time and seeing the force with which I kicked it, I was promoted to the defender's position for the main team. Then, we all were made to do penalty shootouts. Surprisingly, all my shots were bang on target! I was in such an enthusiastic and positive frame of mind that I performed to the best of my ability. This made me realise my inner strengths—power and accuracy, both! My team even thought I was fit to be the main striker.

I did a lot to improve on my skills. Every day, I played with my dad, and he guided me. I watched matches, played with my friends, and kept working on how accurately I could kick a ball. My brother taught me lots of soccer tricks too and I got to know the ball better. I even watched *Bend it Like Beckham* and felt a burst of inspiration!

Soon enough, it was time for the Sintex Cup matches. We drew our very first game. I was disappointed because I could not score a goal. We said, 'Never mind,' but it was this attitude of carelessness that led us to lose in the next match!

Instead of moping, we analysed the reasons for the loss. We worked on our attitudes and our team spirit. We practiced a lot and . . . we won the next match 2-0 and that took us to the finals!

And you know what? We won the finals too! I even scored a goal and saw my name in so many papers! What a feeling!

But this piece is not about how I helped win this match. It's about what happened to me and what I learnt from football . . .

The Sintex Cup win was great for our confidence. We continued playing and practicing. A professional coach started to come by to help us train. Everything was great, and fun to boot!

It was while playing a casual match that something happened to me. I was playing without shin guards and during a tough tackle, my shins were kicked at (unintentionally, I know). I heard a sound like a crack and fell down in agony. I had broken my shinbone. My leg was in a cast for five whole months and not only was it painful, it was almost impossible to walk. When I was finally allowed to play again, and only after being warned that my shinbones were now fragile and 'easily breakable', I played for three whole hours! How much I'd missed the game!

Soccer went on as usual, with my passion for it increasing day by day. Then, our coach told us that selections for the Gujarat U-17 team were coming up. We were all very excited and the whole team went for tryouts. Seven of us were selected!

The coaching camp and subsequent matches were to be held in another city. Other U-17 State teams would be joining us there too. When we reached the camp, we were escorted to what was to be our living quarters for our entire duration there. The place was like a shack: big, with twenty mattresses on the floor. There was an all-pervading smell of ghee coming in through the window, which we could not close because it was jammed. The washrooms were not only tiny, but also dirtier than I had ever imagined possible. There weren't any showers and instead, we had to put our heads under the taps, at a height of three feet. We would walk three kilometers for food—and to say that it was terrible would be an understatement. The chapattis were like rubber and we had to use both our hands to tear them. All this was tough to adjust to, even for me. I thanked God every single day, for blessing me with all the luxuries of life and missed home, my parents, my brother. I missed Mom tucking me into bed, her hugs, everything about her . . . but my love for football kept me going.

We practised six hours a day, with breaks for meals and sleep. There was simply no time for enjoyment.

In our very first match, we beat Himachal Pradesh 3-2. But the second match, against Uttarakhand, was an absolute disaster! We lost by 16-0! We realised that practice alone was not enough, but skill, endurance and pushing ourselves to be better than what we are, also mattered.

A few months later, the Gujarat U-14 selections were held. We went for that too. A team-mate of mine and I were selected. I was so happy that all the hard work and training had amounted to something.

A few weeks ago, I received a letter confirming that I was the new captain of the Girls U-14 Gujarat team! I was so happy, excited and thankful that I had got this far. Then, I thought about the journey that helped me reach here . . . and wrote this.

I hope it inspires someone to take up challenges and to go after a dream the way I am going after mine!

Namrata Jaykrishna

Mind Your Ps & Ms

Have you ever chickened out of a situation which needed time and effort to tackle? Have you ever given up on a relationship because you did not have the heart to sort out the mess it had got into, or maybe because your ego would not let you? Have you ever hoped that things would change and you would find the courage to set things right but you cared too much of what others might think and then stopped short of trying? Have you blamed destiny for your cowardice and neglected to acknowledge your own fault?

If you haven't, then I am a little jealous of you. People have such fond memories of their schooldays that it irks me, sometimes, because I don't have much happiness to reminisce about. Most of the things that happened have left a wound somewhere on my psyche and I am still in the healing process.

I was a shy child. Since I was an average student, being part of a group of friends who scored high and won accolades wasn't an easy task. An introverted and thoroughly confused soul, I followed rather than led. I often did things that I thought would help me fit in with the 'cooler' lot. No points for guessing that I let myself be manipulated quite a few times. One such incident was what I now call the 'gang war'. I was fourteen then and my coveted group was ruminating over adding a new member to 'the family'.

The complication however was that the name of the group was 'MACKS'. MACKS stood for the initials of the names of the existing group members, so a new addition to the group would compromise the nomenclature. Also, my friends debated whether I was worthy of retaining my initial, 'M', in the title, over that of the new candidate, 'P'.

'M' being dispensable, I was going to be given a 'fair chance' to prove that I truly belonged to the gang.

In their excitement the group members scrutinised my every move and that of my opponent. I was stupefied by insecurity and felt wretched. I remember going home depressed and coming to school with only half a heart in the proceedings. I remember sitting alone in lunch hour, trying to avoid everybody else. I would hardly speak to anyone, humiliated as I'd been for no apparent reason.

I found relief in my dreams. I dreamt of being a really confident, clever and witty girl. I would often play whole situations in my head over and over and think of smart, cutting things to say that would ensure no over ever dared to be unkind to me again. In real life I remained tongue-tied.

However, I found solace in writing. Since I felt uncomfortable about talking to anyone about my dilemma, I started conversing with my diary. Penning down poems and describing my experiences in prose made me understand myself better. I enjoyed this time spent with myself; here I was honest and free of any prejudices that held me back elsewhere.

It never occurred me to that this indulgence would help me in many other situations.

To make up for it I wrote her a poem as a belated birthday wish and as a present. She replied from the US, where she was then, saying, 'Mani, that was beautiful. I felt every word reach my heart. That leads me to another thing. You write beautifully. You have talent, kid!' That was a turning point in my life. Since then I have tried my hand at everything that interests me, pottery, fashion, make-up or making documentaries. I realised there was much to discover about myself and my strengths.

As far as the 'MACKS' story goes, a group meeting was called, but I gave it a miss. Seemed to me I didn't need to go since I was still considered a part of the group—along with the new entrant.

In retrospect I realise that I was not totally innocent myself. In my attempt to deal with the chaos around me, I, too, hurt people. To some I was dreadfully malicious, something I am terribly ashamed of. After the MACKS episode, I started valuing people for their goodness and not for of their popularity.

That was my lesson: to believe in what I think is right, and stick with it. Everybody has a battle to fight, to forge their own identity, to find their individual path. It's been a struggle for me for I have been my own enemy. As my perspective changed, my faith in myself increased, and I was able to bend situations to my will.

Manika Bansal

Musings on Solitude

From a protected childhood in Delhi, I was displaced to a more tumultuous life in what is now called Kolkata; it was Calcutta back then though, when I was thirteen, and I always think of it as Cal.

In Delhi, I had friends— both in the colony and in the co-ed school I was in. I was always one of the toppers in class, and in the evenings, always on the streets, playing with one group or another.

I came to Cal, to long power cuts—popularly called load shedding. I entered an all-girls' school, where students predominantly spoke Bengali—a language I had no clue about. In the colony, I could see no girls my age. From a sprawling colony in Delhi, I had moved to a high-rise—I could not even see the roads from my eighth floor flat. The streets were full of houses huddled together so all I could see were shabby rooftops.

In class, from being near the top, my rank plummeted to rock bottom. The teachers were new, the class was new, the language was new, and even the syllabus was new!

And something else was new. My feeling miserable. Till then, I had been a happy-go-lucky girl. But shifting to Cal gave me the worst jolt a teenager could experience. That of loneliness. My brothers had moved to Mumbai and Chennai to pursue higher studies, so even the family set-up was new, with it just being my parents and me at home.

I would cry when it was time to go to school, telling my mother I hated everything about Cal—like a preschooler! I insisted that she wave to me from the balcony as I left because I superstitiously thought that if she did, my day would be better.

I was so down in the dumps that if someone rang the bell, I thought it would be death, come to claim me. Perhaps I was not actively suicidal, but I was willing to be a passive ally to death.

I would stand in front of the mirror and test out the theory that time flies in the blink of the eye. It didn't. It lay heavily on my hands as I struggled to readjust.

When the ninth standard final results came, I howled, refusing to go to school and meet the headmistress, positive that I had flunked. My mother went alone as I fretted and fumed back at home.

I had been promoted, but provisionally. It was a shame I could not bear. But I survived as my parents told me to take it up as a challenge.

I returned to school after summer, and a new girl had joined. For some reason, she and I became friends. She was always cheerful, and because she claimed she was a palmist, people flocked to her. I was amused, but I realised what a handy skill that was. There I was, struggling to call at least one person my friend after a whole year, and here she was, walking in and having people flocking to her on day two!

Then my colony friends expanded. I had always been good with people any age—younger, contemporaries and older people. And suddenly, I had friends who were a lot older than me.

The one who was nine years older threw a bombshell one day. She was a survivor of dowry harassment and in the process of getting a divorce. I looked at her. Though she had scars that showed, emotionally, she was a fighter. And interacting with her for close to a year had not made me suspect even once that she was struggling so much with her personal life.

The one who was five years older was always cheerful and cracking jokes. One evening, when I was pretending to study, she walked into my room and started crying. Her father had a violent temper, and she had just had to face one of his outbursts. That evening she cried, but the next day, she was back on her feet and there we were, walking down the market, showing each other cards that swore friendship to each other.

I learnt that day that misfortune befalls all. But how we react to it is what decides our personality.

When I shifted to Chennai for college, I remembered my lesson well. Relocation needs adjustment, and one needs time to find and make friends. It does not happen instantly. Patience and faith in oneself are important to keep a sane head. But most importantly, being content with oneself is the key to happiness—especially in today's world where there are many acquaintances but few friends.

S. Meera

My Hardest Days

Blood is soothing, pain is drunk with realisation
That anxiety will not leave you, it will extract
The last drop, the last gleam, the last hope.

I wrote this during the hardest days of my life. No earthquakes, no typhoons, nothing on the outside. The turmoil was all inside me. Inside something whose existence I had totally disregarded all my life—the mind.

University exams were knocking at the door and I was oblivious of my predicament till, like an amateur exorcist with his first success, I became aware of the vile spirit befogging my mind. I realised something was changing within me, something was happening to me—that something was very wrong with me.

It was not that I was a vivacious outgoing leader, I had always been one to keep to myself, speak to selected people, make few friends, but this something brought a flow of negative energy into me, with which I seethed, day in and day out. I found it impossible to sit in one place, look at one thing, read or study, and concentrate for long. My eyes were perpetually wet, I did not know why. The hardest challenge I faced was when my concerned near and dear ones asked me what was wrong. I knew I could not explain and their quizzical expression angered me even further. The words in my books swam before my eyes. I prayed every day, though I was confused about God too.

The psychologist confirmed my mother's suspicions. I had been torn in the tension between two worlds: the 'good girl' world—of studies, acceptance, obedience, and the world of 'fun and rule-breaking'—rebellious, which beckoned me with its delights. And I had lost my balance.

Medication followed, with drowsy side-effects. Studies were at a total standstill. My mental ordeal had left such a huge impact on my appearance that neighbours and relatives enquired after my health. I was a tree struck by lightning, abandoned even by the crows. The first weeks of medication yielded no results, I plunged into darkness and fear; passing each day was a punishment to me. Eating, sleeping, bathing were tedious exercises.

I had counselling sessions. And more medication. There was much probing and delving into my life, which till then I had thought pretty mundane. But now, several issues came up: parental pressure, peer pressure, low confidence, a distorted value system.

Something, or all of it, made me calmer. And since there are no absolutes, at least I am now in search of none. I have learnt things the hard way. The mind as an organ has a routed existence in our system. We are blessed with it and we are responsible for it. I never understood the otherness that exists in its dark recesses until now. In my humdrum existence, I never felt I was capable of such curious . . . power. No other word comes to me that describes the new feeling that came to me. I succumbed to it, was paralysed by it, worshipped it day in day out, until it decided to wear out.

I have also learnt that it is not always possible to think about others. I had tried to be nice, and turned out to be a showpiece. I was false about the secret liaisons I had with some boys, just to spice up my morose life and ended up hurting my conscience. I tried to 'help' a 'friend', who I thought was going down the wrong path, loving the wrong person, and was wronged myself. It was hilarious really, when I come to think of it now—the only hitch in the tale is that I cried whole evenings locked up in my room. Then came college, and came a friend who explained to me my problem and its solution in straight, simple words: 'Help only those who need your help' and in the process, help yourself. After the mental ordeal I had gone through these words were a blessing to me. I realised something which I was trying hard not to realize—that 'helping' to me had become playacting, not the genuine thing. It was not honest.

A little selfishness is precious in this world!

Sreemanti Sengupta

New @ Work

Last summer, I was quite crushed when, even fifteen days into the holidays, I could not bag an internship. After a lot of running around, I managed one with a national daily. The first few days were quite boring; the only relief was that I could sneak out with my boyfriend (Mr Know-All) almost every evening. I would walk all the way from ITO to Connaught Place to hang out with him. I had so much time in hand that I could do anything I wanted. But I didn't like getting home early; I wanted to strike an attitude that said, '*Look, I'm working*.'

But the job was bugging me. I spent entire days with little or sometimes no work to do. I wanted it to be thrilling; that was the least you expect of a reporter's life.

One day I had a terrible fight with Mr Know-All. He sometimes freaks me out with his attitude of omniscience. So I sat in front of my computer in a pensive mood, disinclined to go out. I watched a senior on an adjacent seat blowing puffs of smoke, imagining them to be the many dreams I had, that dissolved into thin air.

I stayed in office longer than usual. Later, when I was about to leave, my boss came in to tell me that I had an assignment to cover. It felt totally insane. I mean, I had been sitting in the office since 10 in the morning, with nothing on my hands. And now, just as I was to step out, an assignment had materialised. Whatever! Better late than never . . . at least now I had something to do. So I asked for the details and he told me that it was a farewell party at the Australian High Commission for the outgoing high commissioner.

It was a big occasion, with a group performance by children and an exchange of greetings. On this, my first assignment, I didn't know what to report. Also, I felt completely out of place in my casuals, with a backpack like a school bag gummed to me, certainly not dressed to attend a formal function like this one.

I looked around, lost, when there came a friendly pat on my shoulder, and I heard a bubbly voice saying, 'Dude, do you know where the loo is?' I turned to greet a real *patrakar* in a khadi suit and carrying the trademark *jhola*. She smiled and the heavy kohl in her eyes shone. I didn't know the way to the toilet, but she asked me to accompany her to the door, all the same. We found the way, and also a new friendship.

I told her how nervous I was about being in a new job. And Gunjan, in her cheerful way, told me to take a chill-pill and wait for things to unfold. She said the most important thing in the field of journalism was to observe minutely and report interestingly. We hung around together; we shared a drink too.

The event unveiled at its own pace, a series of amusing incidents. An odd-looking man with long, curly hair went to perform *aarti* before the high commissioner, an unusual ceremony to conduct when someone was departing. Anyway, the absurd creature stepped back abruptly, smoke rising from him. He had burnt his hair in the flame of the ritual *deepak*. I controlled my laughter with great difficulty.

After the ceremony we moved on to interview the high commissioner. I was standing in the queue of her well-wishers, growing restless. Suddenly, there was the sound of a loud splash, and droplets of water fell on us. It took us a few seconds to realise what had happened. A drunk gentleman, in his hurry to meet the high commissioner, had fallen into the pool. This time we rolled about laughing. A photographer clicked in time to capture the gorgeous moment. These incidents, and Gunjan's trenchant commentary on the ways of party animals, made the evening rock for me. We both had a good story to report when we went back to work.

I learnt to observe, to wait and let things unroll on their own, and also that humour can lighten a serious situation as well as your workload.

And I did patch up with Mr Know-All when he agreed that to know all, one has to observe all.

Palak Malik

Teenagers' Tale

The 'younger generation'
Has a thrilling sensation
When you enter your teens
You're addicted to jeans
Movies, parties, discos—the like
Singing in the bathroom—who needs a mike?
Kicking the pedal of my new dirt bike
Strolling along, singing a song
Walkman on full blast all day long
Pigging out on pizza, burger and chip
Wearing only clothes that are in fashion—'hip'
Teenage crushes—you feel like floating on air
The teasing of pals you learn to bear
All this is a teenager's fantasy
But hold it right there – what about the pain and agony?
Breaking out into rashes, pimples and acne
If I don't study, Mom's gonna smack me!
We mug up all day and burn the midnight oil
To score good marks we sweat, study and toil
Exams, tests, periodicals – what a *bore*!
All this drives me nuts, how about a nap and a snore?
Fights with Mom, rows with Dad
'You will *not* go to that party!'

'But Mom, it's so cool . . . so RAD!'
You finally give up and slam the door
Then the vacations start and exams are no more
You shout in glee and rush to the new store
Fun days are here, I'm surfing the Net
And playing with Fluffy, my new virtual pet!
I do love my teenage, free-age life!
I accept it with all its troubles and strife
So what are you waiting for, my friend?
Go sailing thro' these years and party till the end!

Nandini Swaminathan

The Funny Side of Poetry

When I went to school that day, a bunch of students were gathered around the school notice board which is placed in the main entrance hall. I edged my way to the front and, among the mass of notices on display, what caught my eye was this one: 'Inter-School Poetry Recitation and Writing Competition—1995'. I was studying in a reputed public school in New Delhi and rather fancied myself as a writer. Though sixteen years old, I had never participated in a debate, elocution or a recitation competition before, but I thought I should try my hand at this one.

The competition was being organised by Cambridge School. During the break, I walked up to the activity coordinator, Mrs Bhanu, to make further enquiries. She told me that the subject chosen for poetry writing and recitation was 'Growing up in English'.

'This topic doesn't make sense, ma'am,' I observed.

'It must have to do with the spread of the English language in our country,' she replied. 'You know, even Hindi is not spoken these days without a few words of English thrown in.'

The teacher's explanation was not convincing, but I let it pass. Later, at home, I discussed the theme with my father. 'How can anyone grow up in a language?' I asked him. 'And with all the top Delhi schools participating, the competition is going to be beastly.' How was I ever going to write on such a strange topic?

Dad resolved the dilemma in typical military fashion. (He was a lieutenant-colonel at that time and was posted at the army headquarters.) 'The topic is strange,' he said, 'but that gives you greater poetic licence. You follow the dictates of your heart, young lady, and write that poem. Once you're ready, I'll help you rehearse it.'

The next few days went by in a flurry of poetry writing and excitement. Finally, the poem was completed. I read it out to my younger siblings and they were enthralled. More importantly, Dad liked it too. 'Well done, kid,' he said. 'Your poem is a simple, fun-filled and touching portrayal of a child's fascination with the complexities of the English language. It should pass muster. Let's start rehearsing now.'

When Dad would return from office, the whole family would gather for what we called 'poem rehearsal time'. It was great fun and my family was most supportive. When the day of the competition arrived, I felt I could not have been better prepared.

We had assembled by the school bus when the activity coordinator gave us the competition invites. When I read the invite, a cold fear gripped my heart. The topic for the poem was 'Growing Up' and not 'Growing up in English'. I thought of all the painstaking work put in to write the poem, the time spent by my family in rehearsals; all reduced to naught because of somebody's error. Soon the cold fear was replaced by an even colder fury. I brought the anomaly to the notice of Mrs Bhanu.

The teacher was initially annoyed with me but mellowed down when she realised that the mistake was hers. 'Oh well!' she exclaimed. 'Maybe I got confused when the teacher from Cambridge told me the English and Hindi topics over the phone. She must have meant that the topic for English poetry writing was "Growing up" and it all got mixed up. Anyway,' she continued, 'as your poem is on the wrong topic, I suggest you go back to your class and forget about the competition.'

I stared incredulously at Mrs Bhanu; she spoke without remorse and with complete nonchalance. I was outraged. 'I am not going back to class!' I exclaimed, with vehemence. 'My family is waiting to hear how I performed and perform I will.' The passion in my voice made the teacher do an instant reversal of her earlier decision. 'Go if you must,' she said coldly. 'Your entry might get disqualified, though.'

At the Cambridge School auditorium, there was a palpable buzz of excitement amongst participating students assembled from all over Delhi. The flow of adrenaline amongst the competitors was evident as each moved in turn on to the stage to present her or his poem. And then my name was announced. I took a deep breath, and walked up on to the stage. Many were the times that Dad talked of obstacles as opportunities given a different name. Well, the hypothesis was soon to be tested.

'A very good morning to everyone,' I started, looking boldly at the audience. 'Growing up has been a wonderful experience for me but the aspect that I would like to present to you is how I grew up learning a language alien to me . . . so here goes 'Growing Up in English'. With my opening statement, the faux pas of writing on a wrong subject had been covered. I suddenly got this incredible feeling that the audience was with me and so I continued with growing confidence.

When I was little, small and young,
I grew up in my mother tongue
A simple language soft and sweet,
Melodious, musical beat

A language that I loved to learn,
Each word of which my tongue would churn
A language to open one's mind,
To lofty thoughts, ideas sublime.

Those fun-filled baby days of yore
Continued till the age of four
And then to nursery school I went
To learn something quite different
A foreign language was to be
Used to mould the thoughts in me
It's English, dear, my teacher said,
A language I had never read.

After I finished the second verse I looked at the audience and was pleased to see the look of rapt attention on their faces. It seemed as if they were hanging on to my words. I continued through the next few stanzas. In that big hall, I felt a million eyes stare at me, but they were all supportive. I looked at the judges and they seemed to give an encouraging nod. I plunged euphorically into the final verse:

These quirks are what make English be
A language so extraordinary
A noble tongue, clear and sublime
An ideal tool to shape one's mind
Growing up in English I can say
Enriched my life in many ways
And though I love my mother tongue
Growing up in English has been fun.

The applause that ensued when I took my final bow was exhilarating. I knew the audience was with me but what would the judges say?

Many years have passed since that young girl walked up on stage to deliver a poem which was not even on the right subject. But she followed her heart and the dictates of her conscience. Since then, many accolades have come my way. But the joy which I experienced when I walked up to receive the first prize that day was of a different kind. Truly, problems we face are opportunities given a different name. Thanks, Dad! This one's for you.

Aarti K. Pathak

There are No Mistakes in Life, Only Lessons

If there was one thing to distinguish Amar from the rest of the students of the twelfth standard—easygoing young things all, pursuing by-and-large pure science courses, concerned about what life would be like after school—it was his passion for computers.

Owning a personal computer was still considered a luxury in India early this century, and the Internet was yet to spread its wings in most second-tier cities. So Amar, and fellow star student Dheeraj—a calm and composed young man from the same class—made computer laboratory classes their playground.

Their computer teacher held the two boys in high esteem. To everyone's constant amazement, both could produce flawless computer codes in response to almost any problem asked in class. And they made full use of the laboratory classes to test their computer programmes.

Passion isn't always a good thing—as with anything else, an excess of it can spell trouble.

One weekend, both friends were appearing for a day-long mock entrance test conducted in another school in the city. Like most engineering entrance tests in India, it had two breaks of an hour each. The school was a prestigious one and taking a round of its premises during the first break didn't seem a bad proposal to either of the boys. While others kept themselves busy studying, Amar and Dheeraj roamed the campus, naturally inquisitive about everything there that was different from their own school. They discussed what they saw—the small temple in the middle of the schoolground, the impressive basketball court which they didn't have in their own school, the not-so-good-looking girls so contrary to their expectations, the bakery within the premises and its delicacies, the laboratory for a subject like mathematics.

Then they found their treasure. The letters on the door in bold and read 'Computer Laboratory'. Their legs moved almost involuntarily towards it. Their faces were flushed and their hearts pumping feverishly from the excitement of seeing what was inside. Who knew, the school might have equipment and systems they had only dreamed of! The lock on the door was a minor impediment. A simple twist to the door latch with an iron rod kept in the nearby janitor's cabinet was something which wasn't spoken about or planned. The action was done as if both had a tacit agreement on it, as if what was happening was perfectly natural—no second thoughts; rather, no thoughts whatsoever.

A new world opened up in front of them. Colour monitors, projectors, multimedia devices, switches, hubs, actual speakers, optical devices—they touched, lifted and felt everything to make sure they were real. Suddenly, their own computer laboratory, consisting of monochrome monitors and CPUs still running 5¼-inch diskettes, seemed like an antique!

Then it struck them. Why not take some of this home? A ridiculous thought, a sane person would have said, a theft actually. But their minds had stopped working temporarily, overcome by the moment; as if they had forgotten the basic distinction between right and wrong. And so they did it.

It then dawned on them that they might be in trouble. They

kept some of the stolen components in one of the classrooms back in their own school, and threw some in the dustbins in the evening. But the inevitable followed. News had flown in from the other school and, the next morning, Amar found himself standing in the principal's office. He was told that Dheeraj had already accepted his role in the 'crime'. Crime! He was being accused of being a criminal! He was a child, *again*. Tears flowed profusely from his eyes. His mother, called there by a special request from the principal, sat next to him. There were tears in her eyes as well. Amar saw them, and the reason behind them.

'Once character is lost, everything is lost,' he thought. *'I am a thief,'* he kept telling himself with self-loathing. He detested himself. No one understood what came over him in the following few months, because no one knew the truth—the principal was kind enough to keep anyone from knowing.

Amar didn't even feel the final blow which came when he finished school—he was denied a character certificate.

Time heals all scars. Academics provided the only respite from his nagging fears about himself. His focus, made stronger by the experience, landed him in one of the top-notch engineering and management institutes in India.

Amar learnt the hard way. So did Dheeraj. They realised that wanting something badly was no reason for stealing it. That an immature passion was no excuse for doing wrong.

Kumar Vivek

8

ON HEARTBREAK

'Do not dwell in the past, do not dream of the future, concentrate the mind on the present.'

—Gautama Buddha

A Little Bottle Reminds Me . . .

Too tall and thin for Indian tastes, Anupama was well suited to walk the ramp. We were not the best of friends but shared a simple 'hi-bye' relationship in college. She always had a pleasant smile and an affectionate pat for me. But she had her own gang of pals and I had mine.

I remember that day pretty well. The bell had rung and all the girls were scampering out of the gates. I had to go to the loo and as I approached the door, I heard a sob. I peeped in and was shocked to see Anupama in tears.

'Hey, what's up?' I asked. She lifted her head, saw me and turned away.

'Go away! I want to be alone,' she said. Her voice was low and broken and it was terrible to see that sweet grinning face in so much sorrow. I felt my own tears coming.

Slowly, she came near me. Soon, we both were holding each other and she was crying on my shoulder. In between sobs, her story came out. She had fallen in love with a guy and let things go too far. She suspected she was pregnant as she had missed her period that month. As soon as she'd raised the issue with her boyfriend, he'd completely vanished from her life. He had never given her his address or other details. He changed his mobile number and simply disappeared. She'd confided in her 'close' friends, who were harsh and judgmental of her. They didn't want to have anything to do with a girl with 'loose morals'.

She didn't want her parents to know anything. She didn't know what to do. I was just a seventeen-year-old girl myself, but I wanted to do something for her.

'Don't worry, you're not pregnant. It's just a suspicion, right? We'll wait!'

'But what if I am? My parents will die of shame,' she cried and struck her forehead in sorrow. I blurted out the first thing that came to my mind.

'No, they won't! We'll arrange for a secret abortion. Don't worry, okay? No one will know . . . now, stop crying, please . . .'

'It's not so easy. It's illegal. Those fellows may charge something like ten or twenty thousand. Where will we get the money?

I removed my gold chain and my diamond ring and pressed it into her palm. 'I will be there for you whatever happens,' I promised.

Both of those ornaments were expensive, and had been gifts from my parents, and I'd felt a small pang removing them.

I wondered how I would explain their loss to my parents, and then decided to make up a story when the time came.

I went home and prayed hard to God. The next day, Anupama came running to me.

'I got my period! Hurray!' she said. I smiled and heaved a sigh of relief.

The three years of college sped by. Anupama made new friends and so did I. But, there was a special silent bond between us always. Then, on the day of our convocation, Anupama pulled me aside and showed me something she was holding in her hand. It was a small bottle of pills.

'I was going to swallow those just before you entered the

toilet. My life, this certificate and all—I owe to you. "Thank you" sounds so inadequate,' she said. 'I'm keeping this with me to remind me that angels like you do exist.'

I was shaken. I couldn't believe that a simple gesture of help and hope had saved a life. I realised the power of unconditional and unjudgemental love.

'I want something from you,' I asked Anupama. 'That little bottle.'

'Why?' she asked.

'Just to remind me that I can be an angel too,' I said. 'Sometimes, everyday life makes me forget that . . .'

Once again we hugged, this time without tears.

Archana Sarat

Exchange Programme

At the time of writing, I study at Doon school, in Dehra Dun. I have been here since the 7th grade and am currently pursuing my 10th standard.

My school has a student exchange programme and afffiliations with many countries abroad, South Africa, Canada, USA and Australia being the major ones. Getting selected for the exchange programme is one of the most prestigious things to happen in a student's life at Doon. It requires major homework too. We have to fill in application forms listing details of our academic, sports and other co-curricular achievements along with essays which talk about why we want to go for the programme, what we can contribute through it, and what we think we will achieve from it.

Making it to the exchange was to me my way of proving to myself what I was made of. When the time to apply came, I gave it all I had. I pored over every word, thought of the smallest details, wrote and re-wrote till I was satisfied with what I had done. My friends and parents were impressed with my work, as were the few seniors I'd shown it to.

I was amongst the first few to reach the board when the shortlist was put up. To my delight, most of my closest friends were on the list. As I read on, I saw that I was not. My first reaction was that there had been a mistake. Perhaps they would release a revised list later . . .

When hopes of that shattered, I pretty much felt the same on the inside—shattered. Something I had hoped for ever since I could remember was now being denied to me for reasons unknown to me. I knew I couldn't let go of it so easily and so I did what at that point of time I thought was best. I decided to go to my headmaster and ask him directly to reconsider my application.

I went to the office along with a friend who was also in the same boat. What we feared most happened. The headmaster said a categorical 'No'. At that moment it seemed like my whole life was done for.

A few days later the school came up with a revised list, but my name wasn't in that list either. With it faded my last ray of hope and never in my life have I felt as insecure of my abilities as I did then. My exams were round the corner, but my negative mindset made it impossible for me to concentrate on anything. I found myself close to tears, lost my sense of humour and all the gaiety that had once made me popular.

One fine morning, after about two weeks of self-castigation, it hit me. What had I turned myself into? Why was I acting like this—this was not me! I understood that the world hadn't fallen apart. My life did not end there. It was a setback, just one little setback. I should have bounced back long ago instead of whining about it like a child. I had been immature at accepting defeat.

Instantly, I felt rejuvenated. I understood that I shouldn't treat a temporary disappointment as a hard and permanent truth that stared me in the face every day, but as a learning experience. As these thoughts found their way to me, so did my confidence and cheerfulness.

The paradox of the entire situation was that when the interviews were over and the final list drawn, I was the one consoling the ones who hadn't made it. As far as I know, all the students I spoke to bounced back just the way I had done.

Yes, I couldn't go for the student exchange after all, but I do think I learnt a very valuable lesson. Losing self-confidence is close to killing yourself; only you can convince yourself against it.

Ankit Chowdhary

I Miss You, Dad

Why did you have to go, Dad?
Why did you have to die?
Why did you leave me behind?
With nothing to do but cry?

I miss you terribly, Dad
I can't believe that you're gone
I can't believe this has happened
I don't know how life will go on.

Those times we had together
Keep coming back to me
Those shopping sprees, eat-outs
And all the movies we went to see.

I miss all our talks and walks
And I miss the love you showed
I miss the amazing guidance
And all the stories told.

I miss every time I wrote a poem
And showed it to you
I remember how proud you were
And you also told me so.

I remember the pains you took
To make sure I was okay
No one can ever again
Love me in that same way.

You were the best, Dad
You had a heart of gold
And what hurts me now
Is the things I left untold.

My love for you, Dad
Will never go away
In fact it only grows
Intenser each day.

I hope that somewhere
Wherever you may be
You can hear me now
And read this poem and see.

This poem doesn't do you justice, Dad
Nothing ever will
But do you wonder the reason
Why I'm writing it still?

I wrote it, Dad, because
I know how you loved the sight
I wrote to tell you
That I will continue to write.

I will continue to make you proud
I'll continue to shine
I will always remember that
Your heart rests with mine.

Nithya Ramachandran

It's Okay to Be Sorry

'I am so sorry, please forgive me,' he said guiltily.

Sorry.

So, this is it, I thought. This is all he can manage to say after all that he has done. After all the pain and misery he made me undergo, all he can come up is the word 'Sorry'. For the first time, I felt angry. I wanted to hit him, hit him and keep on hitting him until he could feel the pain I felt. Until I could avenge my hurt. Until I felt better. He put his hand over mine and I instinctively pulled it back, with nothing but feelings of hatred for him.

It's just so easy to get away with everything that one does with a single word, as if it frees us from all our sins and wrongdoings. I looked at him, wondering how I should react. Forgive him? Forgive him just like that and pretend that nothing happened? Why shouldn't I make him suffer just as he made me suffer?

I couldn't say anything. I just looked at him with an expression of bewilderment. He made eye contact and, as if reading my thoughts, he began speaking again.

'It's not easy for me to come here and acknowledge each and every wrong that I have done you and to accept that I have been unfair, and that it has hurt you in more ways than I thought it would. I could have gone away without doing it.

I could have not bothered to come here. But I am here, asking you to give me another chance.'

I was still angry. But I felt bad for him, too. He looked miserable—and he was right. At least he was repenting. I had every right to scream at him to get out of my life. I had every right to never forgive him. But what if, when I'm in the wrong, no one forgives me? If I don't forgive now, can I expect to be forgiven?

Sorry.

It's that magic word that makes all the wrongs right. It makes the sinner an angel. It gives hope. It is the start of a new beginning. The same old thing could happen again but at least I wouldn't regret not having given him a chance. Chances bring change—the change we all want. Giving others chances increases our own chances of a better life.

'Forgive me?' he asked apprehensively. He took my hand in his—and this time I didn't pull back.

Rajaa Qadri

Lessons in Biology

I

A friend called me up to say that Manasi had died in an accident. Her friends could see her for the last time at her house. I walked the ten-minute distance there.

Manasi's corpse lay on a bed in the big hall. People were crying in different groups. In my short life I had never experienced the death of anyone I knew. I'd seen it only in the movies—the loud lamenting of people—and I lived with the notion that they rather overdo it on the big screen.

I endeavoured to cry—shed a few drops of my own—in vain. Was my heart made of stone, or was it just normal for a man not to cry?

The males present were mostly looking down at the tiles of the floor. I hung my head and did the same. The situation was very awkward for me; my friends had not yet arrived.

There were 513 tiles in the hall—no mistake—I counted them twice.

Manasi was my classmate in the senior secondary school. She was a merry soul and talked a lot. Her countenance passed my beauty test with distinction. The most attractive thing about her was her mouth, her lips as red as blood.

The first few days in school, Manasi hardly spoke a word.

By the second month I found that she was a brilliant student and that her favourite subject, like mine, was biology. The third month, I asked her to sit beside me. She accepted.

We developed a friendship—the relative closeness of our houses playing a major role in it—and started spending most of our time together.

II

One day, in the library, I was practising the schematic diagram of mitosis.

Manasi asked me why. 'There was a question on it in last year's paper,' she said.

'Oh! Was there?' I said. Manasi was correct. Questions from the last year were never repeated. There was no point in studying mitosis closely for this one.

I gradually got accustomed to the chatterbox by my side. Our friendship grew and we developed feelings for each other.

She told me all about herself, her mother, her father, how her cousin poured a bucket of water on the sleeping cat, her fear of cockroaches. I told her that I was afraid Argentina might not have the right combination to win the World Cup Football that year.

If she was absent for a day I felt horribly alone. If I did not show up, she would ask after my health with concern the next day.

III

Viruses are clearly more complex than chemical molecules, yet simpler than the most basic single-cell organism. It is very difficult to answer the question whether viruses are living or non-living.

'What do you think viruses are?' I asked Manasi. 'Living or non-living?'

She thought for a moment and answered, 'They are in-between living and non-living.'

There were two textbooks in biology, one by Choudhuri & Sen, the other by Dasgupta & Dasgupta. We all had the first book, but when the time came to read the chapter on nutrition, I felt that I needed to have a peep into the second one too.

I asked my father to buy me the book, but he said he could not afford it that month. So when Manasi brought 'Dasgupta & Dasgupta' to school I stared at it with greedy eyes.

'Take it home to read,' she said casually.

'No,' I objected. 'There's a class test next week. You'll need it.'

'I don't mind.'

'I do.'

She tore off half the pages of the book and handed them to me.

'What have you done?' I shouted. 'You spoilt a brand-new biology textbook.'

'Idiot. Now we can *both* read the book. You finish your half and then we can exchange.'

I was angry with Manasi. A new book was one of my biggest weaknesses. Its fresh smell, the smoothness of the pages, the secrets it contained, gladdened my heart. Under no circumstances should she have torn one up.

'Adaptation is the heritable feature of an individual's phenotype that improves its chances of survival and reproduction in the existing environment,' taught our teacher in the class.

Manasi whispered, 'We all need to adapt for survival—physically or mentally.'

IV

The gossip spread that Manasi and I were 'life partners'. For most of the boys in our small town, just talking to girls is considered a great achievement. We could not think of an actual romance. Love affairs, I supposed, were for movie stars. They could not happen in real life. They could be conducted, at most, by the smart guys, those city hunks, not by a lower-middle-class, feeble boy like me.

The thought of asking Manasi for her hand, like they do in the movies, terrified me. I was just so ordinary. In some part of my heart resided the fear of rejection.

So I joked about it. I told her, many times, 'I love you Manasi. Do you love me?' Each time I made sure to follow up the statement with laughter in full throttle. 'How good was the joke?'

The biggest bursts of laughter were called upon the days I asked her, 'Will you marry me?' I seemed to be suggesting, 'Was this not an even better joke?' I laughed on the outside, inside my soul burned. Every time I comically proposed to her, I waited impatiently for her to reply seriously. She never did.

I kept a mental list of our meetings: Central Park twice; first time on 2 January, 1998, then 17 June, 1998. We saw movies together on 25 April (my birthday), 8 August (her birthday), 23 November and 2 February, 1999. We sat by the lakeside nineteen times.

One afternoon on the school balcony, in flew a cockroach. Manasi ran to me, held me tightly and screamed, '*Cockro-o-o-o-ach!*' In our small township, and with the kind of mentality people had, if anybody had seen us in that pose, her reputation would have been reduced to ashes.

Personally, I lived a lifetime in that moment, saw the ocean in a drop of life.

That night, I sleeplessly asked myself the question, what could our relationship be called? It was not an affair, and it was not just friendship either. It hung somewhere in the middle of the two, like the virus, the organism that hung between living and non-living.

V

Four years later, I had passed the Board examinations with a mouth-watering score and enrolled myself in an engineering college.

Manasi, to my surprise, fared poorly. I don't think she'd touched her books once in the three-month preparatory holidays. Her marks were so miserable that she could not take up science. She studied English Honours instead.

A stupid, skinny young man now occupied the seat beside me in class, once the throne of a queen.

For the first few months, I missed her a lot. Later, I adapted. No, I did not go to her and propose formally. Life, I was convinced, in the sewer of lower-middle-class society, had nothing to do with a feature film.

One evening, my friend Manasi was run over and killed.

I went and sat in her room, made up of 130 tiles. A lizard loitered on the walls.

My eyes travelled across a small case full of different showpieces, a calendar, and a painting of a marriage celebration.

On the table there were many books of English literature—Shakespeare, Shelley, Hugo, Austen, Bronte, Coleridge.

And what was the other one?

Textbook of Biology by Dasgupta & Dasgupta. What was this book doing there, four years later?

I picked it up in my hand and inquisitively started turning the pages.

Most of the book was very untidy—underlined hither and thither in ink. A lot of notes had been made on the right and left margins. The pages torn away four years ago were missing.

Then I saw it, the shocking thing that blew me away. In the chapter on the human heart, in each of the pages was written multiple times in block letters: 'I LOVE YOU TOO.' My first name followed each inscription.

An earthquake erupted under my feet and I wept like a child, the same way actors do in identical scenes.

VI

My life was ravaged in the aftermath of Manasi's death.To overcome the sorrow and lead a normal life again was tough, but I tried. I read religious books, listened to spiritual speakers, proposed to another girl.

The process was time-consuming, but I had to succeed. I could not afford to waste the rest of my life. I definitely could not afford to. Not for any selfish reasons, for Manasi.

She was the lady who taught me, 'We all need to adapt—physically or mentally.'

I knew she would be happy if I did. If she is happy with me, then when I die and go to her, she will give me a kiss, with those deep red lips.

It makes me shy even to talk of it.

Bilwadal Roy

Not the Answer You Want

'An error doesn't become a mistake until you refuse to correct it.'

—Orlando Battista

This story is about the transformation of a bubbly teenager into a creature her parents did not recognise and what she did in that persona.

The change in Namita, a clever student in Class 12 of a reputed school, was glaring. From outgoing and warm, she became withdrawn and reclusive. Her parents' worried questions were always brushed aside with a brusque 'I'm fine'. And then, Namita failed her Board exams. This came as a shock to all who knew her. Namita? Bright, intelligent Namita—had failed?

After this upset, her parents rigorously interrogated her, at the same time reassuring her she would not fall in their eyes if she revealed the true nature of her problems. Despite their encouragement, Namita remained unresponsive.

Imagine her parents' surprise when they found a cell phone hidden in her school bag. Where had it come from? They hadn't given it to her.

The story tumbled out. Namita had become part of a group of boys and girls in school whose motto seemed to be: 'Live it up, no matter what the consequences are.' These children bunked classes to go to movies, shirked all responsibilities, and engaged in sex with multiple partners.

Namita had initially turned down their invitations to join the gang, but she was teased mercilessly for being a prude and a *behenji*. She finally succumbed and started spending all her time with the group, abandoning old friends and lying to her loved ones.

One boy had taken a particular fancy to Namita. He was the one who'd presented her with the cell phone, so that they could chat with each other late into the night. Namita revelled in the intoxicating sensations of her crush. Soon enough, the boy started trying to coerce her into having a physical relationship with him. He told her 'everybody' was doing it, so it was 'okay'. When she refused, he threatened to send 'nude' photographs of her to her parents, friends and classmates, and even post them on the Internet. Namita was confused. Where had he even gotten such photographs? The boy told her that he had taken pictures of her on his mobile and then had had them digitally altered. To make matters worse, he started abusing her in public places, slapping her on many an occasion. The boy tried every trick in the book to get Namita into bed with him, even dragging her poor mother's name into the mess by saying that she, too, had affairs.

Not able to bear the shame, and fearful of the outcome of his threats, Namita contemplated taking her own life. She went to the terrace of her parents' apartment building and was about to jump, when something happened . . . she thought of her mother and father. She wondered how her parents would ever cope without her, and with the pain of not knowing what had gone wrong. What right did she have to inflict such agony upon two people who had loved her so unconditionally?

Mercifully, Namita stopped herself from taking that drastic step and decided, instead, to open up to her mother. She told her everything and trustingly unburdened herself totally to this woman who loved her so much. Her mother patiently heard her out and reassured her that she would take care of everything. She swung into action immediately. First, she got rid of the dreaded cell phone and next, she confronted the boy, threatening him with police action if he didn't leave Namita alone. The CD with Namita's pictures turned out to be non-existent, too!

Some time after this incident, when I met Namita, I noted that she had regained her lost self-esteem. She had lost a year academically, but she had learnt a bitter lesson at a tender age. She was now ready to face the world, backed by the unwavering love of her parents.

It's never too late to do the right thing. Suicide is not the answer to anything . . . never has been and never will be.

Gaurangi Patel

Stepping Out of My Skin

I'm standing in the hallway
Of my strange new school
People laugh and chatter
Oh—to be so cool!
They go into the classroom
In groups of threes and twos
I feel like falling through the floor
As I stare down at my shoes.
My life—the one I lived before
Has changed completely
I've gone from smart, popular prefect
To insignificant newbie.
My sadness turns to anger
As someone shoves me out of their way
Why should they have all the happiness
That I left behind one day?
I decide I do not care
Let them be who they are
I love to read, I have my books
That can take me to worlds afar.
But I become more bitter
My grades begin to fall
What would my old friends think of me now?

I feel really small.
Sitting up in a leafy tree one day
Staring at the sea
Going over things in my head
A thought comes to me.
They haven't rejected me yet
What if I took a chance?
What if I tried to make some friends?
They might spare me a glance.
And suddenly, I've made a choice
Life will be okay again
I'll turn over a new leaf
And step out of my old skin.

Tara Kaushik

Teenache

'I got a Facebook message,' he says, leaning against the door for support.

'She's . . . gone.'

A teardrop rolls down his stubbly cheek.

I am reminded of a grey morning long ago. Sweat-beads of rain on my window pane. A heavy nimbus cloud inside my heart.

How sunnily it had begun, how everlasting it had promised to be. Looking back, the naïveté of my youth seems so heartbreakingly beautiful, so achingly innocent . . . but back then, it was just the way I was.

He had walked into my life like a Mills & Boon hero, hair fluffing, flesh roiling beneath his size XXL shirt. (So what if he dismounted a battered bike instead of a horse.) All I knew was that something in my heart shifted each time he flashed that crooked dimpled smile at me. And when he quoted Richard Sheridan, 'Why don't you come into my garden, I would like my roses to see you,' I was his for life.

At long last (eight whole days after me met, to be precise), he whispered Those Three Words to me. So what if they were followed by 'because of your new haircut . . .' I was too busy worshipping the way he just wheeled around and left, as if overcome by the intensity of what he had felt in that moment.

So Amitabh Bachchan.

That night, I couldn't sleep. Tomorrow, he would bring me my first rose. We would hold hands and gaze into each other's eyes. And never again would a boy dare tease me on the streets.

The next evening, he came, minus a rose, or even a smile. 'Ready?,' he asked, and I nodded, thinking he was talking about badminton—which was our daily excuse to meet after school, in the court located conveniently close to the Junior School corridor.

'Good,' he murmured.

We did not play. Instead, he took my hand and propelled me into the corridor.

I stood there, pinned against the wall, feeling his heart beat against mine. Our badminton racquets fell to the floor, and the sounds of our breathing rose. *Now*, I thought, closing my eyes.

And that's when the dream broke. Those Mills & Boons heroes, for all their muscled manliness, had been tender, considerate creatures. This was crude, callous, and getting nearly violent now that I was resisting him with all my might.

I dug my teeth into his arm, and he yowled in pain. The next sound was a sharp 'Crack' as his palm connected with my cheek. Hot tears spilled down my burning face. 'What did you think,' he bit out. 'I wanted to play Ludo with you or what? Stupid b . . .'

He picked up his racquet and slammed it against the wall, breaking its frame, and my heart, into two. Long after he had stormed off, I stood there, trying to pull together my clothes and my dignity.

For the next few days, I walked about in a daze. There was no one I could talk to about the hurt and the humiliation. What would my friends think? How shameless I had been!

How utterly idiotic! By now, it had struck me that the real reason he left that day after declaring his 'love' for me had been the sound of the watchman's footsteps.

My father returned from his tour, and determined as I was to not to let him suspect a thing, I greeted him with my cheerful smile and snuggled up beside him as he lay down to rest. Soon, his shirt sleeve was soaked with my tears. I felt his warm hand ruffle my hair. 'What happened?' he asked.

In response, I just tightened my arm around his chest, seeking the comfort I had always known.

'It's alright,' he said, 'I think I know, but you don't have to talk about it. Don't be afraid to cry it all out. I understand your pain.'

With that last sentence, he squeezed the cloud inside my heart. I cried until I was cleansed.

I did not know it then, but my first heartbreak did me a lot of good. It hardened me, and tenderised me. It blessed me with the deep comfort that comes from knowing that no matter what, your parents will always love you, always be there for you.

So, I walk up to my son, freshly jilted on Facebook.

I cradle his head on my shoulder, stroke his hair, and murmur, 'It's okay, son. I understand . . .'

Shubhra Krishan

The Road Not Taken

'I understand,' was all she said.

Why doesn't she say anything more? Does she not realise the enormity of my mad, beseeching words? Does she not comprehend that everything is coming to an end? Is she so devoid of emotion that she can't shed even a tear? Why is she so unfazed by the things I'm trying to tell her? Why is she not fighting for *us?*

If only she would say something . . . anything . . .

The cold wind was blowing so hard, it cut like a knife through to his heavily muffled face. He did not know which was causing more pain, whether it was the wind, or whether it was her standing there saying nothing when he said they could not go on . . .

They had known each other almost all their lives and had been through a gamut of experiences together, each bound to the other by loyalty. But now their paths had diverged forever. Sometimes in life, roads do diverge, for no fault of anyone. It just happens to be that way.

If only he could hear the thoughts running through her head behind that stoic mask. They were not coherent; they were not even relevant to what he was saying because she couldn't hear them anymore. The things that were ringing in her ears were conversations that they had with each other when they were kids.

'You'll be okay, he won't bother you any more,' she'd said when the big bully of the school had snatched Sid's water bottle away from him. Seeing him sprawled across the hallway, she had gone up to the bigger boy, punched him right in the face and retrieved Sid's property.

A stone had hit her head in the playground. Blood was oozing from her forehead and the next thing she knew she was at the hospital with Sid by her side saying, 'Don't worry, you're perfectly fine . . . I've made copies of all the notes I took in class today.'

She had just had a fight with her best friend in college. The fault was all hers—and she knew it—but as she cried on Sid's shoulder, all that he said was, 'Don't let her hurt you. I know you're always right.' They had implicit faith in each other.

And now he was leaving on a journey that she knew she would not accompany him. She didn't know if she would ever get over him or would forever in the shadows of the past, but she knew that if she let fall a single tear, he could never go ahead and pursue what he had decided to.

You know it's love when all you want is that person to be happy, even if you're not part of the happiness.

Anuradha Chandrasekaran

plan they won't like.

You'll be okay, he would tell her—you are more [illegible] and wiser. A big bully of the school had [illegible] her pretty water [illegible] away from her and [illegible] across the hallway; she had gone up to the bigger girl, punched her right in the face and retrieved her property.

A [illegible] had hit her head in the playground. Blood was oozing from her forehead [illegible] the next day she knew she wasn't [illegible] the hospital [illegible] by her side [illegible] very [illegible] took in class today.

She had just [illegible] faith with her best friend in college. Their faith was all lost—and she knew it—but [illegible] on his shoulder all that he had [illegible]. Don't let it hurt you. I know you're always right. They had implicit faith in each other.

And now she was leaving on a journey that she knew he could not accompany [illegible]. She didn't know if she would ever get over him or would forever [illegible] in the shadows of the past. But she knew that if she let fall a single tear, he could never go in peace and [illegible] as if he had [illegible].

You know we love you and all you need is that you need to be happy, even at your nearest [illegible] of the happiness.

~ [illegible] Chandra [illegible]

9

ON FRIENDSHIP

'Friends are God's way of taking care of us.'

—Unknown

Aisha

I was in the tenth grade when my six-year-old pet was afflicted by cancer. The doctors told us he had only a couple of months to live. I was heartbroken. Durga Puja was nearing and all my friends were excited and planning for the festival, as well they should. Whenever I went out with them, I felt forlorn, constantly praying for my pet. My friends did inquire after my mood and I told them about my dog. They listened to what I said but quickly forgot all about it and went on with their celebrations.

Just after the Puja holidays, my pet passed away. The pain of losing him was unbearable. Everyone in my house was sad. I couldn't come to terms with the fact that I had lost such a dear friend. Crying uncontrollably did not lessen the pain. I needed a shoulder to cry on, but had none. My family themselves needed help so I could not expect any from them. None of my friends, despite knowing what had happened, had bothered to even call me. I was used to receiving numerous calls from them for help at studies as I've always been a good student, but for once, when I needed help, no one was there. I felt alone without any friends. Not only had I lost something I loved deeply, but was dismayed by their indifference to my loss.

I was angry, depressed, irritated and frustrated. One day,

as I sat in my room crying my heart out, my cell phone rang. It was a classmate of mine. My sister had accidentally called her from my cell and so she had called back, out of politeness. I was sobbing as I said 'hello'.

She asked me, 'Hey, what's wrong? Why are you crying?' I did not want to pour my bruised heart out but everything bottled up inside just kind of purged itself. I told her about the death of my pet and the fact that none of my friends had even bothered to call. They had been to my place before and had even petted him a couple of times. I told her that I had messaged one of them and was pretty sure that they all knew about his death. By then, I was crying so hard that I was almost stammering.

Aisha calmed me with her soothing words. She said, 'Ummmm . . . maybe they think you don't want to talk right now. If you like, I can come over to your place. Don't worry, I won't be giving you lectures on how not to cry because I can't even imagine your sorrow. No one can compensate for what you have lost, so I won't even try to do it. But I can be beside you and help you through this.'

We spoke for close to an hour. After I hung up, I was still crying but there was a difference. Yes . . . I was still grieving but was somewhere content to know that at least someone cared. I had never been close to Aisha, as I had my so-called 'friends' to hang out with. When Aisha approached me, I would be curt and dismissive of her overtures, just because she did not 'fit' into my group.

My parents took me out of town to help me get over my grief, and all that while, Aisha called me every day to know how I was doing. When I needed a friend the most, it was Aisha who stood by me through it all.

More than a year has passed since then. Aisha and I have become very close friends. It does not matter which friend comes first in your life or whom you have known the longest.

What matters is who stands beside you in hard times. My other friends did apologise to me later and I really do not have any grudge against them anymore. I guess they were not mature enough to deal with the situation. Neither was I. What I have learnt most importantly is that even if you cannot help, you should at least try to be there for others in times of hardship, irrespective of whether they are close to you or not. Thanks to Aisha, I know the difference a small gesture can make in someone's life. Aisha brought a ray of happiness, a glimpse of hope in my life when things were at their very worst, and I hope to do the same for others.

Atasi Ghosh

At the End of a Pen

This is a tale about friendship. A friendship that spanned distance and grew in depth and love over the years, all through the old-world device of letters. Yes, those now redundant pieces of paper with hand-written bits of news stuffed into envelopes and sent near and far, carrying tales trivial, tremendous, big and small.

The two protagonists of this story are Madhavi and Nivedita, and they were brought together by a delightful fortnightly for children called *N'Joy*, short for Newsjoy. They found each other when they were only ten years old in the 'Pen Pals' column.

Nivedita still remembers how excited she was when she received her first letter. 'I was very proud, and enjoyed the fact that my dad wasn't the only one getting mail! I had long-distance friends now, friends whom I had never met!' But, she admits, 'As is usual with friends, some would gradually fade away while others would remain in my life.'

Even when e-mails became the trend, Madhavi and Nivedita preferred the traditional way of writing. It's not as though they were averse to technology—they would e-mail each other, too, chat on the Net and even natter on the phone. But both agreed that letters retain a classic charm that the e-world can never replace. Their letters would contain little doodles in the corners and funny sketches. Their different handwriting, one beautiful and flowing, the other a scribbly scrawl, was all a part of knowing each other.

The rifts in this story came in the form of Time, Studies and Exams. For a long time these close friends had no contact with each other. School Board examinations, entrance tests and college preparations took their toll, and they could not keep in touch as often as they liked. Something or the other would always be in the way.

One day, while Madhavi was clearing out some old junk, she accidentally threw away her old address book. By the time she discovered what she'd done, she was beyond gloom and dejection, as she now had no way of contacting Nivedita. For over a year they had no contact.

Then, Friendship Day arrived. The thought that she could not wish her friend made Madhavi feel even more depressed. She continued to receive Nivedita's letters, but couldn't reply as they had long given up writing their addresses in every letter.

Now Madhavi hit upon an idea. She wrote a piece in the 'Voices' column in the *Statesman* in the Friendship Day special issue. She poured her heart out about her special friend and how much their friendship meant to her.

It worked! Nivedita read the piece and called the very next day. They were both so happy to speak again, and took up from where they had left off.

The tale continues to this day. In 2006, Madhavi wrote a moving piece about her exceptional friendship in the *Statesman*: 'She lives in Mumbai and is currently in college and yet I never got round to meeting her personally. Somehow it never happened . . . I didn't go to Mumbai and she didn't come down to Kolkata; yet we share and care and will be there for each other. Some might say that the whole concept is silly—but don't people have "Net pals"? Hasn't the tradition carried on via the new media?

'This Friendship Day, I just want to tell Nivedita, "I knew you when I was ten; I still know you . . . doesn't it speak volumes?"'

Moved to tears, Nivedita wrote back to the newspaper. This is what she wanted to share with the world. 'I would like to point out through this letter that for each and every person in this world there exists a friend . . . you meet them in circumstances that leave you baffled, but at the same time happy, that you found a friend for the rest of your life.'

There is always a special friend waiting for you. That friend might be next door, in your school, waiting in college, or just a letter or e-mail away. That one true friend is just waiting to be met. True and ever-lasting friendship *does* exist. Just ask Madhavi and Nivedita.

Madhavi Chandak

Ms Congeniality

'Here,' Diya said as she handed me an invitation to her thirteenth birthday party to be held at a popular bowling alley. We hadn't talked much during the first two weeks of school, and getting an invite from her was a complete surprise. She was part of the 'popular group' in my class. Even though she and her circle ignored me and didn't like me because I am the topper in class, I didn't have a boyfriend, flash an iPod or cell phone at school, I decided to go to her party because I thought that she was trying to make amends. So I arrived at the party, dressed in a short kurta and jeans, at 11 am sharp, ready to bowl.

As soon as I spotted Diya chatting with her three friends I walked towards them waving and smiling. She didn't even notice me and just walked past to greet someone else behind me, so I followed her to wish her and give her the birthday gift.

'Happy Birthday Diya,' I called out to Diya as I approached her from the back. 'Oh, thanks, just put it on that bench,' she replied with her body half-turned and then walked off without even making eye contact. *That was rude*, I thought as I placed her present with the others and went to where she and her friends were talking. I saw some space in the circle they had formed but as I walked towards it, I saw Kirti tell Diya something while looking at me, and then almost immediately, they closed the circle so I couldn't get in! I stood behind them for a couple of seconds and then went and sat down on another bench and waited for them to start bowling. As far as I was concerned, those girls were really unkind and ill-mannered.

Sitting, I observed the girls in the charmed circle. They all looked alike—dressed in tight tops and black mini skirts (*How could they bowl in that*, I thought!). All had straightened their hair for the party. They all carried a purse containing a cell phone, iPod, and flavoured lip gloss. They were all acting alike too, taking pictures of each other and playing music loudly.

Then it hit me: they *always* behaved like that, even in school. They copied their leader. Everything they did had to be approved by their leader. What they should wear, what their ideal weight should be, where they should go, what they should do during break in school . . . nobody in that group dared to be different!

I realised that I am special because I am different. I like being smart and don't want someone else deciding what I should wear or do. I don't want to change just to belong in one big group.

Does being 'popular' mean that you are not allowed to have your own identity? If being popular means not to be friendly towards others outside the group, then in my book, being popular isn't the best!

Mahika Dubey

Music Created the Universe

My roommate in college was a quiet, silent and plump boy, from Nagaland. He hardly talked to anyone, and mostly kept to himself. For the first couple of days, we hardly saw each other, and if we did bump into each other, we would just nod and maybe say hello.

I play the guitar, and was waiting for my guitar to arrive from home when one day, suddenly, I heard music coming from my room. I walked slowly towards my room, slightly curious, slightly excited. I opened the door, and there he was, sitting on my bed, playing my guitar! He was playing a piece that I had been trying to play just before I shifted to my hostel. He looked at me, and smiled, almost apologetically, since he was playing my guitar which had, it seems, just arrived half hour before. I smiled back, and waved a 'don't worry about it' hand, asking him to continue playing. I sat there and watched my quiet, silent and plump friend from Nagaland play for a very long time.

Sure, he started to speak a little more than he did before, but that was not it. From that day on, we would sit together with our guitars (we bought one more) for hours, creating elusive melodies and delicate harmonies. Later on, we even went on to participate in many competitions, even winning some of them.

But, regardless of any of that, I learnt, that no matter where you are from, or how different you look and what you speak, music is beyond all of that. We did not create music, music created us. Every rhythm, every shape, every colour in the world is made out of music. It is then our choice whether to use race, culture and nationality to divide us, or to listen to this music of nature and let it bring us together.

Are we not formed, as notes of music are,
For one another, though dissimilar?

—Percy B. Shelley

Kabeer Kathpalia

Puppy Love

A really companionable and indispensable dog is an accident of nature. You can't get it by breeding for it, and you can't buy it with money. It just happens along.

—E.B. White

Like it did for me.

I am a single child. I had always longed for a sibling, someone who could walk back home with me when we finished play in the society gardens, someone with whom I could snuggle up under the same blanket and share whatever made me happy or sad. Years passed, and I was still a single child. But God had something precious in store for me.

My longing for a sibling was fulfilled on my twelfth birthday, when my parents gave me a dog. Little did I know then that Sheru, as we named him, would change my life completely.

Being a single child, I got more than I required of my parents' love and affection. A small scratch on my knee and they would be in tears; a little late coming back from school and my mom would be pacing up and down the porch steps; a small whimper from me and they'd give up their evening's party plans. Everyone knew I was by far the most precious thing in their life. This made me a little arrogant, at times unfeeling, too. Moreover, since I'd never had to share my stuff with anyone, I knew more about the joys of taking than giving.

Sheru became my tutor, and how naturally I learnt life's little but important lessons from him!

Through him I learnt to be responsible. Since I was the one who fed him always, he soon got into the habit of eating food served only by my hands. One evening I went café-hopping with my friends and forgot to bring him his dinner before that. When I got home it was well past his mealtime. Sheru did not reproach me for this neglect, but ran towards his food bowl and started wagging his tail. I never forgot to feed him again.

Through him I learnt about giving happiness. Sheru loved our long walks. He loved being stroked and petted. He loved playing with me whether it was fetch-the-ball or antics at my bidding. Through him I learnt the pleasure that comes when you shower your love and affection on another.

Through him I learnt how to share. Earlier, when a visiting cousin would eye my teddy or other toys, I would go into a panic attack. But when Sheru took a fancy to my favourite bear, would have nothing short of half my bed-space or hog my soft green blanket, refusing to budge without those, I let him have them. In sharing things with him I experienced joy and not irritation. Now I readily share my things with friends and cousins.

Sheru, with his unconditional love, imbued me with a sense of confidence. Unlike others, he would sit beside me and give an ear to what I was saying. I didn't share my sorrows with anyone, sometimes not even my parents. But I always saw a look of concern in Sheru's eyes when there were tears in mine. Somehow, it was a lot easier to give vent to those tears in front of Sheru. This gave me a feeling that there really was someone in this world who loved me more than he loved himself. This changed my perception towards myself. I started loving myself. This made me an upbeat person, who looked at things in a positive manner.

Today, I am a student of journalism, studying in London. When my colleagues appreciate me for my maturity and understanding, I thank God for the gift of Sheru. He, a dumb animal, taught me the real value of life.

Aanal Shah

This Time it's a Different Gift

This time last month I wondered: Now that I'm 1,829 miles away
What would I give you on your sixteenth birthday?
I racked my brains for something that's different and special
Then I wondered whether all gifts had to essentially be physical.
I realised that there's something more precious I can give my friend
My very own fist-sized yet magnanimous heart to lend.
So I decided to doodle my thoughts about you—and of course, us.
Though these are things you already knew, I wanted to make it obvious.
This poem is an outlet for the things I want to express
A friend's euphoric remembrances and I hope they aren't a mess.
For starters, let me remind you about the day I got to know you in grade tenth.
We unceremoniously began our friendship on a stereotypically girlie bent.
Our eyes met, our mouths couldn't stay shut and we began jabbering away.
Our twaddle was silly, though at times it did make sense.

But hey, the lack of sensibility did nothing to make us babble less.
Our topics were usually parents, clothes, boys, school and the world of glamour.
And oh yes, if someone created a scene in class, we made sure
We were part of the clamour.
I remember the day you told me about your first crush
That day I resolved to find out what makes cheeks blush.

Well, you know what makes our friendship so special?
Well, it's because our love for each other is not superficial.
Unlike with my other friends, I can so easily relate to you
Maybe because with me you are so frank and true.

If I were a boy I would most willingly ask you out
But hey, I'm sure you'll find a special guy
And about this you don't have to harbour doubt.
It's a downright shame that I had to meet you so late.
However, I can't find a more perfect and freakish friend, so you were worth the wait.
We have seeds of love, pleasure, success and money yet to sow
Sure, but it's going take a helluva lot of time to grow.
But meanwhile on this eventful journey, we can lean on each other's shoulders;
With patience, strength, and confidence, we can push away all the boulders.
In my heart of hearts, I can't imagine a future without you
Because you're the kind of girl who'd wipe my tears without making it an issue
To round it all up I just want say, 'You're indeed the sister of my heart'
We can't or rather should not be ever too long apart.

Happy Birthday,

Vinothini Subramanian

Via con Dios

When we first moved to Spain, and I started school, I'd felt different from the rest. I was Indian, a vegetarian and on the small side. This made me easy prey for the few bullies that roamed the school. But Carla and Andrea always stuck by me.

Once, a boy made a racial comment. Carla and Andrea told a teacher and a few days later I received a note from the boy apologising and asking if he could do anything to make up for what he'd said.

The loyal friends that they were, they did their best to ward off the bullies. They got me involved in extracurricular activities before, after and during school.

With Carla and Andrea, I discovered the many artists and architects who had lived in Spain, their works.

They helped me learn Spanish during their free time, thanks to which I'm now fluent.

We bonded well during those three happy years. Get-togethers, movies, meals and sleepovers were planned for every weekend.

I tasted authentic Spanish food, admired their way of life, at work and at play. With the help of these willing friends, I discovered two things: Spain, and how much good friends can help with anything.

With the help of Carla and Andrea I was soon accepted by the rest, and I began to blossom in my favourite subjects and hobbies. Now I believe that friendship is a gift of God, to be truly treasured.

God makes friends, you make friendships.

Deepti Narayanan

Welcome to the Club!

I sat staring at the back of Arjun's head. It was bent. I noticed the precision of the hairline at the nape, indicating a fresh haircut. His shoulders seemed to sag. Looking at his crestfallen profile, I could feel a certain rage build up inside me. The insides of my eardrums felt hot with the blood gushing to my head as I braced myself to contain my emotions.

I'd joined the school in the seventh grade. It was quite stressful in the initial weeks. The boys ogled most of the time and made fun of anything I said or did. They were a raucous bunch; pretty disorderly in their class work, and audacious when reprimanded by the teachers. I learnt quite a few cusswords from them and enjoyed my mum's wide-eyed expression when I recited my new dialect to her each evening.

As the exams approached and all of us struggled together with the new course, we became a group commonly terrorised by scalene and isosceles triangles. We were bonded by a common enemy . . . trigonometry!

Arjun had been kinder to me than the others. He spoke only when all suggestive body language failed to convey the message. So it would be appropriate to say that he used his vocal cords sparingly. When Sir Dubey actually paired us to sit together in class, I was most relieved.

Back to what had sent the hot flow of blood to my head.

It was the maths period and Ms Iyer, our class teacher, abruptly asked Arjun if his parents were separating. Silence suddenly descended on our fish market of a class. The uncomfortable hush could actually be sliced into thin strips and fed to the crocodiles. Arjun stood there meekly, flushed and silent. Ms Iyer probed deeper. 'What is the reason for the divorce, Arjun?' she persisted.

We gaped at Ms Iyer. Had no one taught her social etiquette? Where was the human kindness our principal talked about endlessly each morning during prayers? How could Ms Iyer deport herself like this?

Each of us could see Arjun's look of defeat, except Ms Iyer!

As the class got over, I quickly slid to Arjun's side and, shaking his hand, said, 'Welcome to the club; my parents are divorced too!'

I can bet you the entire contents of my piggy bank that my smile salvaged Arjun's shredded confidence. His eyes searched mine, wanting me to share more. And I did. Not because I enjoy talking about my parents' separation. But I owed it to all the kids who are like me. Somebody needed to tell them that they were not alone.

I saw myself in Arjun when Sister Sangita had asked me similar questions three years ago.

Priyanka Kadam

10

ON KINDNESS

'Be kind whenever possible. It is always possible.'

—The Dalai Lama

On the Wings of a Prayer

My mother and I nervously walked to the gate wondering what to say. We rang the bell and a woman in her early fifties welcomed us with a smile, oblivious to the apprehension that we felt. There was a certain awkward pause in her own voice as she ushered us in, but that was only because she didn't know our names. However, that did not stop her from being warm and friendly. The house was a small, cozy bungalow with an attractive lawn. Our eyes searched for the one person we were impatient to see: Dadaji. He wasn't really *my* dadaji, but I had lovingly christened him so. We 'met' him on a day that neither he nor my mum and I would ever forget.

I remember it like it was yesterday. Mum and I had gone shopping right after my Board exams. We went to Fashion Street in Churchgate. Fashion Street, in Mumbai, is a shopper's paradise. It has an endless number of shops overflowing with heaps of clothes selling at really affordable prices. We picked out two or three t-shirts and then decided to return home as it was getting very late. We were just heading to the railway station when we saw an old man lying on the road with his leg bent at such a gruesome angle that it defied the laws of biology. The sight was not only horrifying, it was heart-wrenching! What made the situation even more appalling was that hundreds of people were just passing this elderly man by, pretending they didn't see him. Forget about calling for an ambulance, no one even bothered to ask him if he was in pain or needed help.

I must admit that at first, when my mum and I passed by, we glanced at his leg and walked away. Five steps later we looked at one another and, reading each other's thoughts, walked back to the gentleman. Bending down we asked him if we could help him in any way. His blue eyes searched ours questioningly for a while before he pointed to his ear. We realised that he was trying to tell us that he was hard of hearing. He indicated a chit of paper he was carrying on which a landline number had been scribbled. He requested us to call up his daughter to inform her about his injury and to say that he was getting a paralytic attack. Mum thought his leg looked broken rather than paralysed. He told us that he had fallen down while getting off a bus. He was eighty-five years old and had been lying there for two hours, without a scream or a request for help.

Two hours, 120 minutes, 7,200 seconds. No one had cared how long that must have been for the victim, or his family who might have been waiting for him.

When we explained to his daughter what had happened to him, she asked us to bring him to his house in Kandivali. The old man reluctantly allowed us to help, emptying his pockets to hand us the taxi fare.

A huge crowd gathered around us, and even those callous people who had been standing at the bus stop all the while, began helping us. With the aid of three men we carried him to the taxi. His leg was swelling up fast and by now it had turned a colour of hazy purple. Mum and I sat in the front seat, next to the taxi driver. Not once did the old gentleman utter a word or exclamation of pain along the way, and whenever we both looked back to see if he was all right, he would wave his hand in reassurance.

In a little over an hour we reached his home. His family had been waiting for us, sick with worry. The doctor had been called. He took just one look at the leg and said, 'This is an emergency; we need to rush him to hospital.' And he was taken away in the same taxi.

Mum and I went home. When we called later, we were told that he had suffered multiple fractures and had been admitted to the ICU. They told us that he had strongly fought against entering the hospital, saying that he only wanted to go back home. He had never been admitted to hospital before and was scared. All the blood tests, medical formalities, doctors' check-ups and nurses armed with medication irritated him no end. His reasoning was that since he would die soon anyway; there was no need to for him to go through all that.

Well, surgery and three months of intensive physiotherapy later, he is very much alive. It has been eight months since the accident, and he goes for walks everyday. Now he is even allowed to go anywhere he wishes unaccompanied.

It was around this time that my mum and I went to see him. A thin man wearing square-rimmed spectacles walked into the room, a confused look in his eyes as he tried hard to place us. The lady, who happened to be his daughter, loudly asked him if he recognised us. She pointed to us, then at him, and then she mimed a taxi and pointed to his leg. He looked at us, awestruck, and with tears in his eyes. Seeing him walk in, Mum and I stood up, surprised, emotional and also delighted.

He had been an author of literature in Sindhi in his youth and, as a token of his gratitude, presented me with, what else, some of his cherished books. But more importantly, he gave Mum and me his blessings and assured me that I would get into the best college in Bombay. Within a month I received my admission letter and instinctively knew that God had heard his and my prayers. In my heart I believe I would not have got into college without his intercession with God.

Shachi Udeshi

Debt Unpaid

The hardest thing that happened early in my life was the death of my beloved grandmother.

She had been there as far back as I could remember, being a mom to me after the death of my mother. She took good, tender care of me and when the time came for me to go to school, she helped me with my studies. After my dad's death she took up the responsibilities of a father, too, carefully planning our future. She also helped my brother and me get admission to the boarding schools we wanted to go to, visiting us every alternative weekend with a special gift each time.

One vacation, my grandma, my aunt, my brother and I went to Delhi. It was May-end and scorching hot when we went to visit the National Railway Museum. After being outside in the sun for some time, she told us that she was not feeling well. We took her inside and found a couch where she could lie down. My aunt wanted to take her to a doctor. But my grandma said she would be fine and insisted that we carry on exploring the museum while she rested. When we returned to her, she said she was not feeling great and would go home with the driver and send him back for us. By the time we returned home she seemed fine. The rest of the trip went well, and when we returned to Mumbai she took a long rest.

Two days before we were to leave for school, it was decided that my brother and I needed a haircut. My grandmother had an appointment with her doctor that day, but she postponed it to the next. The next day, too, was a busy one, what with the preparations of departure for school and she put off her meeting with the doctor once more. Late in the evening, when we remembered, she put us at ease by saying that she would visit him first thing in the morning.

Late that night I was woken up by my aunt to massage my grandmother's feet. Soon my aunt took her away to the hospital. I was so tired that I went to sleep and started dreaming about my new school. When I woke up and asked my brother why he hadn't got me up in time to leave for school, he told me that our aunt had called to say our grandma was critically ill in hospital. Not much later my aunt came in. By the look on her face I could see that the worst had just happened. She hugged us and softly broke the sad news. My heart felt like it was being crushed.

I knew then how much my grandmother had loved me, and I her. I wished I had insisted on her being taken to the doctor the day we got our haircut. Or on the day when we were at the museum. I wished I had the opportunity of paying back all the care and affection she'd showered on me. To this day, I mourn for her every time I see someone else's grandmother.

Sanskar Bhattacharya

I Cry with the Crying Child

I woke up with a start. The bus had stopped suddenly and jerked me out of dream world. I didn't completely come out of it, though. My eyes were still closed and my mind was desperately assimilating the broken pieces of the dream that I had been having. I was neither inside it nor outside. A fraction of my senses perceived what was going on around me and a fraction was slowly lulling me back to sleep.

My eyes were tired but my ears were alert. There was a slight commotion . . . the sound of scampering feet . . . hushed voices, all tensed. Something was wrong . . . or was it in my imagination? Was I hearing voices in my dream? It was a confused state.

I was awake and something was definitely wrong.

'An accident . . .'

'Where?'

'When?'

'Oh, my God.'

'Somebody, help . . .'

'Call up the police . . .'

'We need to get out . . .'

I shook my head to fend off the tiredness and the confusion. I peeked out of the window. Evidently, there had been an accident in the middle of the road. A bus had crashed into a mini-truck (later I was told that it was a dumper). The front half of the bus was totally crushed and the exit was blocked. However, as always, human genius had divined a solution and a rescue operation was being carried out through the windows.

I slumped back onto my seat. *Damn! This means we'll be delayed. Now we'll have to wait till all this mess is cleared up.* I was frustrated and very angry. Typically, I was thinking only about myself. *Where's the driver? Why don't we leave?*

Apparently he had joined the rescue team.

The fool! I was seething. I was selfish. I was not sorry that I was selfish.

And then I saw something which knocked the wind out of my lungs. A woman was lying on the road, unattended. She was unconscious and yet no one approached her. She was bleeding and yet no one tended her. She needed someone . . .

I got off the bus and rushed towards her. A man intercepted my path. He was half-carrying a moaning man. 'Help me carry him,' he said to me.

'But what about that woman lying there? Shouldn't we attend to her? She's unconscious.'

'No point.'

'What do you mean "No point"?'

'She's dead. Been dead for quite some time now.'

'Dead,' I uttered in a hushed voice. I stood there frozen. My hands were trembling.

'Will you please help me with this man?' he asked, exasperatedly.

My mind had gone numb although it was not because I hadn't seen a dead body before. Even a moment ago, I was sure the woman was alive, and that she needed my help. And now, all of a sudden, the cold fact hit me like a blast of icy wind. I felt choked up and weak. She was dead . . .

I grabbed hold of the injured man's legs and carried him

into the bus. I worked like a machine, without emotion, without feeling, without knowing where I was, without knowing what I was supposed to do, without knowing where I was supposed to go . . . I could see only one thing—death.

It was leering at me obscenely. Oh, the ugly face it had . . . the blood spilling out of the open wounds . . . the nasty crooning of the moans of people around me . . . the tears . . .

We gently laid the injured man across some seats in the bus. More victims were being carried in. All of them were desperately injured. Some had their foreheads split open; some were caressing their broken limbs.

The man I had carried in grabbed hold of my sleeve. He was trying to say something to me. I was repulsed by the dirt on his attire and the blood on his face. I tried to break away but he did not let go. He gave a faint tug and, to my wonder, I obliged. I bent towards him.

'Thank you,' he said in an almost inaudible whisper.

I tried to smile.

'While the world cried with all its pain, I smiled, for the pain did not touch me. I was happy because the pain of other people did not concern me. I was only grateful that my own children did not have to experience that pain. But now I am crying, and all the pain is flowing down my cheek,' he said.

That was the last thing that I heard from him. He slipped into unconsciousness.

If there was ever a hell on earth then it was here, it was here. So much sorrow . . . so much pain . . . how can a human heart hold so much pain inside it? Why doesn't it explode? Maybe we are made to suffer. We define our lives through suffering.

'The sufferings that befall us are not the test of our inner strength, they are proof that we are already strong enough to bear them,' I tried to tell myself.

But how could I bear this? A child was crying. He was

hardly ten. And he was crying.

'Baba . . . Baba . . . Baba . . .' he shrieked for his father.

'Where is my mother?' someone implored from behind me, 'Mother? Mother?'

It was a woman in her twenties. Her eyes were pouring torment.

'I am here,' a woman called from the rear. She was an old woman.

The younger woman heaved a sigh of relief and said, 'Thank God you are safe.' She rushed to embrace her mother.

'Baba . . . Baba . . . Baba . . .' The boy still cried.

'Where is his father?' someone called out to the conductor.

'We don't know. But we must leave immediately. We have two critical patients on board.'

The engine of the bus roared but it couldn't drown the cry of the child. 'Baba . . . Baba . . . Baba . . .'

'Does any one know where Bidhannagore Hospital is?' a man asked from the front.

I recognised him as the one who had carried the injured man in with me.

'Does anyone know where it is?' he asked again.

No one responded. No one knew where it was.

I did not respond. I knew where it was. But I did not remember that I knew.

'Let's move,' the driver said, 'we'll ask anyone on the way. Surely someone will know.'

The bus lurched forward. Perhaps, the jerk this time brought me back to my senses, for I cried out, 'I know where the hospital is. I will direct you there.'

'Please come to the front,' the driver said.

The bus moved on, the driver following my directions.

The child was not crying anymore. He was asleep. His face was calm. His face was wet. It was a mask, hiding the turbulence inside.

Let him sleep . . . let him dream . . . let him live . . .

I got off the bus as soon as it reached the hospital. There was no need for me there. The hospital had staff to take care of the injured ones. I could not take it anymore. I felt nauseated and terribly weakened. I walked away slowly. I had done what I could. I had played my part. And so I walked away.

As I walked I sensed a feeling rising through me. It was warm and oddly comforting. I was weak, but I was still not totally broken . . . there was still hope. I hoped that the child would find his father, I hoped that the man would live, I hoped . . .

And it is this hope that keeps us alive. A hope for a new day . . . a hope for a new sun . . . a hope for a new life . . .

I had to believe that it was possible . . . I had to remember that life is beautiful . . .

I walked on . . .

Shubhabrata Dutta

P.S. I Love You

And none will hear the postman's knock
Without a quickening of the heart.
For who can bear to feel himself forgotten?

—W.H. Auden

An aluminium letterbox hanging inconspicuously near the electricity meter . . . an address book on a shelf . . . my writing pad and my favourite Parker . . . the post office opposite my school . . . the five-rupee postage stamp with a picture of a leopard on it . . . my Camlin gluestick which I never left for school without . . . bits of paper . . . memories . . . 'Dearest Anu . . .'

When teenage turmoil had thrown me into the deep, these letters were paper boats that withstood the roughest storms and delivered me to the shore. At a time when the flock around me was alienating me, a few birds chose to take me under their wing and helped me fly higher than ever before. At a time when most were frogs in the well, I found bits of paper fluttering in with perspectives of different worlds . . . each a Hitchhiker's Galaxy . . . each a small universe on its own.

I received a plethora of letters in envelopes of all shapes

and sizes—some small and blue, others white and businesslike, khaki, pretty Hallmark or Archies envelopes. Over time I learnt to recognise the handwriting on them and know who had written to me just by looking at my name through the dirty glass window of the letterbox. Over time I realised who had time to sit and write to miles-away-me and sign it off 'Affectionately'. Over time I found true affection through that dirty pane.

I learnt more through my letters than through all my textbooks. I discovered the existence of neutrinos, heard the latest buzz from colleges in Chandigarh, learnt how to spot embassy cars, and about life in Saudi Arabia and Japan, copied out my name in Arabic, peeped into the cultures of Lakshadweep, Manipur, Goa, Pondicherry and the Andamans, poured out teenage angst in my letters and learnt how to deal with those crises. I grew up with some of these friends—through school, through junior and senior college—without meeting them more than twice in about seven years, yet relating better to them than to anyone else around. I found true friends through the India Post seal.

I was sixteen and just out of school, dealing with the novelty of college, when my father suffered kidney failure and was in the hospital for days together. For the first time in my life I was afraid that I might lose him. I was torn between having to pretend to be brave, being the older child, and yet longing for someone to hold me and let me cry.

When the friends I had around me heard the news, I don't remember anyone even placing a hand on my shoulder just to say that they were there. But I do remember two of my far-away friends sending letters by express mail offering comfort, relating similar experiences when one of their parents fell ill, and how they dealt with them. They called frequently to check how I was doing and I was able to stand tall in that period of my life only because I had my friends backing me irrespective of where they were on the map. I owe them more than they know, and their letters have been the pillars of my life. It was the time I found strength in fragile paper . . .

Today, with the entry of e-mail and instant chat, I'm able to keep in constant touch with these friends. Yet, in the flurry of 'HRUs?' and 'BRBs', I miss those days when I used to be up till three in the morning writing letters, drafting and redrafting my replies, sending and receiving pictures and Christmas gifts, saving money to buy the best paper cards to send to my beloved friends and preserving the ones that they had sent. I miss fishing out old letters to read, to warm myself when I'm down with a cold and fever. I miss craning out of the balcony at three every afternoon to see if the postman had come, and running down to my aluminium letterbox as soon as he left to see if someone has written to me. And I miss the words, 'Dearest Anu . . .'

Anupama Kondayya

Pass It On

In high school, there were many of us who adored Mabi, hanging on her every word as if it was the gospel truth. She was tall and handsome, not pretty. And despite the bulk, there was elegance in her expressive hands, whether they explained a point or swept the long bangs of hair off her broad forehead.

Among the many poems and prose chapters she taught us, there were also gems of distilled life. One in particular remains with me to this day, more than four decades later.

I came across her one afternoon in Main Street.

'Where have you been?' she wanted to know.

'To see the Queen,' I responded pertly and then giggled. 'Actually, I'd gone with Rita to get a gift for Mira. We got her a lovely book.'

'I didn't know you three were such good friends.'

'Nor did I, till recently,' I admitted. 'Remember the accident Rita met with just before the last paper? She was really blanked out and would have opted out of the exam had it not been for Mira. She spent two whole days going over the whole course with Rita, revising everything and pepping her up to make sure that she sat for the exam and did not lose her rank. Rita thought the book would be a good way to say thank you.'

'Certainly, it's a good way to say thank you, but remember one thing always: one can never return a favour.' Mabi wasn't making sense.

'Why not? When someone does us a favour, one can return it in some form or the other.'

'When someone helps you in a time of need, you know the impact of that help on the crisis at hand. By merely saying thank you, presenting a gift or performing some small service, can you equal the importance of the original favour?'

'Things can't all be equal.'

'Exactly. Favours can never be equal as no two situations are ever the same. So the best thing to do, if your wish to honour the person who did you a favour, is to pass on the favour to someone else.'

I looked suitably blank.

'Nearly every day,' she continued, 'you will meet people facing some sort of crisis. Whenever you can, help them as your friend had helped you. Pass on the good deed and tell the receiver to pass it on too when the times comes. Create circles of goodwill wherever you are and see how they come back to you.'

I hope that is what I have done.

Kusum Choppra

More Chicken Soup?

Share your heart with the rest of the world. If you have a story, poem or article (your own or someone else's) that you feel belongs in a future volume of Chicken Soup for the Indian Soul, please email us at cs.indiansoul@westland-tata.com or send it to:

Westland Ltd
S-35A, 3rd Floor
Green Park Main Market
New Delhi 110 016

We will make sure that you and the author are credited for the contribution. Thank you!

Contributors

Aanal Shah, a nineteen-year-old media aspirant, is pursuing her Bachelor's in journalism in London. The dog-lover that she is, Aanal believes in respecting each and every person in life. She can be reached at aanalnshah@gmail.com.

Aarti Pathak is a professor of economics and a freelance writer. She can be contacted at aartikpat@gmail.com.

Aekta was reborn at the age of thirty when she suddenly realised that she had two kids and lots of things to do before she died. She's now rushing to catch up on lost time. She lives in New Delhi and is currently an editor in a women's magazine.

Aishwarya Bharadia studies in the eighth grade in Anand Niketan, Ahmedabad. Her hobbies are reading, dancing and being with her friends. She has over 1200 books in her personal library and they are her true treasure, apart from her I-pod and laptop. She can be reached at aishwarya-b@hotmail.com.

Amit Shankar Saha was born and bred in Calcutta. He is currently pursuing PhD research work in English Literature at Calcutta University. His interests lie in academic research and creative writing. He blogs at http://amitss6.blogspot.com and www.amitss6.sulekha.com

Amita Dalal is a sitar player attached with Saptak School of Music. A regular on All India Radio and TV, she has performed in Japan,

Russia and Germany. A graduate in B.A, L.L.B, she is also involved in hand block printing on fabrics. She can be reached at amberishdalal@hotmail.com.

Amitabh Shah, a Yale MBA, is founder of Yuva Unstoppable, a volunteer movement in 12 cities with over 4000 members who are helping 100 NGOs. Yuva gives youth an opportunity to volunteer for two hours a week and inspires them to do random acts of kindness.

Anjali Ambani is an avid reader, loves swimming and dancing, and plays the flute and piano. A student at Ahmedabad International School, she has founded booksandballs.org, which donates sports equipment and books to municipal schools throughout India, and worlpeace2040.com. She hopes to be a doctor one day. She can be accessed at jixi92bookworm@gmail.com.

Ankit Chowdhary studies at the Doon School, Dehra Dun. He has represented his school on a trek to the base camp of Mt. Everest and also to a worldwide conference in Canada. He can be reached at ankitchowdhary@gmail.com.

Anupama Kondayya is a software consultant by profession and a traveller, photographer, musician and book-lover. But she is a writer above all, as writing helps her express all that she experiences while engaging in either her profession or her passions. She is based in Bangalore and can be reached at anupamakondayya@gmail.com.

Anuradha Gupta studied at BITS, Pilani, and after her MBA at IIFT, Delhi, worked at Hindustan Lever for seven years. She has over ten years' experience in the corporate sector but derives maximum satisfaction from her current hobby, writing. She has written a book on environmental issues called *The Green Dragon* and writes regularly for various websites and the BITS alumni magazine, *Sandpaper*. She can be reached at anusharma86@yahoo.com.

Anuradha Chandrasekaran works as Software engineer in HCL. She is currently doing her Master's in computer science. She is sometimes a mystery, at times a well-known story, always on a cloud of dreams, forever on a quest, occasionally a social butterfly, many a times a closed clam, above all a true Piscean.

Anurita Rathore is assistant editor with the *Times of India*'s *Ahmedabad Mirror*. Prior to this, she has been with the *Indian Express* followed by a year at a radio station, MY FM, as programming head. She likes writing on art, culture, people, lifestyle, behaviour, life patterns and everything that has something worth a thought. She can be reached at anuritarathore@gmail.com.

Archana Sarat is a freelance writer who remembers wheezing through her chartered accountancy sometime back in history. Her website, www.archanasarat.com, boasts of her experience on a variety of subjects from stock markets to mesothelioma, podcasting to diapering. Apart from the hundreds of online articles to her credit, her works have appeared in various popular newspapers and magazines including the *Times of India, Economic Times, SEBI and Corporate Laws Journal* and *Me Magazine*.

Arpita Bohra is a student of English literature at Lady Shri Ram College, Delhi. An incurable Indophile, she spent most of her childhood abroad. Apart from writing, her interests include dance, reading, travel, art, environmentalism, spirituality and psychology. She can be reached at arpita311@gmail.com.

Arun Gandhi is president of the M.K. Gandhi Institute for Nonviolence, University of Rochester, Rochester, NY. He is a grandson of Mahatma Gandhi.

Seventeen-year-old **Atasi Ghosh** is currently in the 12th standard. She actively takes part in debates and extempore, loves any public speaking event where she can interact with others. She is also into sports, especially tennis and would like to become a sports manager in future. She enjoys reading authors like Erich Segal, J.K. Rowling, Charles Dickens and Agatha Christie. She can be reached at atashi24@gmail.com.

Ayesha Sindhu is a sports anchor and reporter with the English news channel NewsX where she's been working for the last year and a half. She's a graduate in English literature from Lady Shri Ram College and a postgraduate in journalism from AJKMCRC, Jamia Millia Islamia. She has lived in various parts of the country and abroad but is now based in Gurgaon, where she lives with her family and dog.

B.S. Keshav is an architect, currently residing in Navi Mumbai with his wife Vinita and their twelve-year-old son Prithvi. A graduate of Sir JJ College of Architecture, Mumbai, he works for an IT major looking after their architectural and interior design projects across the country. Writing is his passion and he has one book published, titled *Subbu Chronicles*, apart from short stories and essays published in various magazines.

Baisali Chatterjee Dutt has an MA in French from JNU, New Delhi, which she doesn't quite know what to do with, as she's been and still is rather busy with diaper duty. She has two boys who are not just the centre of her universe, but her entire universe. When she's not busy being nurse, chef, storyteller and teacher to them, she can be seen with her precious computer . . . or sleeping, standing up! She can be reached at bchattdutt@gmail.com.

Bilwadal Roy is an engineer by profession. He was born in Kolkata, West Bengal, to a middle class family. Writing is more of a passion, which he mostly pursues in his free time. His focus is mainly short stories and articles with an occasional poem. He can be reached at bilwadal.roy@gmail.com.

Bipasha Roy has a PhD in political sociology and a degree in law from Utkal University, Orissa. She has worked with the nautch girls of Kolkata and is currently involved in the movement to eradicate 'ragging' from the academic institutions of our country. She is a board member of the Juvenile Justice Board, Kolkata District. She is an ardent lover of nature and believes that nature is our best teacher. She can be reached at bipasha_roy5@rediffmail.com.

Biswadeep Ghosh is a Pune-based journalist, presently editing *Pune Times*, the daily supplement accompanying The *Times of India*. He has worked with the Indian Express Group, *Outlook* and The

Hindustan Times in New Delhi; Zee and Magna in Mumbai. He has also written a book of poems (mediocre) and four biographies (equally mediocre). He has degrees in literature and music, both of which are statistical realities today.

Crystal is a dreamer, philosopher and an optimist. She likes poetry, nature, and books. If you have been through the same experiences, or need help dealing with domestic abuse/depression, she would like to help. You can mail her at indigomermaid@gmail.com.

Dawood Ali McCallum lives in the UK with his wife and two children. He is the author of *The Lords of Alijah* and *Taz*.

Deepa Venkatraghvan, a chartered accountant, loves to write. She works in the media, and when she is not writing about smart investing, she pens her thoughts about life's experiences. She would be happy to share her treasure trove of memories with you at deepa.venkatraghvan@gmail.com.

Deepti Narayanan is a student of class eight, and lives in Mumbai with her parents and a younger sister. She has studied in six different schools in four different cities. A voracious reader who devours books, she is fluent in Spanish and is one of the youngest students from India to have cleared the Spanish proficiency test conducted by the University of Cervantes, Spain. She can be reached at deeptithegreat@gmail.com.

Dhanalakshmi Sashidharan is a quiet, cheerful person who enjoys spending time with her friends and family. She is married and resides in Bangalore with her husband Santhosh, where she works for a software concern. She fills her leisure time with her favourite books, music and movies. She is also an ardent window shopper who loves shopping in the narrow crowded streets of old Bangalore. She can be reached at Dhanalakshmi.S@honeywell.com.

Divisha Mehta is thirteen and a half and lives in the beautiful heritage city of Jaipur, Rajasthan. She enjoys reading books, watching movies and listening to music. She has an opinion on many things and any discussion generally finds a willing participant in her. She can be reached at divisha_24@rediffmail.com.

Reading inspires **Divya Nair Hinge** to write, writing spurs her to think in new ways and thinking keeps her going on. Born and brought up in Mumbai, her marriage to a Naval officer gives her an opportunity to travel far and wide. Twenty-six years old, a double post graduate by qualification and a journalist by profession, she is presently working as Assistant Manager in the Corporate Communications Division of a leading organisation. She can be reached at divyarkn@rediffmail.com.

Ekta Bhandari is a gold medallist in Electronics and Communications and is currently working as a software engineer in an MNC. Writing has always been her love and her life. Her poems have been published in a compilation series named 'Sisters in Rhyme'. She is working on her first fiction novel. She can be reached at ektathegreat@gmail.com.

Gaurangi Patel believes that books are tiny windows which introduce you to the 'world out there', and takes you places you never imagined exist. After completing her M.Phil, she founded a Pre-School, 'Baby-Pearl', which keeps her in constant touch with children, and thus, innocence! She writes poems and real-life based articles in English, Hindi and Gujarati. Her email ID is gaurangi_patel2000@yahoo.co.in.

Janani Rajagopal is MBA Finance, who discovered somewhere down the line that she has a flair for the written word. Believing that you excel at something you love doing, she switched careers to pursue her journey with words. She enjoys and cherishes life, love and everything in between . . . meeting new people, reading and music are her passion.

Jane Bhandari has lived in India for 40 years and is a writer and occasional painter. She co-ordinates 'Loquations', a Mumbai poetry reading group, and has authored two volumes of poetry, *Single Bed* and *Aquarius*. She has also written two collections of short stories for children, *The Round Square Chapatti* and *The Long Thin Jungle*. She can be reached at janarun@yahoo.co.uk.

Jairaj Singh is a journalist in New Delhi. He worked with the *Hindustan Times* for three-and-a-half years, and is now working for the news channel, News X. He is 21. His email id is jairajsinghht@gmail.com

Kabeer Kathpalia is presently a university student in his first year. He is filled with doubts about his plans for the future and is enjoying every minute of it. He is a very curious person and wants to learn everything. He can be reached at kabeerkathpalia@hotmail.com.

Kahan Chandrani was born and raised in Ahmedabad. He is passionate about holistic and inclusive socio economic progress and environmental sustainability through education and action. He has worked towards his high school scholarships. He is currently studying at Chapman University, USA. He can be reached at kahan0409@gmail.com

Kumar Vivek is a second year student of the Post Graduate Programme in Management at IIM Kozhikode. He also holds an undergraduate degree in Electronics Engineering from ISM Dhanbad. An amateur Hindi poet, he blogs sporadically at http://krvivek.blogspot.com and can be reached at kvmaheshwari@gmail.com.

Kusum Choppra is a writer, journalist trying to distill the experiences of a life time into fluent words which will reveal the emotional quotient, rather than action or thriller. She can be reached at kusumchoppra@yahoo.com.

Madhavi Chandak is a college student studying Graphic Designing and Advertising in Kolkata. Her interests in writing heartfelt pieces of real-life incidents go back to her secondary school days when she started writing for her school magazine. Soon after, she joined Voices, a weekly teen supplement published by a reputed news daily, The Statesman. She can be reached at madhavichandak@gmail.com.

Mahika Dubey is a student at Monta Vista High School in Cupertino, CA. She has done part of her schooling in India and part in the United States. For the past eight years she has been training in

Odissi. Mahika also has a deep interest in art and her artwork has been showcased and displayed in various venues in Cupertino including the FUHSD Art Showcase 2009.

Malcolm George graduated from St. Stephen's College, DU, in 2002, and now works as a radio journalist with the BBC World Service in New Delhi. You could write to him at malcolmgeorge@gmail.com.

'Everything else takes effort but writing is something that rejuvenates my soul.' **Manika Bansal** loves to experiment with anything that catches her fancy. A movie buff and a true Gemini who completely believes in destiny, she can be reached at mani.destiny@gmail.com.

Max Babi is a multi-lingual writer, metallurgist and plasma technologist. Born in Cambay, he grew up in Baroda, Ahmedabad and Pune. He is working seriously on 'transcreations' to ensure nothing is lost in translation. He has been published extensively. He can be reached at maxbabi@gmail.com.

Meghna Sethy has done her Bachelors in Mass Media from St. Xavier's college Mumbai. She is a media professional. She can be reached at meghnasethy@gmail.com.

Mehul Mittra is presently studying in DPS Ahmedabad in the 12th grade. His dream is to become a film-maker. He loves to sing, dance, paint, write poems, stories and songs. He also loves to compose music. He can be reached at mehul_mittra@yahoo.co.uk.

S. Meera is an editorial consultant, based out of Chennai. A work-from-home mother of two, she is also a classical dancer with several performances to her credit. She has been in the field of writing and editing since 1993. She can be reached at meerasampath@hotmail.com

Mrinal Pande is an author, journalist and television personality. She studied in Nainital, at Allahabad University and at the Corcoran College of Art and Design, Washington DC. She is Chief Editor of *Hindustan*, a Hindi daily.

Namrata Jaykrishna is a student of Riverside School, Ahmedabad. She is a voracious reader, writer and soccer player. Soccer is her passion and she has captained her state U-14 soccer team. She also holds many honours in swimming and loves adventure sports and travelling. Reach her via email at glamdiva.namrata@gmail.com.

Nandini Swaminathan is a twenty-year-old student of English literature at Lady Shri Ram College, Delhi University. She has been writing since the age of ten. She writes poetry, occasional stories, songs and cartoons. She also dabbles in amateur photography. She can be reached at nandini.swaminathan@gmail.com.

Natasha Ramarathnam was born in Delhi, had a dream-like childhood in a small township in Jharkhand, and spent her formative years in Kolkata. After an under-graduation in physics, and a degree from IIM-Ahmedabad, she was an investment banker for five years before moving to the development sector. She lives with her husband and two pre-school sons in Mumbai and can be reached at nuts246@yahoo.com.

Music is **Nikhil Sundar**'s passion, he loves playing the guitar. His other passion is football. He loves to play as well as watch football matches. He loves good food and enjoys experimenting with all kinds of cuisines. He is in grade 10, studying in NAFL, Bangalore.

Nimisha Sinha is fifteen and is the daughter of a defence officer. Her hobbies include reading books, playing, swimming and making friends. She loves to talk. Her usual pastime is to chat with her friends, shopping and hanging out with friends. She is a friendly and naughty teenager, difficult with parents but cool with friends.

Nithya Ramachandran is a seventeen year old from Chennai. She is the chief editor of her school's online newspaper. Poetry is not her profession, but her destiny. She believes 'life is like an ice cream—eat it before it melts'. She is deeply passionate about the English language, the environment, babies and that crazy little thing called love. She blogs on http://kissbliss.blogspot.com.

After writing a tell-all book about advertising, *Welcome to Advertising! Now Get Lost*, **Omkar Sane** has made certain he will never be given a job in advertising again, but that knowledge leaves him unfazed.

He proposes to join—and similarly demolish—a string of other professions.

Palak Malik is still engrossed in discovering her passions. She observes, learns and explores as the tales of her journey through life unfold. She can be reached at palakmalik1@gmail.com.

Prasoon Agarwal is a student at the Indian Institute of Management, Ahmedabad. He is a graduate Mechanical Engineer from Banaras Hindu University, with work experience in the energy sector. He is an energetic weekend biker and likes travelling, writing and graphology. He can be contacted on prasoon@iimahd.ernet.in or +91-79-66324714.

Priya Kaur Gill, twenty-five, is a journalist, currently based in India. She grew up in America and New Zealand, where she completed her postgraduation in journalism, and returned to her roots last year to live and work in her field.

Priya Krishnan was born in 1982 and raised in Chennai, India. She loves to dance, write and finds meaning in astronomy. She currently works as Marketing Manager in Delhi and blogs on her uniquely weird corporate experiences. Visit www.priyakrishnan.com for a true likeness of her. She can be reached at krishnan.priya@gmail.com.

Priyanka Kadam is a self-professed nature freak who struggles in the concrete environs of Mumbai, India. Writing for her has been a therapeutic exercise to express and treasure the impressions and experiences of life as it unfolds each day. She can be reached at priyankasonia2002@yahoo.co.in.

Priya Pathiyan, currently editor of *Mother & Baby*, India's premier parenting magazine, has been a lifestyle journalist with mainstream media for twelve years. She has also co-authored India's first comprehensive wedding guide *Wedding Belles*. She has travelled extensively, loves movies, music, dancing, reading, wildlife and trying out different cuisines. She can be reached at priya.pathiyan@gmail.com.

Rachana Mirpuri was born in the Philippines and grew up in Chicago, Africa, and the Caribbean. After acquiring BFA in Writing,

Literature and Publishing in Boston, she moved to Hong Kong and is currently the founding publishing editor of *Beyond Sindh*, a magazine targeted to Sindhi Indians all around the world. She can be reached at m_rachana@hotmail.com.

Rajaa Qadri is doing her Bachelor's in sociology and has been writing for as long as she can remember. She loves to read and photography is another one of her interests. On a personal note, she is an easy-going, laid back girl who enjoys long conversations over coffee. She can be reached at rqadri28@gmail.com.

Rambler is a software engineer by profession. Amidst the professional chaos, he discovered blogging and the power of writing one day. It helps him come out with his feelings, thoughts and emotions, which he could not have otherwise expressed in front of real people. More of his writings can be read at http://virtualrambling.wordpress.com/

Resmi Jaimon is an international freelance writer with over 400 published clips in 62 print and online publications on varied topics including travel, trade, technology, career, business, company profiles, real estate, lifestyle and food, and several content and corporate writing projects. She is open to syndicating her published works, pitching ideas for publications, working on commissioned assignments and writing columns. She lives with her husband, Jaimon, in Kochi, Kerala. Website: www.resmijaimon.com; Blog: http://resmi-jaimon.blogsot.com; email: resmi.writer@gmail.com.

A journalist and freelancer by profession, **Ritu Goyal Harish** has been writing for more than 10 years. Principal amongst her writing interests are human interest stories and civic issues. She contributes to a wide number of magazines and local editions of newspapers such as *Times of India* and *DNA*. A mother of two, she lives in Pune with her family. She can be reached at ritugoyalharish@gmail.com.

Roshan Shanker has been an avid blogger for the last 5 years and enjoys creative writing. Apart from writing, he also loves to sketch and create cartoons. Roshan is currently pursuing an MBA from the Darden School of Business at Virginia. He can be reached at roshanker@yahoo.com.

Rumana Shanker is a graduate in Apparel Designing from NIFT, New Delhi. After working in Pantaloons for two years as a designer for their in house label 'Bare Denim', she is presently freelancing and simultaneously preparing for further studies abroad. She has designed for the National Team of Special Olympics Bharath and is also taking initiatives to coach the future aspirants of NIFT.

Salil Desai makes management training videos and short films through his production firm Re-Living (www.relivingindia.com). His short film *To Khayega Kya* was selected for the Hyderabad International Film Festival 2008. He has over 200 published pieces in *Times of India, Indian Express, DNA Me, Alive* etc. His stories have also been published in anthologies like *Stories at The Coffee Table* (2007) and *The Shrinking Woman and other Stories* (2009). He can be contacted at salil.des@gmail.com

Sandeep Shete is a Pune-based professional and has worked in fields such as sales, marketing and product management. He's now trying to revive his yen for creative writing that he'd put on the backburner for many years in the pursuit of a livelihood, which took him from Vadodara to Mumbai and then to Pune. He is a voracious reader, a driving enthusiast and a beach lover. He can be reached at sandeepshete@yahoo.com.

Sandhya Gupta can be reached at sandhyagupta02@gmail.com.

Sanskar Bhattacharya resides in the beautiful hills of Mussoorie (the abode of Mr Ruskin Bond), studying in the famous Woodstock School. Being a great fan of books, he has improved his writing skills and put them all together in this story. There will be many more to come as he is only thirteen.

Shachi Udeshi, eighteen, lives in Mumbai and communicates with Dadaji when she visits him using a pen and paper because of his age.

Sharmishtha Bhattacharjee graduated from the University of Leeds in 2004. Currently working as a writer in an advertising agency, she pens her thoughts about culture chaos and compassion fatigue in her blog titled Petrichor. On and off, she pursues her hobbies of working with children, music and dance. She can be contacted at sharmishtha.b@gmail.com.

Shobhaa Dé is a noted writer and columnist. She attended St Xavier's College, Mumbai and later became the founder-editor of a number of magazines, including *Stardust* and *Society*. She is the author of such bestsellers as *Spouse* and *Superstar India*.

Writing has been **Shubhabrata Dutta**'s passion since he was in the sixth standard. Today he stopped at the first station . . . but the engine is hooting already. He can be reached at email.to.shubha@gmail.com.

Shubhra Krishan is a writer and journalist based in Delhi, where she is an assistant editor with *DNA* newspaper's *ME* magazine. She has previously worked in Doordarshan, *Cosmo* and *Femina*. Krishan has written two books published in the US: *Essential Ayurveda: What It is and What It Can Do For You*, and *Radiant Body, Restful Mind: A Woman's Book of Comfort*. She is currently scripting a thriller and writing a novel. She loves books, coffee, music, travel, food. And she still believes in love.

Most people call **Soumyarka Gupta** Shom because they find his full name too cumbersome to pronounce. He is a copywriter by profession. Writing has been a passion with him for longer than he can remember. He likes to read and believes that to be a good writer, one has to be aware of the world and how people's minds work. The story included here is a piece of his life, which has helped him grow along the years to become what he is today. He can be reached at 9958417407 / 9999476466.

Sreemanti Sengupta is a poet by dreams, a copywriter by choice and a writer by ambition. Her dreams are more or less encapsulated at www.mistywhimsofelicity.blogspot.com. She can be reached at sreemanti.sengupta7@gmail.com

Suma Rao is a freelance writer. Creating magic with her words is something she enjoys. She has been fortunate enough to be able to work from home and get the best of both worlds—my writing, and my family. You can reach her at sumabhats@yahoo.com

Sunil Robert is an Indian professional who is now recognised as one of the finest communication professionals worldwide. In 2006, he won the Stevie International Award, considered by many the Pulitzer for corporate communications. Sunil lives with his wife and son in the United States. He recently wrote his memoirs, *I Will Survive: Comeback Stories of a Corporate Warrior*.

Tara Kaushik lives in Mumbai, and studies in class VII at The Cathedral and John Connon School. She was born in Kenya, and has lived in Nairobi, Bangalore, Kolkata and now Mumbai. In fact, at the end of this year, she might be moving to Delhi! She loves reading, writing stories, art, drama, guitar, and playing with her dog Jasper.

Vatsala Kaul Banerjee has been a journalist-writer-editor, starting with *Target*, the children's magazine and going on to *Teens Today*, of which she was chief editor. Both magazines were of the India Today Group. She then went to work as commissioning editor, Puffin, at Penguin Books India. She edited a parenting magazine, *Child*, at Media Transasia India Limited before coming back to her abiding love—books. Currently, she is editorial director, children's and reference books, Hachette India. She lives in Delhi with her cartoonist-illustrator husband and two daughters.

Vikas Hotwani is a Mumbai-based journalist and photographer. When not chasing stories, he loves travelling, blogging, studying different cultures and gorging on rajma chawal. His all-encompassing philosophy of life is to keep it simple and stupid. He can be reached at vikas.hotwani@gmail.com.

Vinith Aerat is a Naval architect who endeavours to put down life's experiences on paper. He firmly believes that a good story is necessarily 'good' when it inspires a reader to become a better person. It is a lofty dream indeed, to make the world a better place, but he knows that his contribution counts, as does everyone else's.

If Vinith's stories made a difference, then let him know at aerat_v@hotmail.com that he's on the right path.

Vinothini Subrmananian has the courage of her convictions. Two things come her way easily: dreaming and sarcastic humour. She has built enough castles in the air to love life. Writing is her choice of an outlet for the crazy emotions that swarm in her. She sees herself in her work and nothing beats that feeling! You can read her work on her blog: mypennings_mynourishment.blogspot.com.

Yashvardhan Jain is sixteen years old and studies at the Doon School, Dehradun. He is the secretary of the Doon School Music Society, and the music captain of his House and has just started recording songs independently. He is the editor-in-chief of the DSIR (Doon School Information Review).

Permissions

Becoming Indian. Reprinted by permission of Priya Kaur Gill. © 2009 Priya Kaur Gill

Celebration. Reprinted by permission of Malcolm George. © 2009 Malcolm George

Colour Me Everything. Reprinted by permission of Sandhya Gupta. © 2009 Sandhya Gupta

My Taste of India. Reprinted by permission of Anjali Ambani. © 2009 Anjali Ambani

Oporojita. Reprinted by permission of Shubhabrata Dutta. © 2009 Shubhabrata Dutta

Personal Style. Reprinted by permission of Anurita Rathore. © 2009 Anurita Rathore

So Very Young. Reprinted by permission of Anurita Rathore. © 2009 Anurita Rathore

So, What's New? Reprinted by permission of Aekta. © 2009 Aekta

There's Always a First Time. Reprinted by permission of Sharmishtha Bhattacharjee. © 2009 Sharmishtha Bhattacharjee

Music to Help You Grow. Reprinted by permission of Mrinal Pande. © 2009 Mrinal Pande

All Grown Up. Reprinted by permission of Janani Rajagopal. © 2009 Janani Rajagopal

Fact & Fiction. Reprinted by permission of Soumyarka Gupta. © 2009 Soumyarka Gupta

How My Father Taught Me Non-Violence. Reprinted by permission of Arun Gandhi. © 2007 Arun Gandhi

In a Lighter Vein. Reprinted by permission of Ayesha Sindhu. © 2009 Ayesha Sindhu

It's My Happy Heart You Hear. Reprinted by permission of Yashvardhan Jain. © 2009 Yashvardhan Jain

Not This, That. Not That, This. Reprinted by permission of Omkar Sane. © 2009 Omkar Sane

The Boy Who Taught Me. Reprinted by permission of Biswadeep Ghosh. © 2009 Biswadeep Ghosh

The Year I Turned Macho. Reprinted by permission of Dawood Ali McCallum. © 2009 Dawood Ali McCallum

Your Own Jigsaw Puzzle. Reprinted by permission of Vatsala Kaul Banerjee. © 2009 Vatsala Kaul Banerjee

Your Smile in New York. Reprinted by permission of Rachana Mirpuri. © 2009 Rachana Mirpuri

A Complete Individual. Reprinted by permission of Rambler. © 2009 Rambler

Grades Don't Define You. Reprinted by permission of Resmi Jaimon. © 2009 Resmi Jaimon

It's All About the CV. Reprinted by permission of Arpita Bohra. © 2009 Arpita Bohra

Minus Three Plus One. Reprinted by permission of Aishwarya Bharadia. © 2009 Aishwarya Bharadia

Only in Your Dreams. Reprinted by permission of Ekta Bhandari. © 2009 Ekta Bhandari

Reaching Out. Reprinted by permission of Kahan Chandrani. © 2009 Kahan Chandrani

Cinderella Lives On. Published online under the title 'Small Town Girl' in 2005. Reprinted by permission of Natasha Ramarathnam. © 2005 Natasha Ramarathnam

The Astute Teacher. Reprinted by permission of Max Babi. © 2009 Max Babi

The Eleventh Hour. Reprinted by permission of Sandeep Shete. © 2009 Sandeep Shete

The 'It' Girl. Reprinted by permission of Baisali Chatterjee. © 2009 Baisali Chatterjee

To Be Words-worthy. Reprinted by permission of Jairaj Singh. © 2009 Jairaj Singh

Win-Win. Reprinted by permission of Divya Nair Hinge. © 2009 Divya Nair Hinge

An Answer to a Question. Reprinted by permission of Suma Rao. © 2009 Suma Rao

Angst with Pimples. Reprinted by permission of Kabeer Kathpalia. © 2009 Kabeer Kathpalia

Bad Boy Joy. Reprinted by permission of Salil Desai. © 2009 Salil Desai

Down the Road. Reprinted by permission of Sunil Robert. © 2009 Sunil Robert

Healing. Reprinted by permission of Crystal. © 2009 Crystal

His Heartstrings. Reprinted by permission of Amita A, Dalal. © 2009 Amita A. Dalal

Love, Actually. Reprinted by permission of Divisha Mehta. © 2009 Divisha Mehta

Remembering a Room and an Age. Reprinted by permission of Amit Shankar Saha. © 2009 Amit Shankar Saha

Ruben. Reprinted by permission of Priya Krishnan. © 2009 Priya Krishnan

Rude is Crude. Reprinted by permission of Nikhil Sundar. © 2009 Nikhil Sundar

Smoke. Reprinted by permission of Jane Bhandari. © 2009 Jane Bhandari

'So, What is Your Son Up To?' Reprinted by permission of Vikas Hotwani. © 2009 Vikas Hotwani

The Name Board. Reprinted by permission of Archana Sarat. © 2009 Archana Sarat

Why? Reprinted by permission of Roshan Shanker. © 2009 Roshan Shanker

Never Again. Reprinted by permission of Anuradha Gupta. © 2009 Anuradha Gupta

Safe At Home. Reprinted by permission of Mehul Mittra. © 2009 Mehul Mittra

With a Cigarette in My Hand. Reprinted by permission of Prasoon Agarwal. © 2009 Prasoon Agarwal

My Arithmetic Lessons. Reprinted by permission of Bipasha Roy. © 2009 Bipasha Roy

Forgiving Father. Reprinted by permission of Ritu Goyal Harish. © 2009 Ritu Goyal Harish

Miracles Follow Faith. Reprinted by permission of Deepa Venkatraghavan. © 2009 Deepa Venkatraghavan

My Brother Adi. Reprinted by permission of Atasi Ghosh. © 2009 Atasi Ghosh

My Dad, My Hero. Reprinted by permission of Nimisha Sinha. © 2009 Nimisha Sinha

Only By Accident. Reprinted by permission of Meghna Sethy. © 2009 Meghna Sethy

Pancakes. Reprinted by permission of Arpita Bohra. © 2009 Arpita Bohra

Security Blanket. Reprinted by permission of Anurita Rathore. © 2009 Anurita Rathore

Shake the Rain. Reprinted by permission of Dhanalakshmi Sashidharan. © 2009 Dhanalakshmi Sashidharan

Skeletons in My Cupboard. Reprinted by permission of Anupama Kondayya. © 2009 Anupama Kondayya

Someone to Watch Over Me. Reprinted by permission of Vinith Aerat. © 2009 Vinith Aerat

Watch Out For It. Reprinted by permission of Bilwadal Roy. © 2009 Bilwadal Roy

A Winner All the Way. Reprinted by permission of Rumana Shanker. © 2009 Rumana Shanker

Alka Came Out Tops. Reprinted by permission of B.S. Keshav. © 2009 B.S. Keshav

The Girl in the White Gi. Reprinted by permission of Priya Pathiyan. © 2009 Priya Pathiyan

Hold Your Tongue. Reprinted by permission of Amitabh Shah. © 2009 Amitabh Shah

Lessons in Football. Reprinted by permission of Namrata Jaykrishna. © 2009 Namrata Jaykrishna

Mind Your Ps & Ms. Reprinted by permission of Manika Bansal. © 2009 Manika Bansal

Musings on Solitude. Reprinted by permission of S. Meera. © 2009 S. Meera

My Hardest Days. Reprinted by permission of Sreemanti Sengupta. © 2009 Sreemanti Sengupta

New @ Work. Reprinted by permission of Palak Malik. © 2009 Palak Malik

Teenager's Tale. Reprinted by permission of Nandini Swaminathan. © 2009 Nandini Swaminathan

The Funny Side of Poetry. Reprinted by permission of Aarti K. Pathak. © 2009 Aarti K. Pathak

There are No Mistakes in Life, Only Lessons. Reprinted by permission of Kumar Vivek. © 2009 Kumar Vivek

A Little Bottle Reminds Me.... Reprinted by permission of Archana Sarat. © 2009 Archana Sarat

Exchange Programme. Reprinted by permission of Ankit Chowdhary. © 2009 Ankit Chowdhary

I Miss You, Dad. Reprinted by permission of Nithya Ramachandran. © 2009 Nithya Ramachandran

It's Okay to be Sorry. Reprinted by permission of Stepping Out of My Skin. © 2009 Raaja Qadri

Lessons in Biology. Reprinted by permission of Bilwadal Roy. © 2009 Bilwadal Roy

Not the Answer You Want. Reprinted by permission of Gaurangi Patel. © 2009 Gaurangi Patel

Stepping Out of My Skin. Reprinted by permission of Tara Kaushik. © 2009 Tara Kaushik

Teenache. Reprinted by permission of Shubhra Krishnan. © 2009 Shubhra Krishnan

The Road Not Taken. Reprinted by permission of Anuradha Chandrasekaran. © 2009 Anuradha Chandrasekaran

Aisha. Reprinted by permission of Atasi Ghosh. © 2009 Atasi Ghosh

At the End of a Pen. Reprinted by permission of Madhavi Chandak. © 2009 Madhavi Chandak

Ms Congeniality. Reprinted by permission of Mahika Dubey. © 2009 Mahika Dubey

Music Created the Universe. Reprinted by permission of Kabeer Kathpalia. © 2009 Kabeer Kathpalia

Puppy Love. Reprinted by permission of Aanal Shah. © 2009 Aanal Shah

This Time it's a Different Gift. Reprinted by permission of Vinothini Subramanian. © 2009 Vinothini Subramanian

Via con Dios. Reprinted by permission of Deepti Narayanan. © 2009 Deepti Narayanan

Welcome to the Club! Reprinted by permission of Priyanka Kadam. © 2009 Priyanka Kadam

On the Wings of a Prayer. Reprinted by permission of Shachi Udeshi. © 2009 Shachi Udeshi

Debt Unpaid. Reprinted by permission of Sanskar Bhattacharya. © 2009 Sanskar Bhattacharya

I Cry With the Crying Child. Reprinted by permission of Shubhabrata Dutta. © 2009 Shubhabrata Dutta

P.S. I Love You. Reprinted by permission of Anupama Kondayya. © 2009 Anupama Kondayya

Pass it On. Reprinted by permission of Kusum Choppra. © 2009 Kusum Choppra